My Experiences in
Astrology

Books on Astrology by Dr. B.V. Raman

A Catechism of Astrology
A Manual of Hindu Astrology
Ashtakavarga System of Prediction
Astrology for Beginners
Bhavartha Ratnakara
Graha and Bhava Balas
Hindu Astrology and the West
Hindu Predictive Astrology
How to Judge a Horoscope Vol. I
How to Judge a Horoscope Vol. II
Klachakra Dasa
My Experiences in Astrology
Muhurta or Electional Astrology
Nirayana Tables of Houses
Notable Horoscopes
Planetary Influences on Human Affairs
Prasna Marga Vol. I
Prasna Marga Vol. II
Prasna Tantra
Raman's One Hundred Ten Years Ephemeris (1891-2000)
Studies in Jaimini Astrology
Three Hundred Important Combinations
Varshaphal or The Hindu Progressed Horoscope

My Experiences in Astrology

BANGALORE VENKATA RAMAN
Editor : THE ASTROLOGICAL MAGAZINE

📖 **UBSPD**
UBS Publishers' Distributors Pvt. Ltd.
New Delhi • Bangalore • Kolkata • Chennai • Patna • Bhopal
Ernakulam • Mumbai • Lucknow • Pune • Hyderabad

UBS Publishers' Distributors Pvt. Ltd.

5 Ansari Road, New Delhi-110 002
Phones: 011-23273601-4, 23266645-47

10 First Main Road, Gandhi Nagar, Bangalore-560 009
Phones: 080-22253903, 22263901, 22263902, 22255153

8/1-B Chowringhee Lane, Kolkata-700 016
Phones: 033-22521821, 22522910, 22529473

60 Nelson Manickam Road, Aminjikarai, Chennai-600 029
Phones: 044-23746222, 23746351-2

Ground Floor, Western Side, Annaporna Complex, 202 Naya Tola,
Patna-800 004 • Phones: 0612-2672856, 2673973, 2686170

Z-18, M.P. Nagar, Zone-I, Bhopal-462 011
Phones: 0755-4203183, 4203193, 2555228

No. 40/7940-41, Kollemparambil Chambers, Convent Road,
Ernakulam-682 035 • Phones: 0484-2353901, 2363905

2nd Floor, Apeejay Chambers, 5 Wallace Street, Fort,
Mumbai-400 001 • Phones: 022-66376922, 66376923, 56028017

1st Floor, Halwasiya Court Annexe, 11MG Marg, Hazaratganj,
Lucknow-226 001 • Phones: 0522-2294134, 2611128

680 Budhwar Peth, 2nd floor, Near Appa Balwant Chowk, Pune-411 002
Phone: 020-66028921

NVK Towers, 2nd floor, 3-6-272/B, Himayat Nagar,
Hyderabad-500 029 • Phones: 040-23262572, 23262573, 23262574

Visit us at www.ubspd.com & www.gobookshopping.com

© Mrs. Rajeswari Raman

Tenth Edition	1992	Reprint	2003
Reprint	1999	Reprint	2004
Reprint	2000	Reprint	2005
Reprint	2001	Reprint	2006
Reprint	2002		

Printed at: Ram Printograph, Delhi

FOREWORD

Dr. B.V. Raman's elucidation of his "My Experiences in Astrology", as he calls them, is a fascinating chronology of his exceedingly interesting experiences in a sphere in which he commenced to function with remarkable spontaneity at an amazingly early stage.

His vast erudition and superior scholarship in the science of astrology have elevated him to the pinnacle of fame evoking the esteem and regard of eminent thinkers of international fame.

The dazzling astrological convention at Bangalore in December 1983 portrayed the singular adulation which Dr. Raman had earned for himself through undaunted resolution, power of performance and unabated dedication to study, research and dissemination through a multitude of titles.

The Saga discloses Dr. Raman's proud inheritance of distinction and pre-eminence from an ancient and noble family which shone in the blaze and braved the vicissitudes of tempestuous times in the history of our country.

The tutelage of the benevolent aristocrat, the renowned Prof. B. Suryanarain Rao was the most glorious dispensation of Providence which endowed Dr. Raman with abundant wisdom, robust common-sense, capacity for accurate ratiocination and logical deduction. The grandson's firm faith in the efficacy of the *mahamantras* emanated from the same source.

My association with Dr. Raman, during a long tract of more than four decades, generated a rapport of inestimable value flowing from a manifestation of a plurality of rare attributes including those of intellect and intellects, which have projected him as one of our respected representative men aided at all times, in his pursuits by coordination from Mrs. Rajeswari Raman in the riches measure.

And that is what has persuaded this Foreword.

Bangalore   **A.R. SOMNATH IYER**
8-3-1985

PREFACE

This combined volume, of the first part (18 chapters) published earlier and the second part, consisting of an additional sixteen chapters now added as "My Experiences in Astrology", should have two-fold value; one for the trained and academic professional, savant or the student of Astrology in general; and the other, for the non-professional who is interested in understanding a branch of knowledge, unique and profound and the experiences of one, dedicated to its exposition for six decades, to make the educated public astrology-conscious.

For the latter, the book will prove a reference volume and provide information on practical astrology.

There is a further value in the study of astrology by the layman and that is the appreciation of the insights provided by Astrology to understand human psychology and human life in general.

"My Experiences in Astrology" covers a period of immense significance in my early life because of my successful forecasts on the outbreak and progress of the second world war and other historical developments. Several interesting experiences gained by way of examining innumerable horoscopes of people belonging to different temperaments, sections and strata of society who sought my astrological guidance will no doubt evoke the admiration of lovers of Astrology.

This book can also be called an auto-biographical sketch as it takes the reader back 60 years when I first began the study of astrology, a subject I have loved so much.

Anecdotes of human interest also dot the narrative. The book written in simple language is liberally interspersed with my astrological discussions with pandits, scholars and savants and the lessons I learnt from them.

The book is a compilation of "My Early Experiences in Astrology" earlier serialised in THE ASTROLOGICAL MAGAZINE. It is thoroughly revised and re-written at several places.

Chapters 16, 17 and 18 detail my first professional visits to Bombay and Madras, the predictions I gave and my first performance as a public speaker and my first encounter with Nadi astrologers.

The book embodying important astrological principles, methods and their practical application — in brief an astrological text and a human story rolled into one — will no doubt be of great interest and practical use as much to an average educated man as to a student, scholar or connoisseur of astrology.

I take this opportunity of expressing my thanks to Justice A.R. Somnath Iyer — guide, friend and well-wisher, for nearly four decades, for his Foreword; to my wife Rajeswari Raman who gave appropriate suggestions as the book was being written; to my daughter Gayatri Devi, Associate Editor, THE ASTROLOGICAL MAGAZINE, who assisted me in revising the manuscript; to my sons B. Niranjan Babu and B. Sachidananda Babu for their personal attention to details of typing; and to K. Gopinath for the nice job he has done in typing the manuscript.

I must also record my sincere thanks to UBS Publishers' Distributors Ltd. for having brought out this book in an attractive manner.

Bangalore-560 020   **B.V. RAMAN**
1st January 1992

1

After the collapse of the Vijayanagar empire, several Telugu–speaking Brahmin families had to leave Andhra and come down to the then Mysore State in search of livelihood or patronage for their learning. Ours was one such family. Over three hundred and fifty years ago my ancestor Saranavarjulu appears to have migrated from Andhra and settled down in a village near Bangalore. He was a learned Brahmin performing *yajnas* and leading a simple and contented life. So were his son Kondavarjulu and grandson Nagavarjulu and great grandson Mallavadhanalu. The Telugu suffix *garu* appears to have been dropped by Lingappa son of Mallabhattlugaru who was perhaps the last holy Brahmin to perform *yajnas*. Lingappa and Pyarayya devoted themselves to public and private business and service. The family appears to have experienced many vicisitudes until Pyarayya's son Venkataramanayya joined Tippu's army as a commander. He was later on reverted to the civil line and served as Amildar or Tahsildar of Devanahally, Kikkeri and Channarayapatna.

My great grandfather B. Gopal Rao son of Venkataramanayya was well versed in *mantra sastra*. He served in various capacities. For a couple of years he held the post of Dewan of Parlakimundi in Chicacole District and then got back to Mysore and served as a District Sheristedar in Chickmagalur.

By and large we have lived in Bangalore eversince Saranavarjulu migrated to Mysore State, except for about 15 years, when my grandfather B. Suryanarain Rao lived in Bellary and Madras. It is no wonder having lived in Bangalore for over 350 years, the prefix "Bangalore" got attached to our names.

It way my father B. Nanjunda Rao, who added one more prefix—Talamudupulu (T)—and called himself as T.B. Nanjunda Rao. He would say that this was the family name 400 years ago before we left Andhra. But nothing more is known about this.

Beginning from Lingappa our identification with Karnataka was complete. In fact my grandfather's first book *Victoriya Rajniya Charitre* (Life of Queen Victoria) was written in Kannada as also his first book on Astrology *Jyotisha Sudhasaramanjari* (Compendium of Astrology). He was a linguist as he could speak fluently English, Kannada, Telugu, Tamil and even Hindi.

My childhood was not a sheltered one. I was exposed to all the rigors to which the village children were usually exposed to in those times. I had early my education in the village primary and middle schools. I had as my classmates boys drawn mainly from the lower strata of the village and children of farmers from neighbouring villages. It was only after entering the middle school in 1921 that English alphabets were taught to me.

A strictly chronological order has not been followed in writing these experiences and most of the events have been drawn from memory. It will be my endeavour to avoid as far as possible personal matters though sometimes certain details pertaining to my early days may have to be given to provide the readers with a suitable backdrop.

My first formal initiation into Astrology was in my 8th year, when on an auspicious day my grandfather (B.Suryanarain Rao) taught me 2 slokas—*achinthyavyaktarupaya* and *murtitwe parikalpitaha* from *Surya Siddhanta* and *Brihat Jataka* respectively. Then there was practically a complete halt until 1924 or so when I was asked to commit to memory *Jataka Chandrica* which according to grandfather was the best book on the subject for learning Astrology.

Prof. Rao was my father's father. I had lost my mother when I was hardly 20 months old and the responsibility of bringing me up was taken by my grand-parents who never made me feel that I was motherless.. Whenever grandfather went on tours, I used to generally accompany him. This gave me an opportunity to study and understand human nature and gain valuable experience.

The one thing that always stood clear in my mind was the remark often made by grandfather that because of Jupiter's strong position in my horoscope, my future as a "great man" was vouchsafed and that I would have a long and fruitful life.

Various hurdles had to be encountered during the formative years of my life. Though until 1924 grandfather lead a life of aristocracy, his over–generous instincts lead to straitened finances. From about 1927 onwards, the family had to pass through, with decreasing income and increasing expenditure, a phase of poverty the memory of which even at this distance of time I have not been able to shake off completely.

My study of Astrology, *i.e.*, memorizing *slokas* from *Jataka Chandrica* would start at 10 p.m. after everyone had gone to bed and would continue till 12 midnight. There was no electricity and I had to be satisfied with a kerosene lamp. Life was hard as a number of chores had to be attended to. It was my responsibility, voluntarily assumed, to take care of the physical comforts of grandfather apart from acting as his secretary and attend to odd jobs such as walking or cycling everyday to Bettahalsoor—3 miles away from our village —to get the daily post, getti..g drinking water from a nearby well etc.

My father B. Nanjunda Rao never developed interest in Astrology. With great difficulty he was taught to cast a Rasi chart. Casting the Navamsa chart was a very hard nut for him to crack and he bid goodbye to Astrology. His eyesight was not good and he lost his vision in his 40th year.

Father was a pious man, always respectful toward elders, somewhat stubborn, principled and very orthodox. One of my earliest recollections of this stubbornness was when I was in my 7th or 8th year. I forgot to do my lesson in *Amarakosha* and told myself that it was not necessary. Since I had not learnt the *slokas* scheduled for the day, I was made to stand on a bench with my hands tied together. My pleadings were of no avail. After 45 minutes grandmother came to my rescue and I was set free. This sort of punishment was a routine affair until grandfather who came to know about this saw to its end. But I never bore any ill-will towards father to whom I and my wife Rajeswari Raman gave a lot of solace when the responsibility of looking after him fell on us. I must confess however that my knowledge of Amarakosha which in later years was a boon to me to understand astrological and astronomical texts was mainly, if not entirely, due to the discipline, though sometimes, stern, father had imposed on me.

Father was born on 24-7-1883 at 6 a.m. at Bangalore. The planetary positions were: Aries—Ketu; Taurus—Saturn; Gemini— Jupiter; Virgo—the Moon; Libra—Rahu; Capricorn—Venus; Aquarius—Mercury and Mars; and Pisces—Lagna and the Sun. The Moon's position in Virgo aspected by Mars showed reserve, diffidence and a certain amount of coldness. Lord of Lagna unaffected made him affectionate. The mutual aspect of Saturn and Mars explains his stubbornness. The will though changeful was strong, and he could be often content with a noble vengeance. The presence of Jupiter in the 4th is significant. While he was not much educated in the literal sense he had the capacity of intuitional perception and experience. All the sensitive points pertaining to eyesight have been severely afflicted. Unmindful of the tragedy that had befallen him by the loss of sight and indifferent to distractions which an unhappy domestic life had forced on him, father pursued with unabated zeal the task of performing more than 24 lakhs of Gayathri Japam and creating around him a spiritual halo. Frank and outspoken, diplomacy and sycophancy, were completely absent. He died in Mars sub-period in Saturn's Dasa. While grandfather was for me an ideal person, father impressed me as a man of discipline and conviction. The tenth house is free from affliction. If he had no love for many he had hatred for none. His were the qualities of a cultured ego.

After my Upanayanam(investiture of sacred thread) in my 8th year, I underwent a course of study (adhyayana) in the Vedas and the importance of Vedic studies was realised as my studies in science progressed in the college.

In the village school where I studied, the medium of instruction in the primary and middle school classes was Kannada, English being second language. Sanskrit was learnt at home under an elderly Pandit.

Occasionally grandfather would ask me about my "progress" in Astrology but otherwise I had to fend for myself as my studies advanced. Casting of the horoscope on the basis of *Panchangas* or local almanacs gave me little or no trouble. But I had no idea of the ephemerides or western Astrology until I chanced to come across a copy of Butler's *Solar Biology* and Zadkiel's *Primer of Astrology*. A thorough study of these books kindled my interest in mathematical Astrology.

Before I was 13 or 14, I knew by heart 50 *slokas* in *Jataka Chandrica* and a few a chapters in *Brihat Jataka*. I had also digested the Kannada book *Jyotisha Sarvavishayamruta*. I had a very high opinion of my knowledge of Astrology and this egoism prompted me to make forecasts about the longevity of all the members of the household. But *slokas* 23 and 24 in *Jataka Chandrica* on which I mainly relied were also the cause of my own mental anguish.

According to these *slokas*, lord of the 2nd house is stronger than that of the 7th for inflicting death; and the planets occupying the 2nd and 7th are more powerful in causing this event. In my own case, Rahu is in the 2nd and grandfather had Saturn in the 2nd. My Rahu Dasa would end in my 25th year or so and grandfather's Saturn Dasa would commence in his 64th or 65th year. Therefore, it was clear, I then thought, that both of us would die, my death occurring about the end of my Rahu Dasa and his, at the beginning of Saturn's.

The adage "a little learning is a dangerous thing" applied to me in its entirety. When as a lad of 14, I placed my apprehensions before grandfather he flared up and scolded me for my "impertinence and pretensions" in making such predictions. By nature he was somewhat impulsive but his anger would not last long. The next day, when both of us were going in a bullock cart to a nearby village he wanted to know why of all events I was concerned with my and his death. I told him my apprehensions about the 23rd and 24th stanzas of *Jataka Chandrica*. He warned me that longevity should not be predicted without a careful examination of the horoscope — whether it fell into the category of Balarishta (early death), Alpayu (short life), Madhyayu (middle life), or Purnayu (long life) and then, the Dasa and Bhukti lords should be fixed. All this required not only a thorough acquaintance with the essentials of Astrology but also considerable experience and the power of intuition. My query to him as to how I could acquire all this was met with a mild rebuke that I was too young and immature. But my obsession with my own expected death and the death of my grandfather persisted until on one fine day, I watched a discussion going on between grandfather and one Suryanarayana Siddhanti, an astronomer cum astrologer who had come to stay with us for a couple of months. The Siddhanti was arguing that Saturn's sub–period in his own Dasa could prove fatal. But grandfather waving his hand said that Saturn was no doubt *a maraka* but he would kill only about the end of his Dasa and that during Mercury's sub–period he could fall seriously ill and might have to undergo surgery. Grandfather was born on 12–2–1856 at 12–21 p.m. at Chicacole (now Srikakulam), Ganjam district*.

About the middle of 1925 or so grandfather fell seriously ill and all of us went to Devanahally, a Taluk headquarters where my uncle B. Lakshminarain Rao was working as an Inspector of Schools. Grandfather was a well-known man and all the State Officers including the Maharajah of Mysore used to call on him now and then. Sir Albion Banerjee, the then Dewan of Mysore visited us at Devanahally and under his advice, grandfather was shifted to Bangalore, where he was operated on by the then Senior Surgeon Dr. Mylavaghanam. In those days local anaesthesia had not yet become popular. But grandfather's will power was such that as one of the toes in his left foot was being surgically removed, he continued to read a newspaper!

The combination of the three planets Mercury, Jupiter and the Sun in the 10th brought him good reputation and wide influence and made him famous. The *Parivartana* (interchange of houses) between the 2nd and 9th lords (Mercury and Saturn respectively) and the

---

* The Sun 301° 12' ; the Moon 18° 29' ; Mars 180° 53' ; Mercury 308° 27' ; Jupiter 321° 28' ; Venus 260° 33' ; Saturn 63° 20' ; Rahu 6° 9' ; and Ascendant 43° 9'.

disposition of Yogakaraka Saturn in the 2nd enabled him to earn considerable wealth but Saturn in the 2nd and the 12th strongly rendered made him spend all his earnings and rendered the financial situation extremely precarious. His death took place in the sub-period of the Moon in Saturn Dasa.

In 1926-27, we continued to stay at Bangalore and I joined the Government Collegiate High School for my studies. My own ego continued to develop to such an extent that I felt I knew a lot of Astrology; and the obsession that my "attainments" were not given the recognition which in my own opinion they merited had gripped me. I could cast horoscopes and could give textbook interpretations with a daring which, I now feel, was nothing but foolhardiness. Grandfather's frequent admonitions, watch your step, was not being taken very seriously.

		Rahu		Mercury	Ketu	Moon Mandi
	RASI	Jupit.	Venus	NAVAMSA		Sat. Sun
		Moon				
Ascdt Ketu Sat. Mandi		Sun Merc. Venus		Ascdt Rahu		Jupit.

Sir Banerjee used to consult grandfather frequently. Once there was a discussion of his horoscope and I was allowed to be present. Sir Banerjee was born on 10-10-1871 at 2 p.m. at Bristol. At the time he consulted grandfather, he was particular to know whether the term of his Dewanship would continue after 1927. This consultation was in 1926. Grandfather seems to have felt that a "budding astrologer"

like me should not be entirely ignored and he wanted my "opinion".
I figured out that Mercury in Rahu lasted till 23-3-1927. Mercury is
a Yogakaraka because of his association with the Sun and placement
in the 10th. Rahu, the major lord, occupying the 7th which happens
to be Mercury's sign should give the results of Mercury. And I felt I
was fortified in my conclusion by a *sloka* in *Jataka Chandrica,*
according to which, a shadowy planet should give the results of the
lord of the sign he is in. Therefore Sir Banerjee would continue to be
the Dewan not only throughout Mercury's sub-period but also during
Ketu's sub-period as Ketu is in Sagittarius and the dispositor Jupiter
is exalted.

Grandfather cut me to size and said that in the latter part of
Mercury he would cease to be Dewan. I stuck to my guns. He said
that I was young and immature and that my application of text-book
principles verbatim should give place to an appreciation of the exact
import of a combination and how it would express itself. He said :
"Look here, you are intelligent, sincere and persistent but you lack
experience and intuition which you can acquire gradually." He went
on: "Though Mercury has all the qualifications of Raja Yoga, he is in
conjunction with Venus lord of the 6th (and 11th) in the constellation
of the Moon, lord of the 8th."

I interjected: "But the 8th house blemish does not attach to the
Moon." But he silenced me with the remark that the dictum applied
only to *maraka* cases. As anticipated by him, Sir Banerjee had to quit
the Dewanship before the end of Mercury's sub-period. This deflated
my ego to some extent and I began to appreciate the virtues of
humility.

As I progressed in my astrological knowledge I could not easily
reconcile to the dictum that the 8th lordship of the Moon could always
be malefic. And I must say with due deference to grandfather's own
opinion, that after more than five decades of experience I have not
changed my view. The Moon, as lord of the 8th can be harmful if he
is a malefic and if he lacks *pakshabala.* But if he is a benefice and
well-placed, he cannot produce harmful results though owning the 8th.
This 8th lordship is peculiar to Sagittarius. Most persons born in this

sign have had initial disappointments but phenomenal rise especially when Mercury and the Sun are in the 9th or 10th and the Moon occupies the 3rd, 6th, 10th, or 11th.

Sir Banerji's personal life was a tragic one. He married in 1898 and his wife died in 1943. She was a social cock and was said to have been carrying on affairs with all sorts of men. Lord of the 7th Mercury is in the 10th in conjunction with Venus and aspected by Saturn. The 7th house has the maximum affliction centred on it because Rahu is situated there aspected by Saturn and Mars. The Navamsa is equally afflicted. The native himself was said to be a glutton for sexual experiences. He could never adapt himself to the restraints of marriage with the result he went after every woman, respectable or disrespectable, that he could trap through the usual "social" contacts.

When he met me in July 1947, he was a lonely figure, living with two servants. He wanted to know about his longevity as he was then suffering from arthritis. He confessed to me about his and his wife's exploits in extra marital affairs. It appears the couple had agreed between themselves that, each should have his or her own way so far as their private lives were concerned.

My prediction about his longevity was that the end of Jupiter's period (August 1950) would prove fatal. Jupiter is no doubt lord of Lagna but he is in Pushyami, ruled by Saturn, who is a Maraka both from the Ascendant and the Moon. Based on the *Prasna Marga* theory, Saturn would be transiting his own Niryana Rasi about February/March 1950 and this could prove fatal. He died on 26th February 1950.

In 1917 or so, I accompanied grandfather on his visit to His Highness Sri Krishnaraja Wadiyar, the then Maharaja of Mysore, in response to the latter's invitation. The Maharaja was keen to know whether the line of succession in the Mysore Royal family would continue. His dignified bearing and cultivated and polished manners fascinated me. Mr Mirza M. Ismail (who was later knighted), A.D.C. to the Maharaja was also present at the meeting for a couple of minutes and then he withdrew leading me out of the room. Grandfather later told Sir Mirza that His Highness was not particular in getting an issue himself but that he desired that his brother, the Yuvaraja, should get a son. Grandfather not only suggested remedial measures but also had them performed for 9 months. And in 1919, Sri Jayachamaraja Wadiyar was born.

		Sun Merc Sat.		Ascdt Ketu			Mars
Ketu							
	Chart No. 2 RASI		Ascdt Jup. Venus		NAVAMSA		Sun Venus Sat
			Mars Mandi	Merc			
		Moon	Rahu			Moon Jupit.	Rahu

The Maharaja's horoscope interested me much*. When I was about 20 by which time I was supposed to be familiar with the general astrological principles, I was curious to know as to why the Maharaja did not get any children, though the lord of the 5th, viz., Mars was aspecting the 5th from the 2nd. Grandfather's explanation was : The 5th house was much afflicted because of the combined influence on it of three malefics, viz., the Sun, Mercury and Saturn. The 5th lord Mars was rendered weak because of his association with Mandi. From Chandra Lagna lord of the 5th is Saturn and the 5th is aspected both by Saturn and Mars. In the Navamsa again the 5th house is occupied by the Sun and Saturn (and Venus). These are unfavourable combinations preventing birth of children as grandfather explained to me. Moreover all the three houses connected with married life, viz., the 7th the 2nd and 11th are all afflicted. The Maharaja's married life was unhappy. It was rumoured that the husband and wife never had any marital relations.

* He was born on 4-6-1884 at 10-18 a.m. at Mysore.

A couple of months before the Maharaja died, Sir Mirza called on grandfather to ascertain the longevity of the ruler. The prediction was that the end of Mercury in Mercury would be fatal : and the death could be due to some sort of "paralysis". Grandfather's reasoning was : "It is a *yogayus* horoscope, which means when the lord of Lagna is in the 4th and the lord of the 8th is at a place other than a *kendra* or a *thrikona* and the lords of the Lagna and the 8th are disposed in *dwirdwadasa* (2nd and 12th) or *shashtashtaka* (6th and 8th), the

Moon		Ketu	Mars	Ketu	Merc.	Saturn	Mandi
	Chart No. 3 RASI		Sun Jupit.		NAVAMSA		
			Merc. Venus Sat. Mandi				Sun Jupit.
Ascdt.	Rahu						Rahu Moon Venus

maximum longevity could not be more than 60. Mercury in Mercury should prove fatal as Mercury as lord of the 12th is in the 8th from the Moon and occupies the constellation of the Sun, a *maraka*. Mercury occupies Krittika and is blemished by the Sun and Saturn. The native may become afflicted with paralysis". The Maharaja died as predicted.

When Sri Jayachamaraja Wadiyar was born on 18–7–1919 at 6–17 p.m at Mysore, grandfather saw *rajabrastha yogas* in his horoscope and predicted "loss of kingdom". Venus would be the villain of the piece because of his lordship of the 6th and 11th and situation in the 9th. In support of this grandfather quoted a *sloka* from *Garga Samhita*. The association of Venus with Saturn and Mandi, would deprive him of his kingdom. It was in Venus Dasa that the Maharaja lost everything, except his reputation as a righteous and noble man.

His Highness Sri Jayachamaraja Wadiyar, the last Maharaja of Mysore, sought from me astrological guidance on some occasions. In 1963, he presided over two of my special lectures delivered at the Mysore University. He was then the Governor of Madras besides being the Chancellor of the University. In fact His Highness had strongly endorsed my plea for the introduction of Astrology at the Mysore University. We had met several times after 1969. But three years before his death, he sought my advice on an important matter. There was an alleged attempt to poison him. The Maharaja had suspected some of his relatives. A.G. Ramachandra Rao, a former Education Minister who was in the confidence of the Maharaja and another Congressman Siddaveerappa who was till recently a Minister in Karnataka, came all the way from Mysore with a religious head seeking my astrological opinion as to who could be behind the alleged attempt. When I told them that such predictions could be given only to the person concerned, His Highness sent word to me and we had a long discussion at his summer palace. Being himself a keen student of Astrology, he appreciated my arguments and expressed satisfaction that my finding endorsed his suspicion. He did not however wish to pursue the matter further or publicise it. He said that he believed in what he called "Divine dispensation". I had indicated to him then that Mars sub–period in the Sun. Dasa might prove fatal to his life and he was advised remedial measures. But by then he had become a stoic and the flagrant violation by the then Government of India of the assurances given to him (and other Indian rulers) by Sardar Vallabhbhai Patel had made him sorrowful and resigned to his fate.

The fear that I would die at the end of Rahu Dasa persisted until 1932, when on a certain day grandfather, explaining the chapter on Ayurdaya in *Brihat Jataka*, removed my misgivings and said that because of the dispositions of the planets *(in my horoscope) in *Kendras*, the Sun in the 6th and the Lagna, the Sun and the Moon all being aspected by Jupiter, Purnayu or a full term of life was assured. According to him, the Ascendant and the 8th and their lords should

---

*I was born on 8–8–1912 A. D. at Bangalore at 7^h 42^m 44^s P.M. (1ST).

be beneficially disposed receiving the aspect or association of either Jupiter or Venus. He always laid stress on the situation in a *kendra* of the lord of the Lagna or Jupiter or Venus. But in my humble experience, the mere presence of one of these lords in a *Kendra*, should not be the sole criterion for determining the longevity. In the light of experience one has to revise one's views and experience has taught me the basic truth that in Astrology, a literal application of textbook rules should not be done.

2

I distinctly remember that on my twelfth birthday, my grandfather revealed to the members of the family and friends present on the occasion that I would become a great astrologer, due to certain definite planetary patterns obtaining in my horoscope. I was able to gather from him, later on, that the combination which warranted his anticipations about my future were : Gajakesari, *i.e.*, the disposition of the Moon and Jupiter in mutual angles, all planets being confined to angles. He was laying stress on the strength of the Ascendant and the fortification or otherwise of the lord. Grandfather had a flair for uncanny prediction and in analyzing the combinations that indicated a certain event. In my own case, he laid stress on the strong disposition of the tenth house by the conjunction of Jupiter with the meridian point and the strengthening of the Ascendant and the Ascendant lord by the aspect of all the three benefices, *viz.*, Mercury, Jupiter and Venus. He observed about me : "This boy is certain to become a great writer and will, from what I could see from his horoscope, make a name for himself in Astrology."

In 1928 I shifted to Bangalore and joined Intermediate Arts class. For a while I had to stay with a distant relative of ours, who had been indebted to grandfather for securing him a job in the post office. The house was situated in a lane in Cottonpet. I felt very uncomfortable and was waiting for an opportunity to leave the place. An aunt of mine lived in Chamarajapet. I would go to my aunt's place for bath, have coffee and get back to the Cottonpet residence by 8–30 a.m. I would be given food at 10–30 a.m. and would rush to the college so as to be there by 11 a.m. This period of six months from

July to December 1928 was one of agony and financial distress. Every week-end I would go to the village and get back to Bangalore on Monday morning in time for college.

One night while waiting in a Railway Station to catch a train to Mysore, my eyes caught sight of a book with the zodiac drawn on the cover. I immediately bought it. It was a translation into English of a German work on Astrology. As the train started on its journey, I became engrossed in its contents. There were two other occupants— Englishmen — in the carriage who sat opposite me. When my book was finished and as I laid it down, I noticed that the eyes of one of the two persons were fixed on the drawing of the zodiac that adorned the cover. In a bantering way, he said : "You evidently believe in Astrology. I wonder even in the 20th century there should be people reading books on Astrology." "Yes", I answered : "I believe that character and career make themselves manifest as expressions of our previous karma which are indicated in the horoscope. Creation is cosmos, not chaos. If the planetary systems represent the macrocosm or Brahmanda and the individual represents the microcosm or Pindanda, then it is logical to assume that changes taking place in the macrocosm have their vicissitudes on the microcosm also."

He looked amused : "But do the stars tell the future ? That is the point that would appeal to me if I could bring myself to believe in such a thing". "Well," I said, "As far as our future is determined by the tendencies we have inherited, I certainly believe that there is some sort of correlation between the movements of stars and events in life." "Very well," he said, "your point of view has really interested me. Tell me if you can, whether I will be successful in my attempts to start a business in the near future?" I can even now clearly conceive the planetary positions at the time he put the query. I constructed a chart mentally. I explained to him the rationale of Horary Astrology or Prasna and how the birth of an idea was as important as the birth of an individual. I explained the relevant good and bad aspects prevailing at the time of the question and then I called his attention to the position of Saturn in the 10th house in the asterism of destruction and that of Jupiter lord of Ascendant in the 4th house and said that the venture would be a success within six months. But by the time Saturn and Jupiter in the course of their transits would be exactly in conjunction, the business would collapse.

Stretching himself comfortably, the man laughed. By now it was past midnight and I got into my berth. It was in 1940 when both Jupiter and Saturn were retrograde in Aries, that he met with a financial crash and committed suicide. It was then that I realised the significance of the movements of Saturn and the Moon's ascending Node with regard to the Ascendant at the time of a question. This is one of the most important principles in Horary Astrology that has found illustration in a number of cases which I had to deal with subsequently.

The period between 1928 and 1931 was of enormous significance in my life. It was during these years that the real foundation for my future astrological proficiency was laid. While in college, I was more interested in ransacking books available in the library on Logic and History than confining my attention to purely text-books. Logic always intrigued me. I felt logic would be useful in enabling me to get a clear picture of the theory of Astrological knowledge. In studying horoscopes, we arrive at certain inferences. And the inferences can be valid when they are justified by the evidence given in support of them. For example an inference is drawn regarding longevity— this inference being justified by the evidence, i.e., (planetary combinations) given in support of it. It did not occur to me then that an inference could be true only if it expressed the facts as they were. Sometimes we may make inferences which turn out to be true though they may not be justified by the available evidence. Logic is the study of valid inference, not true inference. And in Astrology, the inference must not only be valid but true. The study of the conditions of true inference would mean, an investigation into the truth of all possible premises — an obviously impossible task, and hence the limitations of the logical approach in regard to drawing astrological inferences.

Our logic lecturer, one Thirumalai, was hard of hearing and some what short-tempered. He would insist on our taking copious notes which he would dictate patiently. We were then expected to memorize all that we took down. This was a hard job for me. There were a set of boys who used to faithfully carry out these instructions and who became the favourites of the lecturer. On my part I only tried to understand the subject. In the first terminal examination, the marks got in logic were read aloud in the classroom. My marks were not revealed and I was asked to see the lecturer in his room which I did. The teacher said that my performance in the examination had belied said that my performance in the examination had belied his expectations of my scoring very poor marks. I had not been carrying out his instructions and that he had information that I was devoting more of my time to Astrology than to logic but that he was glad to find that I had got over 60% in a subject which required more of cramming than intelligent understanding. "Of course, Sir", I replied, "I have a mania for astrological studies and one of the reasons why I have selected logic as an optional subject is to enable me to apply logic to Astrology".

"If that is so," retorted Thirumalai," your choice of logic as an aid to the study of Astrology is eminently unsuitable. Logic tells you how to reason but it cannot enable you to arrive at truth. It can even belie truth by clever arguments." I was surprised at these remarks but was wholly unconcerned about my choice of optional subjects. Thirumalai knew something of Astrology. He took up the horoscope of a girl who had died in her 5th year and went on adducing arguments in favour of long life, tearing out my contentions that combinations for infant mortality were present. Youth, want of experience, over–enthusiasm and over–confidence were all on my side. He wound up the discussion with the remarks : "Astrology is not a science in the sense of physics or mathematics, the study of which requires adherence to the conventionalities of common–sense reasoning and ordinary logic. It is not a mere appeal to the reasoning faculty of man but is an appeal to his hidden powers and capacities. A certain amount of intuitive capacity must be brought to bear upon attempts at studying horoscopes. Astrology deals with living beings and not with physical matter. Therefore cold reasoning devoid of intuitive perception will lead you to incorrect conclusions. Try to cultivate your powers of intuition."

This partly opened my eyes to the limitations of the logical approach in the matter of astrological problems.

In narrating my experiences, the reader may perhaps feel that I have studiously omitted making reference to predictions that may not have been fulfilled. There have been instances where my predictions have either gone wrong or have partially come true. And I shall refer to some of them in the subsequent chapters. In the majority of cases I have had the good fortune of making successful predictions.

When I had put in a term of six months or so in the pre–degree class, I had to discontinue my studies, because I was required to assist grandfather in his work. Disappointed and purposeless, I felt I would drift like a rudderless ship. In the meantime, however, I used to be given now and then some instructions in predictive Astrology. I studied astronomy and mathematical Astrology by myself without anybody's guidance and mastered almost the entire range of astrological mathematics. My favourite books were the ancient classics on Astrology and astronomy. Within the period of the next three years, what I lost in general education was more than compensated for by the astrological and astronomical equipment I was able to accumulate.

3

Our family was passing through a crisis. An ulcer in the right foot, operated in 1926, continued to trouble grandfather restricting his physical movements. Father's eye-sight had practically failed. My uncle the late Mr. B. Lakshminarain Rao was in Government educational service, away from Bangalore. I had therefore to chose between continuing my education and my responsibilities to grandfather and the family. Thanks to my own conscience the latter course was chosen. My college studies were discontinued in December 1928.

Frequent visitors to our place ranged from the Maharaja of Mysore to the Dewan, Chief Justice Plummer and members of Council Messrs. K. Chandy, P.G. D'Souza and K.R. Srinivasa Iyengar, not to speak of the lesser fry. My work consisted in receiving the V.I.Ps, providing them with light refreshments and seeing them off after their discussions with grandfather were over. Another important assignment given to me was to keep ready horoscope-castings, working out Dasa etc., upto the time of consultation. I would patiently listen to the analysis made by grandfather and register it in my memory.

Stealing what little time was possible after attending to an endless list of daily chores, I would commit to memory *slokas* from *Jataka Chandrika and Brihat Jataka*.

It so happened around that time, an astronomer Suryanarayana Siddhanti, hailing from Andhra, stayed with us for nearly a year. He spent most of his time computing the *Panchanga* or almanac. My curiosity roused, I started learning these calculations from him. Apart from *Surya Siddhanta*, a hand-written Telugu copy of which he possessed, we studied two other *Karanagranthas* or hand-books, *viz.*,

Ahobaleeyam in Telugu script and *Khachara Darpana* in Kannada script, the latter said to have been written by Adi Sankaracharya. Tedious and cumbersome arithmetical calculations — addition, subtraction, multiplication and division — had to be done taking into consideration, the *ahargana* (the number of days passed from an epoch) and the revolutions in a Mahayuga made by the different planets, to get *madhya grahas* (mean positions) and conversion of *madhya–grahas* into *sphuta grahas* (true positions), by the application of *mandochha* (apogee, aphelion) and *seeghrochha* (perigee, perihelion) etc. I had then no idea of modern astronomy and was ignorant of trigonometry though I had a fairly good knowledge of geometry and algebra. I would marvel then at the intelligence of the ancient astronomers, who, without employing higher mathematics, even though they knew it, devised methods based on arithmetic alone to enable the rank and file to calculate the positions of planets. *Khachara Darpana* was precise, brief and to the point and it appealed to me.

My studies in astronomy progressed fairly well covering *madhyamadhikara* (mean motions), *spashtaahikara* (true places) and *triprasnadhikara* (direction, place and time) in *Surya Siddhanta*.

These chapters covered also such details as *chaya* (shadow), *bhuja* (equinoctial distance), calculation of tithi, yoga, Karana, etc. When we reached *suryagrahanadhyaya* (solar eclipse), the study had to be curtailed for the reason that grandfather took strong objection to what he called my "meddling" with the planets. He said, those who probed into these secrets would eventually become most unfortunate losing their wives and children and that *grihasthas* (family people) should not compute *panchangas*.

During this period one of the occasional visitors to our house was Mahamahopadhyaya Sri Siva Sankara Sastry, a great Sanskrit scholar and astronomer. He was generally good to me and would explain any intricate passages I came across in the two books of my study . Once there was a discussion on the subject of Ayanamsa between Sri Sastry and grandfather. I and the Siddhanti were also present. The discussion hinged on stanza 9 of Chapter III (*trimsat krityo yugebhanam chakram prakparilambate*), especially the words *trimsat krityo* which according to the commentary of Ranganatha means 600 times, which means the equinox oscillates 600 times in a Mahayuga (43,20,000 years) from the fixed point near Zeta Piscium. But Bhaskaracharya in his *Siddhantasiromani* says that according to *Surya Siddhanta* it is *trimsatkritye, i.e.,* the period of retrograde revolution of the equinox is 30 in a Mahayuga, which means the rate of precession is about 9" a year. It was explained that in the version of *Surya Siddhanta* then available to Bhaskara, there might have been an interpolation with the consequence *trimsatkritye* instead of *trimsatkrityo* was found, Bhaskara himself gives the number of revolutions of the equinox as 1,99,669 in a Kalpa (4,320 million years) which gives the yearly rate of precession as 59".9007.

It was suggested by Sri Sastry that 54" should be accepted as the rate of precession, on the basis of the *Surya Siddhanta* definition of the precession of the equinoxes. However grandfather had his own reservations and preferred the modern value of approximately 50" 1/3. This discussion did not interest me much at that time. I had no access to Western ephemerides and all castings were being done according to *panchangas.* Later on as my knowledge of Hindu astronomy progressed, I realised the importance of such a discussion and the justification for preferring 54" as precessional value by the traditional astronomers.

The text–book I used was *Surya Siddhanta* (in Sanskrit) with Ranganatha's commentary published in 1896. My interest in understanding the intricacies of calculating eclipses could be whetted down only after I came into possession of a copy of the English translation of *Surya Siddhanta* by Rev. Burgess. It was said Burgess was a bigotted missionary and some of his remarks were highly prejudiced. But his textual translation, I was told, was quite factual.

When the late Mr. L. Narain Rao, author of "Perpetual Ephemeris", met me in 1942 or so he endorsed grandfather's opinion that *panchanga* calculations should not be done by householders. He cited his own case that he was childless as he had done a lot of 'probing' into the planetary movements. Many beliefs such as this, held by a section of the educated public, cannot of course be given credence. But, it has been within my knowledge that some of the astronomers, whose sole profession was *panchanga* calculation, have met with serious calamities, besides suffering poverty.

My training under Suryanarayana Siddhanti gave me a good grounding in Hindu astronomy which as years passed on enabled me to understand well modern astronomy.

The Siddhanti was also a bit of an astrologer in his own way. Questions by local and other villagers bearing on disappearance of cattle, theft, illness, success and failure in undertakings, missing persons, etc., referred to grandfather used to be generally passed on to the Siddhanti.

He was fairly accurate in his answers. I give below some of the simple methods he used.

Add together the number of the *tithi* (lunar day), *weekday* (beginning from Sunday), *nakshatra* (from Aswini), *yama* (1/8th of a day) and the direction in which the querist stands or sits (east 1, south–east 2, south 3 etc.). Divide the total by 8. If the remainder is 1,3,7, the object in view will be fulfilled in 20 days; 2–8—failure; 4,6, in 3 days; 5, very soon. For example on 15th September 1979 at 2 p.m a person wants to know when the object in view will be fulfilled. Adding the *tithi* (10), weekday (Saturday—7), *nakshatra* (Aridra—6), the *yama* (2–40 p.m.—5) and the direction facing (west—5), the total comes to 33. Dividing this by 8, the remainder is 1, which means the object will be fulfilled within 20 days.

Regarding the return of a person who has gone out of station count from Krittika constellation to the constellation of the day. Divide this by 7. If the remainder is 1, he will be still in the place of visit; if 2, he will return very early; if 3, he will have left the place and gone to some other place; if 4, he will return on the same day the question was put; if 5, his return will be delayed; if 6, he will be ill; and if 7 or 0, he will return in anguish. These methods may seem too simplistic and be dismissed as unscientific. But the village astrologers swear that they work and they are successful in the majority of cases. I give below some more methods for the readers' information.

A query pertaining to the sex of the child to be born can be answered thus : Add together the number of letters in the lady's name, the lunar day, the weekday number and 25. Divide this by 9. If the remainder is an even number, the child is female; if odd, male. In regard to a question bearing on loss of an article : Add together the number of the lunar day, weekday and constellation and 3. Divide it by 5. If the remainder is 1, the article is on the ground or floor in the house; if 2, in water or watery places nearby; if 3, concealed under some debris; if 4, will not be found; and if 5, will be got back after much delay.

I picked up quite a number of such methods bearing on different aspects of life—marriage, birth of children, disease, death, etc. For instance when a person falls ill on the 12th lunar day coinciding with Sunday and the constellation of Makha, he will suffer for a long time. Similarly the following combinations prolong the illness delaying recovery and causing complication; 11th lunar day with Visakha and Thursday; the 5th lunar day, Aridra and Thursday; 3rd lunar day, Uttarashadha and Wednesday; 6th lunar day, Satabhisha and Thursday; 8th lunar day, Aswini and Friday; and 9th lunar day, Poorvashadha and Saturday, especially when these stars happen to be the 1st, 3rd, 5th and 7th from one's birth constellation.

The Chandragarbha and Chakra can also be considered as fairly reliable methods to answer questions pertaining to illness. These methods may have some rationale, some sort of a sequence between numerological and psychological factors.

About 2 miles from out village in a place called Suggatta, there lived an arrogant *mantravadi* (Sorcerer) by name Sangappa, a Lingayat by caste. He was a terror to the villagers all round. He claimed to reveal the past, present and future by a process known as "gazing at the thumb". For this, the nail on the right thumb was to be smeared with a drop of a special oil. Raising the thumb to the level of the eye, one gazed at the oil–smeared nail until he could see enacted before him, as on a television screen the past and future of the querist. I tried this method for a while but found it useless. Sangappa was said to be an expert in this art. By his "mantric power" he claimed to paralyse one's limbs, or damage one's mind or cause misfortunes to the enemy. All such tales about Sangappa did not frighten me. He was the brother–in–law of one Parvatappa who was in charge of our lands at Suggatta.

Once I paid a surprise visit to Sangappa's place which frightened him. It happened in the following circumstance. Two farmers not on good terms with Sangappa complained of the theft of their goats. This was an opportunity for me, I thought, to test the methods I had learnt from the Siddhanti. I figured out that the culprit was Sangappa himself. When I told him that I had looked into the *prasna* and found out he was the thief, he got so upset, he threatened to call into operation all the "spirits" at his command to see that I lost my power of speech. I was not frightened in the least. I told him his *kshudra vidya* would have no effect on me. The police meanwhile found he had stolen the goats but no case was registered. He was let off with a warning. Sangappa offered to initiate me into what he called *karnapisachi mantra* so that I could answer "any question bearing on theft, illness,etc". Though I rejected his offer, the idea that I must also practise some such *mantra* persisted until the happening of another episode described below. Once I had to present myself before the Amildar at Devanahally in response to a notice sent by him to grandfather that all gun–owners should personally appear before him to get their licences renewed. Before meeting the Amildar, I found out astrologically on the basis of the methods I had just learnt, that I would not succeed. This did not dampen my spirits and I decided to meet him all the same. Amildars or (Tahsildars) in those days commanded much respect which today even ministers do not. He said that the licence would be renewed only if the owner, and not anyone on his behalf, came. This was too much for me. Grandfather moved on equal terms with the ministers and maharajas and how could this petty official summon him, so I thought. I lost my temper and declared I would see that the Amildar himself visited our place, apologised and renewed the licence. I left immediately in anger.

After a week, Mr. P.G. D'Souza, a member of the Council, called on grandfather to seek his advice on some matters. I reported to Mr

D'Souza the impertinent and disrespectful behaviour of the Amildar towards grandfather. Within three days, the Amildar came to our place, apologised and renewed the licence. Later on we became friends and met occasionally until 1968 or 1969 when he passed away.

Mr D'Souza, a Mangalore Catholic Christian , was well known

Ascdt.	Rahu					Mars Jupiter	Rahu Sat.
			Moon				
Sat.	RASI		Sun Mars Merc.		NAVAMSA		
		Venus Ketu	Jupit.	Venus Ketu	Moon Ascdt. Sun Mercury		

for his integrity, efficiency and administrative ability. He knew grandfather even from the days of his holding subordinate positions in the State. He was born on 7–9–1874 at about 7-45 p.m., near Mangalore.

He had to face a tough problem involving his reputation about the beginning of 1926, when he was at the fag end of the Sun Dasa. I was asked to find out the problem and what the outcome would be. I figured it out thus : The Sun as lord of the 6th is in the 6th ruling enemies, debts and diseases. He is with Mars (lord of the 2nd and the 9th) and Mercury (lord of the 4th and the 7th). From Chandra Lagna, the Sun as lord of the 2nd is in the 2nd no doubt with Yogakaraka Mars; but the lord of the 3rd and the 12th Mercury is also involved suggesting some financial involvement and displeasure of the ruler. But as the Moon Dasa was about to commence, the native would come out unscathed.

Imagine my happiness when grandfather told me that my analysis was fairly accurate and that one day I would also become a great astrologer. This was my first successful prediction. He was so pleased with my performance that he presented me with a lace *dhoti*.

In Mr. D'Souza's horoscope, the Moon ruling the mind is not afflicted. He was good tempered though somewhat impulsive. Saturn's aspect made him always worried. Lord of the Ascendant in the 7th unafflicted gave him a loving wife, despite the fact that Venus is associated with Ketu and aspected by Saturn. This is a case in point to suggest that merely on the basis of the affliction of *kalatrakaraka*, one should not conclude that one's marriage would be unhappy or one will have a second marriage. Here it will be seen that Venus is in his own house.

In this horoscope *putrakaraka* Jupiter happens to be lord of the Ascendant and is well placed in the 7th. Lord of the 5th, the Moon, is in his own house in the 5th in the constellation of Saturn who also aspects the 5th house. Mr. D'Souza had 18 children. Mrs. D'Souza was indeed proud of what she called "her wealth". I met Mr. D'Souza again in 1959 or 1960, after my return from U.S.A. He expressed his happiness over my successful life. He wanted to know about his longevity. He was told that his 87th year would be critical. And he died at this age.

In the beginning of 1929 a man called Syed Ibrahim who styled himself a fakir came to stay with us to treat father's defective eyesight. He claimed that he was a Syed and hence as good as a Brahmin. He spoke chaste Kannada and knew something of Astrology. But for his name he was all Hindu. He said that he would be able to restore father's vision by some herbal treatment. He claimed to be a *mantric* and herbalist. To whet my appetite he gave me a book in Kannada which described some *mantras* and the miracles they would enable one to perform including the revelation of the past, present and future. This fascinated me. He used to describe the use of the various herbs and how by practising certain *mantras* in a burial place one could control spirits which would always be at one's beck and call enabling one to perform miracles. Ibrahim was a lean anatomical structure, of medium height with a goaty beard and donned a black lungi in the fashion of South Indian Muslims. He persuaded me to undergo "training" in this "art".

The night of a New Moon day was chosen as auspicious to commence this *vidya*. Our watchman was bribed four annas to keep our adventure secret. After everyone at home had gone to sleep, Ibrahim led me to the cremation ground. Actually it was a grave-yard as the majority population in the village were Lingayats and Vokkaligas, and ours was the only Brahmin family.

In those days the surroundings were not quite safe during night times as a gang of robbers was said to be on the prowl attacking passers-by. Generally it was not safe to set out after 10 o'clock in the night. But Ibrahim claimed that he had control over a number of spirits and anyone approaching him with harmful intentions would become unconscious and collapse the moment he invoked his controlled spirit.

I was made to sit facing the south after a bath in a nearby pond. He pretended to be talking to his spirit guide, waved a wand in front of me from right to left and asked me to close my eyes. This done, he murmured in my left ear what he called Karna Pisachi *mantra*. The *mantra* read: *kahakale kalika pinda pisacha hrimphat*. Later on I learnt that the suffix *phat* is used only when the object in view is destructive. He asked me to repeat it 108 times and said that I might even see immediately a small female figure with a dark body, three blood-red eyes, big stomach, white tongue, holding human skulls in two hands and shedding smoke and coloured flame from her body with flowing hair strewn on both the cheeks. All this ritual did not frighten me in the least because of the conviction I had developed that one who regularly recited *Gayatri Mantra* could not be harmed by any spirits.

This exercise to "control spirits" was continued on the next *krishnashtami* and *chaturdasi* (8th and 14th lunar days of the dark half). Ibrahim had instructed me to report to him the moment I saw any vision of the type he had described. I also imagined sometimes that I had begun seeing such an apparition. But on the next New Moon day (*i.e.*, exactly one lunar month after) when the exercise was about to start, our gardener by name Jhampaliga chanced to pass through the grave-yard. He was struck dumb to see me with Ibrahim at such an odd hour at a prohibited place. He immediately reported the matter to grandfather. The next morning I was strongly rebuked and warned that I had taken to a pernicious practice which would ruin my life and family and result in a tragic end to my own life. Ibrahim was asked to quit immediately despite his protests that the treatment of father's eyes was only half-done. It was subsequently discovered that the only treatment he had been giving had been to put two drops of the juice of *nandivardana* flower twice daily into father's eyes.

Grandfather's admonition that one should never resort to *kshudra mantras, ucchista mantras* etc., had the desired effect on me. I bade farewell once for all to my misdirected adventure to secure control over spirits.

Grandfather's advice was that an astrologer should always practise a *mahamantra* to enable him to develop his predictive power. It was decades later after most of my forecasts, whether bearing on nations or individuals, were fulfilled that I was able to understand the meaning and significance of a *mahamantra*.

4

Endless discussions used to go on at *Suryalaya* — this was the name of our residence at the village, during the life time of grandfather — on the relative implications of 'fate' and 'free-will' amongst scholars visiting our place. Still very young in age and intellectually immature, I would silently watch the discussions which sometimes took the form of heated arguments. But grandfather would remark that arguments would not solve fundamental questions. He was not a fatalist. He believed that by right action an indicated evil could be overcome. Such abstruse questions were out of my comprehension, though I now feel that they could have then registered themselves on my subconscious mind, and surfaced as my powers of thinking and comprehension grew.

In support of his thesis that one can neutralise powerful planetary afflictions grandfather would cite a number of practical cases handled by him, the most important of which was the birth of a son to the Yuvaraja of Mysore. To quote his own words from *Royal Horoscopes* : "The Mysore Royal Family lies under a deep curse and for over 2 centuries, the succession has been one legitimate and the next adoption. The present Maharaja had no children. I was desired to get some *santhis* performed for removing that curse and I am happy to observe that through God's grace as per the desire of the ruling Maharaja his brother Yuvaraja got a son, vindicating the efficacy of remedies and the usefulness of the science of Astrology for humanity".

Discontinuance of my college studies and acting as secretary to the great man that grandfather was had its own impact on me. Listening to grandfather's discussions and eloquent speeches contributed not a little to moulding my own thinking and paving the way for my taking a decision that I should champion the cause of our ancient culture in general and Astrology in particular, come what may. My vague so-called scientific ideas of my short-lived college days receded to the background.

In 1928, during my brief sojourn in the Intermediate College (now Government Arts and Science College) in Bangalore I had some interesting experiences. The ancient history teacher M. Pranatharthiharan, a short stout and aggressive gentleman, used to insist on us taking copious notes as he went on lecturing on Myonan civilization, or the rule of Xerxes etc. I resented this imposition but was too timid to assert myself. One day I was asked to meet him in the teachers' room. He had powerful command over the English language and scolded me using choice words for my 'disobedience'. I collected myself and coolly replied that being a student of Astrology, I was observing his gestures, the way he spoke, etc., in the class-room and hence I could not take any notes. "Then you are an astrologer," quipped Haran. "Yes", I replied, "I am a budding astrologer and can see your future." He demanded that I gave him proof. I retorted: "Your Ascendant could be Sagittarius, as you are stout; Rahu could be in the second because of your gestures and style

			Venus
Rahu		10-1-1897	Sun
			Mercury Jupiter Mars Ketu
Ascendant Moon	Saturn		

of speaking, and you have no happiness from your wife." Mr. Haran
cooled down and meekly said that I was correct in every respect. "But
, how could you say all this without a horoscope" he exclaimed. I
gathered some courage within myself and said it was Astrology plus
intuition. Mr. Haran was a brilliant scholar in ancient history. His wife
was always ailing with suspected tuberculosis. We became "friends".
From that day onwards he never took me to task for not taking notes.
In the mid-session examination I got more than 70% in ancient history
and I was complimented.

I have reproduced above the chart given to me by Haran.

Two of my conclusions, viz., the Ascendant and the wife's illness
were correct. Lord of the 7th Mercury is in the 9th with Mars and
Ketu and Jupiter, aspected by Saturn. Though Venus is well placed
in the 7th, lord of that house, Mercury is afflicted. The lady suffered
from a lingering disease. It was only in 1941 or 1942 when I was
struggling against innumerable odds to assert myself as an exponent
of Astrology that I met my old teacher. He was still in service but
was showing signs of premature aging due to domestic problems.

Thirumalai, an M.A. to whom I have referred earlier, was our
logic teacher. His exposition of the dry subject in the class-room was
quite interesting and entertaining. Being a friend of my uncle the late
B. Lakshminarain Rao, Thirumalai began to take some interest not
only in my studies but also in my astrological "activities". He knew
Astrology fairly well and would often put me into embarrassing
situations by quoting from Tamil classics. Once it was my turn to
"challenge" him. It was in the following circumstance.

An elderly colleague of his had a serious health problem. His
Lagna was Leo and Saturn was in the 7th. He was almost at the fag
end of Saturn Dasa. Thirumalai cited Tamil texts in support of his
conclusion that his colleague would not recover from his serious
illness. I controverted his conclusion taking cover under a dictum of
Jataka Chandrika — this was the only text I then knew fairly well
— that "Saturn does not kill the native even if endowed with Maraka
powers" because the Lagna was Leo. Unfortunately for Thirumalai,
his colleague recovered after an operation. I felt that a new feather

had been added to my cap and told my teacher in a haughty tone that since he was a logician he would not be able to make correct forecasts. Pride before fall is as true as dusk after sunset.

From that day onwards I was the object of special attention in the class-room by the logic teacher. The controversy between *adrishta* or *vidhi* (so–called fatalism) and *purushakara* or *ichchasakti* (so called will-power) was being discussed in the teachers' room by other teachers also joining the discussion, sometimes resulting in heated arguments. My intellectual capacity was nominal and inadequate to enter into serious discussions but still I was pressing my point of view, based neither on experience nor on theoretical knowledge, that one could change one's future entirely by effort, remedial measures, etc. Thirumalai would tear my thesis to shreds by his logical arguments. While not owning defeat, I would merely say that logic was no good for Astrology. Thirumalai would assert that logic was an essential ingredient for establishing the truth or otherwise of a proposition.

In Astrology, judgment or inference is essentially a process of synthesis. But there is difference between inference and correct inference. An astrological inference can be considered to be valid if justified by the evidence, *i.e.*, the various planetary juxtapositions in support of it. This was the argument advanced by Thirumalai. I could not make much sense of it then. But in due course I realised that while logic was important in its own way in astrological interpretation, an inference arrived at logically, though valid, need not be true.

For example, according to texts, Venus, as Kalatrakaraka in the 7th house spoils or blemishes the 7th house. Applying this principle to a chart, we are correct in logically inferring that the married life of the native who has this combination may not be happy. This is a valid inference also. But it may not be a true or correct inference, to arrive at which, an intuitional approach is very necessary. When I explained this to Thirumalai in 1952 or so, when he called at my office, he nodded assent and shared my view that logic alone could not lead to correct judgment. Thirumalai lived close to my own residence at Bangalore in the fifties and he was all praise for my work in the field of Astrology.

A Pandit from Andhra, claiming to be an expert in ancient astronomical instruments, visited us in December 1928. I was interested to know how time was reckoned before the introduction of the modern watch. The Pandit stayed with us for about a month during which period he constructed for my edification some instruments, one or two of which I shall describe below.

A hole of the size of a black-gram seed is made in a copper vessel measuring 4 inches wide and 3 inches high and weighing about 18.75 *tolas*. This vessel is floated in another bigger vessel full of clean water. The time required for the copper vessel to sink, after getting filled up to the brim, is one ghati. The experiment was tried three times and the time required for the copper vessel to sink was 23 minutes 58 seconds. A ghati is equal to 24 minutes. Perhaps the slight difference could have been due to the crude method of experimentation employed by us.

This demonstration, though elementary, was thrilling at that time. In fact the method given out by the Pandit to measure a *ghati* is the *kapala yantra* or clepsydra described in *Surya Siddhanta, Siddhanta Siromani,* Pancha Siddhantika*, etc.

He also constructed what he called the gnomon *phalaka yantra, yasti* for finding the *palabha, dhiyantra* etc., with the aid of which, he averred, declinations, latitudes, longitudes, etc., of planets could be correctly found so that the results arrived at on the basis of calculations could be verified. Though simple and primitive looking from the modern point of view it seemed as though these instruments were an essential part of ancient astronomical studies.

Sixty years have passed since I met the Andhra Pandit. I have yet to come across one matching his resourcefulness and expertise in the construction of such instruments.

The same Pandit was also instrumental in kindling my interest in observational astronomy and taught me to identify starts and find time

---

* कुंभार्यकारं ताम्रं पात्रं कार्य मूले छिद्रं
स्वच्छेतोये कुण्डेन्घस्तं तस्मिन् पूर्णे नाडीस्यात् ॥

during nights. To cite an example, if the constellation of Sravana, *i.e.*, its *yogatara* or junction star is at the meridian, ghatis 1-48 would have elapsed in Aries, according to the formula *srona meshaako devaha, eko meaning one* ghati and *deva* meaning 48 vighatis. Similarly if *Swati* is at the meridian, ghatis 2-12 in Capricorn will have elapsed at the horizon. These formulae appear to have been framed taking into consideration the duration of signs in some place in Andhra. Therefore they cannot be universally applicable. At best they could give the approximate longitude of the Lagna though the Lagna itself may be accurate. The formula could be easily committed to memory to enable an astrologer to answer questions any time and anywhere without the need of an ephemeris.

A method in horary employed by the pandit based on the counting of *cowries* was believed to be dependable in answering questions. It was as follows. The astrologer, after purification in the morning with a bath and worship of his family deity, should hand over 25 cowries to the querist after uttering the mantra *Om namo bhagavate chamundeswari malayala swaroopinee sarvasiddhikarinee* . The querist should drop cowries on the floor after shaking them well. The following results are attributed to one or more cowries falling with their heads on: 1— realisation of object, honor and prosperity; 2— worry in the beginning but good tidings later on; 3— happiness and pleasure; 4-affliction, harsh words, loss of money and sorrow; 5— bad news, fear from the state, death of a relative; 6—loss of money, bad news, opposition and quarrels; 7—gain of money, meeting with relatives and good; 8—success over enemies and fulfillment of desires; 9—visit from relatives, good news and honour; 10—happy news and immense good; 11—difficulties; 12—theft, illness and mental worry; 13—increase in status, company of women, gain, and happiness; 14— gain of money, acquisition of lost property and success; 15—ordinary happiness and gain but final success; 16—scandal, quarrels, theft, restriction on movements; 17—realisation of object in view, gain of money and meeting with friends and relatives; 18—success and happiness; 19—realisation of object and honour; 20—disappointment, failure and misery; 21—suspicious deeds and gain; 22—affliction, obituary news and sorrow; 23—fear of theft, opposition, failure and unhappiness; 24— bodily affliction, quarrels and loss of reputation; and 25—loss of money, incarceration, bad news and unhappiness. If no *cowry* falls with its head on, repeat the shuffling and drop the cowries again on the floor.

Who will predecease—husband or wife? A simple method was suggested by the pandit. Count from the star of the wife to that of the husband. Multiply this by 7 and divide the product by 28. Call the remainder x. Similarly count from the star of the husband to that of the wife; multiply the figure by 7 and divide the product by 28. Call it y. If y is greater than x, the wife will predecease. Otherwise the husband will predecease. To take an example : The wife's star is Satabhisha and the husband's Mrigasira. Counting Mrigasira from Satabisha we get 9. Multiplying this by 7 and dividing the product by 28, the remainder (x) will be 7. Reversing the stars, the remainder (y) will be : $(20 \times 7/28)$ 0 or 28. Since y is greater than x, the wife will predecease the husband.

It should not be construed that in giving these simple astrological and quasi–astrological methods, still in vogue amongst a section of village astrologers, I endorse or make use of them. In several instances, the results have been remarkable. It is for the readers to experiment

Moon	Rahu	Ascdt.			Sun Sat.	Venus Rahu	Mars
				Venus			
	RASI				NAVAMSA		
			Mars	Moon			
		Venus Ketu	Sun Merc. Jupit.			Ketu	

with them and decide their utility.

Another important visitor to *Suryalaya* was His Highness Mir Ghulam Ali Khan, ruler of Banganapalle, a small state in Kurnool District. He was born on 26–9–1874 at about 10 p.m. near Kurnool. The Nawab was addicted to cigar–smoking.

I was asked to calculate the longevity of the Nawab by grandfather. My conclusion was :

Lord of the Ascendant Venus is in his own house with Ketu. Lord of the 8th Jupiter is in a trine in association with Mercury and the Sun. Lord of the 3rd from the Moon is in the 8th therefrom while lord of Chandra Lagna aspects Chandra Lagna. Therefore, the native has middle life. Mars as lord of the 7th and the 12th could be Maraka, as he also owns the 2nd from the Moon. Hence Mars Dasa may prove fatal. While appreciating my arguments grandfather disagreed with my conclusion. According to him the Moon could be a Maraka, because as lord of the 3rd he is aspected by Mars, a Maraka; Saturn, a malefic and the Sun (lord of the 6th) and Mercury lord of the 7th (and 4th). He warned the Nawab that his 47th year might prove critical unless he stopped his smoking. The Nawab passed away about the middle of 1929 or so due to congestion of the lungs.

My apprenticeship indirectly under my grandfather and other Pandits who visited *Suryalaya* gave me self-confidence, a fairly good grounding in collateral subjects and the opportunity to learn from those who were experts in their own way. In a sense, what was lost by way of general education was made good by insights into astrological disciplines, which perhaps laid the foundation for my whole hearted acceptance of a career that has made me what I am today.

5

The years 1928 to 1930 were full of significance in my life. It was during this period that I learnt by practical experience the dignity of labour, the pangs of poverty and how, in life, appearance is always different from reality. The Maharaja of Mysore presented grandfather with Rs. 10,000 on the birth of a son to the Yuvaraja after successful performance of remedial measures. Grandfather spent this sum by giving loans to our family dhobi (washerman), priest, maistry and many others hoping that such loans would be paid back or otherwise adjusted.

Those who cried for help while they were in distress never cared to pay back the amounts given to them. The financial position was so bad that I had to visit the debtors scattered in different villages for collection. Once the situation was so grave that we had to somehow manage to get Rs. 50 within two days to pay back a debt. I was sent to a village called Begur, about 10 miles from our own village to collect the money against the loan advanced to one Nanjunda Deekshita. With an escort I walked the distance of 10 miles and met the debtor. His wife pleaded with me pathetically about their own affairs and I had to return empty-handed. I was only 16 years old then. Walking a distance of 20 miles in one day resulted in severe bruises on my soles. My grandmother had to tend me for a week after that.

Though Nanjunda Deekshita sent me back with no money he taught me what he called a snap-shot astrological method according to which one could find out in advance whether or not such a 'mission' as I had undertaken would be successful so that unnecessary physical and mental strain could be avoided.

The method was of course quite simple. Ask for a number of three digits. The unit, the tenth and the hundredth digits respectively represent the future, the present and the past — ruled by the planets of the appropriate number, namely 1—the Sun 7—the, Moon, 2—Mars, 4—Mercury, 3—Jupiter, 5—Venus, 6—Saturn, 8—Rahu and 9—Ketu. Malefic planets denote : the Sun—partly successful, Mars—results in quarrels, Saturn— much effort necessary, Rahu—not beneficial, and benefices denoting : Jupiter—success guaranteed, Venus—success and pleasant happenings, Mercury—much effort necessary and the Moon—not bad.

I was so much in love with Astrology I would put to test every method of prediction that came my way. After a week I had to go to another village called Kadiganahally to collect money from the washerman. I thought of a number the unit–digit of which was 5 ruled by Venus. I became jubilant at the impending success. When I went to the village and asked the washerman to make at least a part payment towards his debt, he pleaded inability due to his own bad circumstances. But he assured me he would pay me back in kind. He gave 200 lemon fruits and a cup of milk. I felt my mission was successful at least partially. Then I reported this to grandfather. He just laughed over the matter.

It was during this period again that I had the opportunity to observe at close quarters the sufferings of those who come under what is now fashionable for politicians to call "weaker sections". About the end of 1929 grandfather was generous enough to write off all the debts and spared me the ordeal of walking long distances to different villages to collect the money.

Years later I discovered that the method given above had been elaborately discussed in *Prasna Marga*, some details pertaining to which I shall giving here.

The number which should consist of any **three** digits is capable of being interpreted in a number of ways even covering medical Astrology. For instance, the number as a whole denotes the entire physical body, the last digit (hundredth) signifying the condition and nature of the body above the neck: the centre digit indicating the body below the neck and above the waist and the unit digit the part of the body below the waist. The nature of the defect or disease would be appropriate to the nature of the planet signified by the number.

For answering questions of day–to–day importance, the hundredth, the tenth and the unit digits may be considered as representing the past, present and future. Multiply the root number by 45 and divide the product by 8. If the remainder is zero or an even number, only failure is to be anticipated. If the remainder is an odd number, good health, recovery from illness, financial gain and success can be predicted. Again reduce the root number to a single digit and find out the planet presiding over it and predict the following results.

If the Sun presides over the number — the object in view will be gained. If the question refers to politics, success will attend and honour will flow. The Moon — mental peace, domestic happiness, plenty of food and acquisition of desired object. The Moon at the time of query should be powerful to give all these results in full measure. Mars — accidents, injuries from fires and weapons, quarrels, head diseases and troubles from enemies. Prasna always refer to immediate future — 1 day to 1 year — and these results are to happen within this period. Mercury — itches, skin eruptions and sores in the body, lingering or intermittent fever, troubles from domestic animals such as dogs, cats, etc., and losses in trade and business. Jupiter — access to wealth, realisation of objects, blessings from preceptors and holy people and smooth sailing in all affairs. Venus — good sexual enjoyments, happiness with wife, good income and acquisition of money and ornaments. Saturn — colic pains, sorrow, misunderstandings, fear from spirits and hobgoblins, rheumatism and bad results in general. Rahu — skin diseases of a virulent type, eye troubles, misunderstandings, fear from poison, snakes and reptiles.

These methods have their own value and they cannot be brushed aside as of no avail. In fact whether in the matter of interpreting horoscopes or numbers, one must possess or cultivate the power of intuition. Otherwise the interpretation may not be quite correct.

The village we lived in had a Mutt headed by a Lingayat religious head by name Nanje Wadiyar. In fact in 1914, Nanje Wadiyar was

put on the *gadi*, thanks to the efforts of grandfather in preventing a
rival group from putting their own nominee on the Gadi. Nanje
Wadiyar was a broad–minded person and tried to keep himself out of
the group rivalries in the village. He showed no difference between
Vaishnavite and Saivite customs and traditions though the Mutt itself
belonged to the Veerasaiva community. In fact he got a temple erected
for Anjaneya near the village precincts. I was much liked by the
Swamiji. I used to spend some time with him every day in the Mutt
premises.

He was about 48 years of age and I was just 17. The age disparity
did not come in the way of our discussions on matters which interested
me then — ritual worship, *mantra* Sastra, etc. Although the head of
a Mutt he was not much interested in the rituals and rites.

Moon Sat. (R)		Sun Merc Sat.				Merc.	Ketu
Jupit. (R)				Ascdt. Mars Venus			
	RASI				NAVAMSA		
Ascdt.				Jup. Sat.			
Rahu		Sun Merc.	Venus	Rahu Sat.		Moon	

One day casually he asked me to tell him whether his horoscope
indicated spiritual progress and whether the mundane matter he was
involved in — administering the mutt, etc., would not come in the
way of his *sadhana*. I figured out thus : Venus, Yogakaraka, is
neechabhanga in the 9th and is not afflicted. The 10th or Karmasthana
is occupied by the Sun and Mercury. There is a *Parivartana* (inter
change) between lords of the 9th and 10th resulting in Dharma

Karmadhipa Yoga. This is highly auspicious for spiritual progress. Rahu in the 12th. *viz.,* mokshasthana is equally propitious. So I concluded that he would progress spiritually. Before giving my finding to the Swamiji, I wanted to have the matter cleared by grandfather. If my memory does not lie, his analysis went more or less on the following lines :

The Karaka of the mind is joined by Saturn in a watery and benefic sign. Saturn is a planet of suffering and has exchanged place with Jupiter. The Saturn–Moon syndrome suggests the tendency of the mind towards gloom, caution, acquisitiveness, restlessness and misgivings. The mental condition could improve with age making him more contemplative, thoughtful and capable of concentration on serious subjects. The Moon in the 3rd gives an inquisitive mind, many journeys, and a desire for new surroundings. This is an unfavourable position for peace of mind. But Jupiter in the 2nd favours success and prosperity in mundane matters. But what about the Moon-Saturn conjunction ? This gives earnestness and caution, capacity for hard work, unlooked for obstacles, delays, rebuffs, disappointments, reversals etc. One with such a combination meets with persecution, slander, difficulties and sorrows through parents and property and even sorrow through death of mother. The strong disposition of Venus in the 9th aspected by the Moon and Saturn gives a tendency for indulgence in pleasures, carelessness in habits and manners and worries and difficulties in matters connected with money and property. The Moon–Saturn in a Kendra from Rahu and Rahu being aspected by Saturn indicates trouble and obstacles for progress in spiritual matters and troubles through the opposite sex. Peculiar changes in emotions, feelings and likes and dislikes are also a feature of this combination.

Saturn aspecting Rahu having reference to the 3rd and 12th houses gives aimless travels and has an injurious effect on the health at some time. Liability to accidents by violent attacks by others, falling objects, etc., is clearly shown by Mars also aspecting Rahu. This mixing up of Mars, Saturn and Rahu influences gives an aggressive attitude and radical views. The horoscope shows inclinations for spirituality but no real progress. The strong disposition of Venus and Mercury gives strong attachments, the slackening of which is an essential ingredient for spiritual progress.

Apologetically, I told the Swamiji that he had a bright horoscope and that he would prosper and leave a mark as a dynamic religious head in his own surroundings. "But — what about spiritual progress ?" questioned the Swamiji. "You will become a highly evolved soul in your next life," I replied. Anyway my reply did not satisfy him.

By nature he was good, helpful, sympathetic and generous. But there were rumors of his illicit association with some women. He hardly ever stayed in the Mutt. Most of the time he was out moving. Once there was an attempt on his life. He was severely injured on his head. But when the accused was brought before him the Swamiji said that the accused be let off as it was God's will that he (the Swamiji) should suffer.

He ascended the Gadi in the beginning of Venus Dasa and the Mutt was quite prosperous until the end of Venus Dasa.

Years later — perhaps in 1951-52 — when I had settled down in Bangalore and had already established a name and reputation he visited me one day and poured out his heart as to what difficulties he was subjected to by the Agent of the Mutt and how he was scandalized etc. He wanted to know how long he would live. I told him Rahu in Rahu could be fatal as Rahu is in the 12th house aspected by Saturn, lord of the 2nd and Mars, lord of the 2nd from the Moon. By the end of 1956 he passed away. He was a great man in his own way and I really felt his loss.

6

One of the ticklish questions that began agitating my minds as I entered my eighteenth year was that of Kuja Dosha. The cause of this agitation was the prediction given to me by one Palaniswamy, an astrologer from Tamil Nadu. He had stayed with us at *Suryalaya* for about 2 weeks. He would go on quoting from Tamil classics explaining to me the several permutations and combinations of what he called *sevvai dosham* or the evil of Mars. He advised me to learn Tamil. But unfortunately I had no inclination for this. I must confess that even today I can neither speak nor write Tamil. I was eager to get a good knowledge of Sanskrit, Kannada and English. I had also been told that what was not found in the Sanskrit astrological literature could not be found in any other language. Palaniswamy who also claimed to know Sanskrit gave the following two *slokas* bearing on Kuja Dosha.

धनव्यये च पाताले जामित्रे चाष्टमेकुजे ।
स्त्रीणां भर्तुं विनाशाय भर्तृणां स्त्री विनाशकृत् ॥१॥
दपंत्योरेक्यकाले धनव्यये हिबुके सप्तमें ।
रन्ध्रलग्ने लग्नाच्चन्द्राश्च शुक्रात् ॥२॥

In both the *slokas* the key-positions are given as 2, 12, 4, 7, 8 and 1. These positions were to be reckoned from the Ascendant, the Moon and Venus. Palaniswamy did not say anything about the neutralizing factors. Nor did it strike me then that there could be antidotes. Moreover the language barrier was also there. He had a smattering of Telugu in which language he tried to explain to me the meanings of Tamil and Sanskrit verses.

The main cause of my interest in Kuja Dosha was the prospect of my getting married soon. Proposals from parents of suitable girls — their ages ranging from 9 to 12 years — were being made to my grandfather. There was no question of grandfather ascertaining my inclinations. He had taken it for granted that whatever he decided about my marriage would be acceptable to me without any murmur or protest from me. Although I had been shown 2 or 3 girls who had all been rejected by me, grandfather had already made up his mind that I should get married to Rajeswari, my father's sister's daughter. He was not really seriously considering any other proposals. Once Palaniswamy told me plainly that Mars, Venus and Mercury spelled disaster in my married life, that I would have a concubine, that I would have two marriages and that my moral character would be questionable etc. He was a fatalist. I now realised how indiscreet he was in making such forecasts. I was scared at these predictions. His main argument was that Mars in the 7th would make the wife aggressive and Venus in the 7th would give me loose character. This set me thinking and I started ransacking all the astrological books in grandfather's library to check the correctness of these dire interpretations. I could not broach the subject before grandfather, lest he should snub me for my impertinence.

Grandfather often suffered from numbness of the knees. It was my daily practice to massage his knees and feet before going to bed. He would lie on a cot in the open veranda. As I massaged his feet he would explain astrological principles or show me how to identify the stars in the heavens or ascertain the time without the aid of a watch. One day while these lessons were going on, availing of the opportunity, I asked grandfather whether Kuja Dosha could make one immoral and bereft of happiness in married life. He explained that no *dosha*, including Kuja Dosha, was exclusively evil. Under certain conditions Kuja Dosha could even be a blessing in disguise as it would ensure a long and happy married life. I just could not reconcile this statement with the fearful interpretations suggested by Palaniswamy.

I said, "But Palaniswamy says that Mars in the 7th gives two marriages, domestic disharmony, profligacy etc.?"

Grandfather lost his temper and retorted, "Palaniswamy is an upstart. He only knows how to quote *slokas* but not how to apply them. We have to go by experience. An ounce of experience is worth ten tons of theory".

I did not feel quite satisfied. Mustering all the courage I could, I felt bold enough to tell him what Palaniswamy had told me about the situation of Mars, Venus and Mercury in the 7th house in my own horoscope. Grandfather cooled down a bit but did not say anything. The discussion ended there.

Somehow I attached too much importance to Palaniswamy's theory. As ill-luck would have it, the headmaster of the local middle school was anxious to know about the health of his wife. He had been married for 30 years. In his chart Taurus was rising with Mars in the 7th from Lagna and in the 8th from the Moon.

When he gave me the Rasi chart I quipped : "Why do you want to know about the health of your wife. The horoscope has powerful Kuja Dosha which means, she must have died long back".

To fortify my interpretation I quoted the above *slokas*. The teacher was flabbergasted and took back the chart cursing me for what I had said. He brought the matter to the notice of grandfather who scolded me for my indiscreet interpretation and warned that giving such interpretations would land me in trouble and bring disgrace to Astrology. From then on, I was more careful in interpreting Kuja Dosha. I decided that I must get to know of this *dosha* in greater detail.

Palaniswamy's prediction that I was destined to lose my first wife, etc., continued to work on my mind. The thought of my becoming a man of loose character weighed heavily on my thinking. I was waiting for another opportunity to broach the same subject with grandfather. I had been brought up with such strict discipline that there was no question of my taking any liberties with him. We youngsters could never think of even sitting in his presence. In fact, my father who was about 45 years old then dared not sit before grandfather. The code of conduct towards elders was very rigid in those days unlike now when the young, in the name of freedom, behave disrespectfully and rudely towards their elders, their own parents not excluded.

We had some lands at a village called Suggatta about 2 miles from where we lived.

One day as grandfather and I were going in a bullockcart to this village, I hesitantly put the question, "What are the combinations for getting married to an aunt's daughter or an uncle's son ?"

He said : "If the lord of the 7th or Venus, whichever is more powerful should be connected with the Sun or the Moon, then marriage will be with a cousin".

Though not quite satisfied I could not show my dissatisfaction. I continued, "In which book is this combination given, please give the *sloka* so that I can commit it to memory". Grandfather did not like what he called "my impertinence". He became furious and answered that Astrology meant experience and not theory. But I did not give up so easily this time.

"If the lord of the 7th happens to be the Sun ?" I quipped. He guessed what was in my mind and smilingly answered : "You are referring to your own case. Do not worry. You will get a good wife. I have already decided that you should get married to Rajeswari".

I gathered some more courage and said that I was too young and I was not inclined to marry then as I had no means of earning. Further Palaniswamy had predicted only bad things. Grandfather allayed my fears and spoke in a serious tone.

He said, "It is not necessary for me to ask you about your marriage. I know what is best for you. Mars in the 7th in Leo is harmless, Venus in the 7th may indicate occasional tension, the wife will be beautiful and affectionate, always devoted to the husband. Mercury's position is equally good. These three planets — Mars lord of the 10th, Venus lord of the 4th and the 9th and Mercury lord of the 5th in the 7th — form a highly favourable combination indicating that you will prosper well after marriage. Jupiter in a *kendra* (quadrant) from this combination adds strength to it. Long after I pass away you will recall my prediction with gratitude. Rajeswari's horoscope is highly fortunate and she brings in luck. Your marriage will be celebrated as soon as you complete your 18th year.

But I still had some misgivings about Kuja Dosha *vis-à-vis* my own horoscope, even after grandfather had assured me that Jupiter in a quadrant or trine from Mars would nullify Kuja Dosha.

I paused for a while and recollecting that grandfather's first wife had died when he was about 46 years old, I asked him why Jupiter's aspect on Mars (occupying the 7th from the Moon) did not nullify the Kuja Dosha in his own case. This was too much for him. Nevertheless, he explained in a grave tone that in the ultimate analysis, the Navamsa chart should be carefully considered. In his own case, Mars was no doubt aspected by Jupiter. But Mars as lord of the 7th was in the 6th (12th from the 7th) with Ketu and the lord of the 6th Venus was in a common sign aspected by Saturn. In the Navamsa, the 7th and Venus were all considerably afflicted. Hence he had two marriages. I nodded with satisfaction.

"Would Jupiter in the 10th in a Kendra from the lord of the 10th, Mars, promote my progress professionally, educationally and financially?" I put this question firmly. He was good enough to allay my fears and assured me "with all the emphasis at my command" that I would outshine him in name, fame, finance and reputation and that if "You have any regard for your grandfather, you must believe me and agree to the marriage." I respectfully gave in and he felt happy.

Rajeswari's father, Dr. M.C Srikanta Pandit, who was serving as a medical officer in the then Mysore Government, who was well known for his power of healing and for his concern for the poor, had readily agreed to grandfather's proposal of her marriage with me. But Dr. Pandit's close relatives were dead against this alliance. They had their own "well founded" objections. I was only an S.S.L.C. I had discontinued my studies and had no means of livelihood. My earnings in future if at all I was "capable of earning" could only be by manipulating a *Panchanga* (almanac). Who would care for Astrology, a degrading profession? Grandfather or father had no property. Throwing Rajeswari into a well would be much better than getting her married to me! They advised Dr. Pandit to consider other boys who were graduates already earning and well-placed economically.

But Dr. Pandit appeared to have had implicit faith in grandfather's prediction of a good future for me and rejected the objections of his close relatives.

With humility I must acknowledge that if at all I have achieved anything in life which has made me what I am today — it is all due to the blessings of my grandfather who had implicit confidence in my capacity to justify his expectations.

My marriage was celebrated grandly at Mysore on 30–10–1930 and as I write these lines 60 years of married life have passed over which I have no regrets. Rajeswari has shared with me with equanimity and remarkable resignation my misfortunes, financial difficulties and all the troubles which were thrust upon me by Destiny. Grandfather had said that her own horoscope had several notable points which would make her a unique personality. Mercury lord of the 9th causing Dharma–Karmadhipati Yoga. Venus is a Yogakaraka for Makara Lagna. Mercury, who is in the 10th from Lagna is aspected powerfully by Saturn lord of Lagna and the 2nd and Dhanakaraka Jupiter. Mercury becomes almost glorified when viewed from Chandra Lagna, as, happening to be lord of the 5th, he occupies the 9th aspected by Jupiter, lord of the 2nd and the 11th and Saturn, lord of Chandra Lagna. These combinations have produced Dhanayogas and Rajayogas.

Born in a middle–class family, married at 12 to a person with hardly any pretensions to education or property, and faced with the tough problems of life, Rajeswari, by dint of luck and determination, overcame all troubles and has earned for herself the affection and admiration of her kith and kin. The husband's financial stability is largely due to the Neecbabhanga of Kalatrakaraka Venus and the *digbala* of Chandra Lagnadhipati Saturn in the 7th therefrom. It was the firm opinion of grandfather that it was not enough if Yogas were merely present. Dasas of planets causing such Yogas must operate in appropriate time. And Rajeswari's horoscope is an illustration of the dawn of prosperity and affluence in accordance with the presence of typical Yogas and the operation of the Dasas of planets causing such Yogas.

Coming back to Kuja Dosha : I started my experiments in right earnest, collecting as many horoscopes as I could lay my hands upon, from the surrounding villages and trying to apply the above quoted *slokas*. I discovered to my surprise that in many cases Mars in the 7th, the 8th, etc., had not killed the wife or husband. In our village we had an Ayurvedic doctor by name Sreenivasapandit. I found in his horoscope Mars and Saturn in the 2nd without any aspects from benefic planets. He and his wife had been leading a happy married life for more than 40 years. It was therefore an enigma for me to reconcile Palaniswamy's *sloka* with actual facts. My doubts were resolved by Mahamahopadhyaya Siva Sankara Sastri. He advised me not to lose my head in calculations or literal application of *slokas*. He explained how Kuja Dosha could get cancelled and quoted the following slokas :

स्वक्षेत्रे ऊच्चराशिस्थे ऊच्छांशोऽवांशशगोऽपिवा

अंगारकानु दोषाय कर्के सिंहाय विद्यते ॥१॥

द्वितीय भौमदोषस्तु युग्मकन्याऽयोर्विना ।

चतुर्यं भौमदोषस्तु मेषवृश्चिकयोर्विना ॥२॥

सप्तमे भौमदोषस्तु नक्र कर्कटयोर्विना ।

अष्टमे भौमदोषस्तु धनुर्मीन द्वयोर्विना ॥३॥

गुरुमंगळ संयोगे भौमदोषं न विद्यते ।

चन्द्रमंगळ संयोग भौमदोषं न विद्यते ॥४॥

राहु केतु समायुक्तः मन्द भौम्य निरीक्षितः ।

मित्रग्रहस्थितो वापि भौमदोषं न विद्यते ॥५॥

During the past 50 years, scores of horoscopes containing the so-called Kuja Dosha have been examined and approved by me for purposes of marriages. The majority of cases has had a happy married life. But in some cases I have failed, perhaps because of factors which escaped my scrutiny.

The Kuja Dosha is a flexible combination. I must record here that the last part of the last *sloka* — Rahu or Ketu conjoining Mars cancels the Dosha — is not borne out in practice. In the large number of horoscopes containing this combination marital disharmony has been caused by the eccentric or even hysterical nature of the husband or the wife.

The subject of Kuja Dosha has been discussed in my book *Muhurtha* to which readers may refer for more details.

It occurs to me that in married life while an understanding between the husband and wife is no doubt essential, in certain important matters the husband must have the upper hand.

The Rahu–Mars syndrome in Lagna or Chandra Lagna appears to be a common factor in the horoscopes of girls who, lacking discretion and independent thinking, allow themselves to be misguided by their own elders to adopt an aggressive and domineering attitude towards their husbands and pressurise them to desert their own parents. Generally such girls hail from families lacking in culture and moral values.

I am obliged to make these remarks in view of the fact that in recent times an increasing number of such cases has been brought to my notice for astrological advice.

I shall be discussing on a subsequent occasion horoscopes of girls whose happy relationship with their husbands were disturbed and broken because of the machinations and intrigues of their own elders.

7

It is natural for one dabbling in astrology to get interested in *mantra sastra*, mantrics and their tribe. I was no exception. *Suryalaya* was the center of attraction for all types of *mantrics*, jugglers, astrologers, palmists, musicians, scholars, etc. Grandfather had the rare ability of enjoying in a relaxed mood performances of jugglers. My interest then was merely academical.

Sangappa, to whom I have referred earlier was highly pretentious about his own "super-natural" powers.

Every year the Dasara celebrations were an important feature of the activities of the villagers. The local religious head was required to visit the *Banni mantapa* on the 9th day of Dasara and then hold some sort of a Darbar on the 10th day. As a leading personality of the place, grandfather would also attend such functions and naturally I would not miss them. There was also the custom of sacrificing a lamb or a goat on Durgashtami day. The vision of an innocent lamb being led to the altar for being killed to "pacify" Durga was so disgusting and inhuman that I determined to have this barbaric custom put an end to. I took up the matter with grandfather and strongly objected to killing animals in the name of Dharma. He appreciated my point of view, but he appeared to have felt it would be difficult to end the practice lest the villagers think that the age-old tradition was being interfered with. I then spoke to the Swamiji with whom I had always been friendly. He was more or less of the same view as grandfather, which meant, he would not actively support me in my efforts to put an end to the annual killings. But the Swamiji said that if Sangappa favoured discontinuance of the practice the villagers might give in.

We had about half a dozen servants in our bungalow. On every Durga Puja day, grandfather would pay Rs. 20/- or so to the head maistry. He would use it for the purpose of sacrificing an animal and then feast upon it with all the servants. I felt charity must begin at home. Therefore just before the commencement of Dasara in 1930 I told grandfather not to give the money for killing, but instead provided the servants with clothes and food. The matter assumed a serious form when grandfather at my persistent persuasion announced that from then on no animal sacrifice would be allowed. The *maistry* accompanied by the *mantric* Sangappa and a number of servants called at our house at about 9 o'clock in the night two days before Durgashtami and went on narrating stories of how evil befell on families and villagers when the goddess Durga was not "appeased" with blood. The code of behaviour those days was such that my interceding when discussions were going on between grandfather and the *mantric–maistry* pair was out of question. I bided for time and accosted Sangappa as soon as he came out of grandfather's room and told him bluntly that from that year onwards I would not allow the evil practice of killing animals on our land, come what may and that if he (Sangappa) tried to frighten our servants with the story that dire consequences would visit them if they went against tradition, I would resort to a more powerful *mantra* to offset his own *kshudra* practices.

Sangappa did not expect that I would be so determined. He was simply flabbergasted at what he called my insolence. I called in the servants and told them that I would use more powerful *mantras* to neutralise Sangappa and that as it was a sin to kill animals in the name of pleasing the goddess, they should stop the practice. Each servant was paid Rs. 3/- and this settled the matter. All of them repaired to the house of Sangappa and declared with one voice that they would use a "pumpkin" and not a lamb as a symbol of sacrifice. Grandfather, the Swamiji, the *patel*, the *shanubhogue* and the villagers were so surprised that they could not believe that an unhealthy tradition had been ended. The next day the Swamiji sent for me and conveyed his appreciation and presented me with an *angavastra* (upper cloth).

The narration of this event has become necessary in the light of the fact that several of these *mantrics* who practised *kshudra mantras* were found to be born in the *vishaghati* area of the constellation in which the Moon was placed and when Rahu and Saturn were in conjunction, opposition or square. It has been invariably found in the majority of such cases that Venus was also afflicted, which meant immoral character.

Soon after this 'achievement' of mine, which I then considered as something significant, I was face to face with another mantric at Bangalore. It was rumoured that the mantric — if my memory does not fail me, his name was Lakshman Sarma — was a *Devi Upasaka* and was capable of performing all sorts of miracles and that people stood in queues to have a glimpse of him. It was also rumoured that he could bring one under his spell by just throwing some *kumkum* (red powder) on one's head.

But fortunately for us, Sarma had one day sent his own emissary inviting grandfather to be present at his *Devi Puja*. His so–called ashram was in a lane in Cubbonpet (Bangalore). There were about a hundred persons who were eagerly waiting to meet him when we were ushered into his August presence one fine evening. He was about 5 1/2 feet tall with a beard and his hair tied at the back. His face looked grotesque. The forehead was smeared with *vibhuti* (sacred ashes) and *kumkum* (red powder). He was wearing rings on all his fingers. He commanded us to sit on a mat spread in the room and started his Puja to the Deity — perhaps Rajarajeswari. Grandfather has seen scores of such miracle–mongers and he had cautioned me in advance not to be carried away either by his claims or his pretensions. I had mentally calculated the chart for the time at which we entered his Puja room. Scorpio was rising aspected by Mars who was in conjunction with Rahu. Earlier I had concluded that he was a propitiator of a *kshudra devata* and had also fortified myself by having performed one thousand *Gayatri Japa*. I had implicit faith in the efficacy of this *mahamantra* lest his spell worked on me. After the Puja, with a grave and fearful look, he dropped some *kumkum* and a small idol of some goddess in my hand and gazed into my eyes. At first I felt a bit uneasy but

immediately recovered my presence of mind. As he was dropping the
idol into my hands, he quipped : "Your grandfather is a great astrologer
and you think you are also an astrologer. Tell me whether your
Astrology confirms that I am a *sadhaka* and have under my control
all sorts of forces. I shall be visiting your place shortly". I was not
surprised at his arrogance and did not feel impressed.

Within a week Sarma visited us. He was closeted with grandfather
for 2 hours and came out of the room perhaps chastened. Before seeing
him off — the parting was somewhat unpleasant — I told him that I
had discovered on the basis of the time at which we had met him at

Sat. (R)		Mars	Ketu	Mars		Ascdt.	Ketu
Jupit. (R)				Merc.			
	RASI				NAVAMSA		Moon
				Venus Sat.			
Ascdt. Moon Rahu		Sun Merc.	Venus	Rahu	Sun	Jupit.	

Balance of Ketu Dasa at birth : years 0.5.10

Bangalore that Scorpio was rising and Mars and Rahu were in
karmasthana (**10th house**) which meant he could do bad Karma and
that he was only a *kshudra mantra* practitioner. This infuriated him
and he threatened to use his powers to disable me physically and
mentally for life. But I did not take his threat seriously.

His horoscope made an interesting study. The Lagna, Sagittarius,
was occupied by the Moon and Rahu and aspected by Mars and Saturn.
Both the Ascendant and the Moon were highly afflicted. I had figured
out — my knowledge of Astrology was not much — but I had also

thought I has mastered the subject — that Sarma's interest in *mantrasastra* and his claim to peep into the future were due to Rahu's position in Lagna. Such a position could also make one appear odd, peculiar and eccentric. Saturn in the fourth is not good for happiness in domestic or home life. Benefic Venus no doubt aspects Saturn, but Venus is debilitated.

This horoscope interested me much for I wanted to show the *mantric* when I met him next that I was an astrologer of "no mean standing" and that I could probe into the innermost recesses of his life, as much as he pretended to do with his mantric powers.

In those days the ego in me had the better of discretion and humility. I was prepared to challenge any person to disprove Astrology and any astrologer, that I was the wisest of all. Probably one may have to go through such psychological aberrations before one's thoughts get settled and make one evaluate oneself sensibly and objectively. What made me assume an all-knowing attitude in Astrology was : I was thorough with at least two classics — *Jataka Chandrica* and *Brihat Jataka*. I could work out *Shadbalas, Ashtakavarga,* and *Pindayurdaya.* I could support my predictions by quoting appropriate authorities. Which professional astrologer, I then thought, could do this ? I was just 18, and were not these attainments adequate to mark me out as an outstanding astrologer, unmatched in astrological learning and predictions ! But to grandfather I was still an upstart with only a smattering of Astrology and without sufficient practical experience. He often emphasised that I must be humble and that arrogance was not only unbecoming of a real scholar but was a sign of immaturity and weakness.

Somehow my ego continued to be strong until the day I was pulled up by a Bengali gentleman, Dr. Chatterjee, with whom I chanced to travel to Mysore by train. He was a Ph. D. of Calcutta University and in the course of a talk made some adverse comments on astrologers. I shot back with all the emphasis at my command that he had no business to make such derogatory remarks and that I could accept any challenge thrown at astrologers. He was touched to the quick and threw a challenge to analyse *putrabhava* in a horoscope

which he took out from his coat pocket. At this distance of time I do
not recollect the chart. But the Lagna was Sagittarius and Saturn and
Rahu were in the 5th house. I said that the native's wife must have
had one or two abortions and that there was no chance of an issue.
The Bengali scholar quipped : "Your analysis is not correct. The person
has a lovely son aged 4. I also know something of Astrology. Lord
of the 5th Mars is exalted and is in conjunction with Jupiter who is
also *putrakaraka*. Jupiter is in his own sign in the Dwadasamsa chart".
But I hit back with the remark that Dwadasamsa had nothing to do
with children. The Bengali gentleman, suave and friendly said : "Look
here. Your spirit of adventure in making snap–shot predictions is
alright.But it will land you in much trouble. Do not be hasty and do
not assume that you are omniscient. Cultivate humility. Study
Parasara Hora . It is due to astrologers like you who interpret
horoscopes as you have done that Astrology has fallen on dark days".

This was not only a shock to me but dealt a death blow to my
arrogance and the feeling of my being infallible.

I narrated this episode to grandfather. He said that he endorsed
every word of the Bengali gentleman and that my reaction should be
sensible and not emotional. From that day onwards — it is 62 years
since this happened — cultivation of humility has become a part of
my existence. Since then much water has flown in the Ganga.
Thousands of horoscopes have been examined by me. Most of my
predictions have come correct. Ofcourse, some have also gone wrong.
But I have always felt and still feel that the ocean of astrological
knowledge is too vast to be fully comprehended by the human intellect
with its limitations.

In my next meeting with Sarma I gave a delineation of his
horoscope in the following terms : "Mars is in the 6th house, giving
disputes, quarrels and peculiar tastes which could impair your health.
Venus in the 10th generally indicates popularity and success in dealing
with women". This interpretation was greeted by him with a
patronizing smile. "But", I declared, "Venus is not free from affliction.
He is *Neecha* (debilitated) in *karmastana* (10th house) and there is no
Neechabhanga. The lord of the 10th Mercury is with debilitated Sun

and combust and Venus is also aspected by Saturn". I paused a little and declared firmly in a low tone, "Venus' affliction indicates intimacy with other women, trouble in marriage, sensuality and doing bad Karma". He became uneasy and shouted in a voice choked with emotion : "Your interpretation is false. I have not married. I am highly spiritual without any sensual feelings. You appear to have come here to assassinate my character. But for my regard for your grandfather I would have cast my 'spell' on you and rendered you speechless. I do not require any more predictions. You can go away".

I pocketed the insults, withdrew from his room and reported the whole matter to grandfather. He smilingly said that the situation of afflicted Venus in *karmastana* was capable of giving the results I had indicated. He felt that on the whole I had a correct grasp of Sarma's horoscope. Grandfather further said that the basic weakness of the horoscope was due to the strong affliction centred on the Lagna, the Moon, the 6th, the 7th and the 10th houses. Mercury being combust could give him a cunning nature, shrewdness and a mind fired with desires. He was also liable to brain and mental troubles. Apt to create enmity he could only be an imposter. Grandfather did not attach much importance to the *Parivarthana Yoga* between Jupiter and Saturn involving the 3rd and 4th houses. On the contrary he felt Rahu with the Moon being aspected by Mars and Saturn could give misfortunes, an eccentric mind, an aggressive nature and indolence catering to sensual life. He felt that the Lagna and the Moon being aspected by Mars and afflicted by Rahu could also give imprisonment. He cautioned me that I should never volunteer to read horoscopes as that would not only cheapen me but also cheapen Astrology, though temporarily my ego might find elation.

Four months later, the local press carried the news that the *mantric* Sarma had disappeared overnight with all the collections and a maid–servant ! Thus ended my experiences with the *mantric*.

Such examples can only warn us not to take such pretenders on their face value. But *mantrasastra* is not a superstition. There are adepts who use their powers only for the good of humanity and not for enriching themselves or playing on the credulity of the ill–informed and the illiterate.

Grandfather used to tell me that his own father born on 17-7-1816 at Bangalore at about midday was an adept in *mantrasastra*. It seems he could, with a blade of grass, stop about 1000 heads of cattle and 30 or 35 cowherds under the effect of *sammohanastra*. In his horoscope Jupiter is in the Ascendant involved in *Gajakesari* Yoga and aspected by *yogakaraka* Saturn from Capricorn. He was a man of high principles, integrity and highly religious.

A study of the horoscopes of all those who claim to be miracle-mongers can enable us to distinguish between the genuine and the spurious. These experiences made me take more interest in *mantrasastra*, with the consequence I became from then on an ardent reader of Sir John Woodroffe's works on Tantra Sastra.

Another interesting outcome of my discussions with Pandits known for their knowledge of and experience in *mantrasastra* was the existence of intimate relationship between Astrology and *mantrasastra*. Grandfather had often stressed the preventive and curative aspects of the remedial measures prescribed in *mantrasastra* for tackling afflictions in a horoscope. In fact, he had undertaken remedial measures with success even in respect of tough health problems given up as hopeless by the medical fraternity. The planets could be "appeased" by *mantras* and *dana—mantrenanena danena grahanee santimrichchati* : But somehow I was not much convinced that such remedial measures could really work in practice. This sort of scepticism, which perhaps was partly due to ignorance and partly due to my own unhappy experiences with some *mantrics*, was gradually overcome until I realised that while ninety percent of those who profess to practise *mantrasastra* could be frauds, at least ten percent could be really genuine ones and that the majority of astrologers under the camouflage of enabling their consultors to get rid of their misfortunes, prescribe remedies, even when not needed, thus taking unprincipled advantages of the sufferings of the consultors. The situation does not appear to be different even today.

I was able to gather some interesting information about remedial measures vis-a-vis planetary combinations which will be dealt with in the subsequent episodes.

8

The existence of divinatory systems other than Astrology from ancient times in India is an eloquent testimony to the fact of the innate longing of man to know his place in the cosmos. It seems clear that ancient Hindus had devised systems of their own in the matter of not only analysing hands but also linking palmistry with Astrology.

In May or June 1930 a palmist from Andhra by name Rama Sastry came to stay with us for about four weeks. My interest in Palmistry was aroused by this Sastry. He studied my palm and predicted that my life–line was well marked and that I would live long and secure prosperity, name and fame. He gave me quite a number of hints on the Hindu system of palmistry. Why not combine Astrology and palmistry and make research was the question I put to Sastry. He said that such a combination was no doubt desirable but it was not practicable. He did not say why. What I admired in him was his ability to quote ancient authorities on hand reading. Given below is a sample of such quotations.

If the nails are of reddish hue, one is healthy and rich, courageous and fortunate — (*aarakta nirmala nakho dhanawaan raajapoojitaha*); if the nails are yellowish, one suffers from indigestion and windy complaints, entertains evil thoughts and is of immoral character — (*haridra nakharo bhooya duraachaara rato naraha*).

He also gave some methods to cast a horoscope from the hand. For example if the *yuva rekha* (a line or mark resembling a rice or wheat grain) is well marked on the first phalanx of the thumb in the right hand, the person's birth will be in the bright half of the lunar month ; if in the left hand, dark half of the lunar month — (*suklapakshe tathajanma dakshinaangushtajaischataihi, Krishnapakshe nrinam janma vaamaangushtagatairyavaihi*). If the sum of one's height and the diameter of his head measured just above the eyebrows (in *angulas* or inches) is divided by 12, the remainder represents the Lagna or the Ascendant — (*angaangulam siro nimnam thashtam dwadasabhisthetha lagnam vignaayate tena sarvam phalamudeerayet*).

Let us take the so-called life-line or *ayushya rekha*. Palmists claim that it is vital for our existence as without it no living hand has been known. It is said to stand for physical constitution, health factors, temper, longevity and resistance to outer conditions. According to Prahlada, it begins between the thumb (*angushtha*) and the forefinger (*tharjani*) and covers the valley of the palm — (*angushtakaram adhye tu rekhaa rujvaayathaa bhavet, sampoornahasta paryaaptaa saa seema paurushaasmritaha*). If this *rekha* starts from the root of the forefinger and is well marked, one lives for hundred years and has a peaceful end — (*ayurbalam bhavedrekhaa tarjaneemoolasamsthita satavarsham bhavedayussukhamrityurnasamyasaha*). This *sloka* is said to be from *Garuda Purana*.

Of course later writers on palmistry deal with this line more exhaustively, but such a discussion is not relevant here. For example, when it originates from a point higher up close to the root of the fore-finger it denotes an urge to rise in life. The native has a strong ambition for power and progress. He is egoistic and dominating, qualities of leadership are well marked, but he will always lack a sense of contentment. If the line begins from a point considerably lower than normal, the native shows a negative approach to life. Quarrelsome and aggressive, irritable and ill-tempered he is inclined to be pessimistic. He wishes to isolate himself and is apt to sulk. A victim of self-pity and inferiority complex he loses opportunities to rise in life.

Taking the head *line* (*atmarekha*) : It starts from the last finger and passing through (below) the Mounts of Mercury, the Sun and Saturn reaches near or the Jupiter Mount — (*Kanishtanguli desaastu rekhagachchati madhyamam ; avichchinnaaturekhasyaadaseetyaayurvinirdiset*).

Why I have given these extracts from ancient sources is to stress the fact that the science of hand-reading was developed in India from the earliest times and carried on to the West, from where, thanks to the interest and zeal of our western friends, a flood of literature on palmistry, containing the same principles is being re-routed to our country. No wonder if some of our palmists declare that they are not aware of the existence of Hindu palmistry in India.

Sastry told me that he had learnt palmistry from his father and that he did not know exactly the source of the *slokas* he quoted, though they were supposed to be from *Bhavishyat Purana, Prahlada* and *Narada.*

I was very disappointed when he had to suddenly leave for his home town. I never met him again. My studies in palmistry continued on the basis of the information gathered from Sastry.

Once probably about the same time when I was asked by grandfather to sort out some old papers, I chanced to come across letters written to him by Cheiro, Zadkeil II, Alan Leo, Goriold (Sepharial) and Robson. When I referred these names to grandfather I was told that Cheiro was a gifted palmist, Zadkiel was well known in England for his correct predictions, Alan Leo was an astrologer and theosophist and Sepharial and Robson were sympathetically disposed towards Hindu Astrology. I was also told that both Alan Leo and Sepharial visited grandfather while he was living at Madras. Alan Leo who had expressed a desire to participate in the Astronomical Conference held in 1911 at Kalady, the birth place of Adi Sankara, under the presidentship of His Holiness Sri Narasimhabharati Swamigalu, the then Sankaracharya of Sringeri, and the Secretaryship of grandfather, was not invited because he being an Englishman, it was felt, he would not be able to adjust himself to local conditions. According to grandfather Alan Leo was somewhat narrow-minded in the sense that while freely borrowing Hindu astrological ideas he never had the fairness to acknowledge his indebtedness to the Hindus. Sepharial on the other hand was a real admirer of the Hindu system, which has received commendable approbation in his writings. Robson of course had started donning the mantle of Zadkiel II (Dr. A.J. Pearce) as Zadkiel had just then died.

With grandfather's permission I wrote a letter to Cheiro, stating that being the grandson of so and so I had "mastered" Astrology and that I was interested in palmistry also which I was studying on the basis of the principles orally imparted to me by a pandit. I sent him my birth details along with my palm impression with a covering letter that I would be interested in having his views on my Life–Line. In those days mail from U.K. and U.S.A. took about 16 and 21 days respectively to reach India. Of course there were no jet planes to carry mail, but there were also no strikes, no go–slow tactics and no agitations as we have today in our country, wedded to a 'socialistic pattern of society'. Postal officials were honest, duty–conscious, efficient and service–minded.

I figured out that I must get a reply within about 45 days from Cheiro. Imagine my happiness when Cheiro wrote to me a friendly letter admiringly referring to our sages as the propounders of the wisdom of Astrology and palmistry and sending me complimentary copies of his *Language of the Hand* and *Book of Numbers*.

In his reply, Cheiro did not say anything specifically about my Life–Line. But there was a brief note. Juggling with the numbers of my birth date, month and year he had written that I would live until my 'fadic' numbers 8 and 2 came together. He figured out that my date of birth being 8 and the total of the day, month and year being 2, 82 would be the length of my life. I thanked him for his prompt reply and our correspondence ceased. In 1931 or 1932, Mrs. Cheiro wrote to me that some talisman which Cheiro used to wear on his body had been lost and that ever since then his predictive powers had ceased.

Fascinated by Cheiro's jugglery with the numbers, I started a serious study of both palmistry and numerology. Cheiro's *Language of the Hand* gave me enough insight into palmistry. I collected palm impressions of a number of people, and tried to interpret the lines on their hands in the light of my newly acquired interest.

One of the hands I took up for study was that of a servant of ours by name Sonnappa. His Life–Line had 'broken' — that was my reading then — at a point coinciding with the age of 35 years. I cautioned him that he might die. He brought this to the notice of grandfather. Sonnappa did not die, but I was reprimanded for my "hasty conclusions". Of course Sonnappa lived for 60 years.

Numerology also engaged my attention for a while. But somehow I had my own misgivings about this subject for the simple reason as to why one should consider only English alphabets. Numerology did work in some cases accurately while in many cases the results were disappointing.

I was waiting for an opportunity to discuss with grandfather the relative merits of Astrology, palmistry and numerology. On a certain lunar eclipse day, when we were together, I brought the subject before him in the following manner.

I said,"Cheiro's book on Numerology which I have carefully studied is revealing. By manipulating numbers we can predict the exact dates of events. I think numerology is superior to Astrology". Grandfather's reaction was as expected. He waved his hand with a gesture of silencing me and said, "Don't be foolish and try to belittle Astrology in which your own knowledge is not much. Numerology and all that stuff are quite useless. Use your time and energy for some better purpose."

"But," I put in, "Numerology according to me is a science. Number of the year of my birth (1912) totals 4. I was married in 1930 which is again 4. Is this not astounding ?" "No", retorted grandfather. "You can justify past events. But the future cannot be so definitely predicted." I could see his dissatisfaction at my persistences as he felt I was not satisfied with his explanation. I continued, "Cheiro says he had predicted events correctly on the basis of numbers and ", — he tried to cut me short with the remark, "Cheiro had mantrasiddhi". He declared : "Look here, I was born on 12-2-1856, the total of my year of birth (1856) being 2. The total of my date of birth is 3. Then my longevity is either 23 or 32, whereas I am 74."

I tried to explain that the name number etc., should all be taken before coming to a conclusion. He dismissed my explanation and advised me to concentrate on Astrology proper and leave "numbers, palms and hands to those who look for easy things".

I felt that in a sense his advice was sound. From then on, while Astrology merited my full energy and time I also tried to pick up as much knowledge as possible in the other two subjects.

In our library I chanced to lay my hands on *The Grammar of Astrology* by "Zadkiel the Seer" published in London in 1833. Vivian Robson with whom I had established correspondence was good enough to send me *A Text Book of Astrology* by Zadkiel II (A. J. Pearce). With these two books my study of western Astrology started. I also decided to collect as many books on the subject as possible. But living as we did in a village and suffering some sort of poverty, I could not dream of buying books. An Englishman by name P.F. Bowring, a retired Inspector General of Police in Mysore, was a frequent visitor to our place, to get astrological counsel from grandfather. When I told him of my desire to acquire some books on western Astrology, he readily agreed to get them for me from England. Two of the books he presented me with were *Mysteries of All Nations* by James Grant, published in 1880 and *The Celestial Science of Astrology* by E. Sibly, F.G.H.S. published in London in 1812 (See appendix). My collection of books on western Astrology was also facilitated by the cooperation of one B.H. Mirza, Proprietor of the Indian Book Depot (now defunct) at Bombay, whom I had met once in Bangalore.

Western Astrology had also its palmy days in the 17th century. Lily, the astrologer, was a great authority in England. He was consulted by the Royalists as to whether the King would escape from Hampton Court and whether he would or should sign the propositions of Parliament. Lily did predict important events. For instance in 1656, when Mars was in Virgo, "there will appear in this Kingdom so strange a revolution of fate, so grand a catastrophe and mutation unto this monarchy and government as never yet appeared". It will be "ominous to London by reason of causing fires and devastating plagues." Many strange circumstances following his predictions went far to support his claim to the prophetic mantle. What Lily observed then., "evil configurations in Virgo are generally attended with bloodshed" is relevant to the present time also.

It **was** not difficult for me to understand the preliminaries in Western Astrology such as the nature and properties of planets, results of planets in houses and signs and similar principles. I was not then interested about the origin of western Astrology and whether it was borrowed from India etc. My main concern was to master the system so that whether in Hindu Astrology or in western Astrology, no one else could match my knowledge!

Grandfather perhaps noticed a streak of omniscient attitude in my posture and he tried his best to dissuade me from entertaining a high opinion of myself. He would say such an attitude would be my undoing. According to him, in matters of learning and knowledge, one should always feel humble recognizing the fact that there could always be persons more learned. In regard to money matters, one should always feel he was better placed when compared to those less fortunate. This sage counsel coming as it did from a learned, pious and experienced personality had a telling effect on me. And as I started facing problems of life and meeting with learned persons, I realised that my own learning was like a drop of water in the ocean of knowledge. Hard experience alone could make one mellow, humble and balanced.

The first ticklish problem that I came across as I progressed in my study of western Astrology was about "houses" in a horoscope. I was no doubt quite familiar with the system of *Bhava sphutas* advocated by Sripathi. But I could not understand the "houses" of western astrology. For instance in *Grammer of Astrology* in the horoscope of Lord Byron's daughter (born 10–12–1815 at 1.00 p.m., London) the longitudes of the meridian and the Ascendant are given as Capricorn 3° and Aries 7° 55' respectively. According to Sripathi the 11th house falls in 4° 38' Aquarius whereas the author of this book has given it as 22° Capricorn. I could not then reconcile this difference. However after I studied some other books on western Astrology, it became evident that they employed a system of house division alien to Sripathi.

More than five decades have rolled by since I first took up study of western Astrology. Though Cyril Fagan a great researcher and

savant says of me : "For one steeped in Eastern Jyotisha, his grasp of
the details and problems of western Astrology is astonishing" I can
only say that I have picked up a fairly good knowledge of the subject.

What I find even today is that the problem of house division —
Equal house, Porphyry, Placidus, Campanus. Regiomontanus, etc., is
still bothering the westerners who, I think, must remember that in
Astrology what may seem theoretically scientific and sound may not
practically work. If the arguments for and against each of the various
house–systems are examined carefully it becomes clear that most of
the systems collapse at higher latitudes. Today it is my considered
view, and I am conscious that my view may not be acceptable to all,
between mathematically sound systems and those based on deep
symbolism perhaps the latter is more preferable. Just as the experience
of generations of astrologers from Parasara to Venkateswara should
not be ignored by us, so also the experience of the astrological savants
from Placidus to Zadkiel should not be ignored by our western friends.

My problem then *i.e.*, house division was solved when I was able
to acquire a Table of Houses and I did not then bother much about
the other contradictions in western Astrology, because I was not yet
aware of such contradictions.

When I started studying the subject of predicting events, western
Astrology posed issues which were important but tough.

9

Western Astrology seemed to me like a glamorous girl, attractive on the surface. The inherent contradictions became evident as I progressed in my studies and started working on the house–divisions and the progressions. For predicting events, different types of directions are to be worked out. A.J. Pearce felt that the most dependable system was the primary directions. These are, of course, arithmetical computations of the apparent motion of any point in the heavens, or of any planet from the situation which it occupied at the moment of birth until it meets with an aspect of some other body or point. Thus the arc of direction is derived and it is converted into time, at the rate of 1 year for 1 degree. Conservative western astrologers measure directions of the midheaven by an arc of right ascension, and directions to the Ascendant in mundo by the semi–arc of the planet directed at the zodiac by oblique ascension. The sum and substance of this system is, all directions are formed within a few hours of the moment of birth.

The techniques of these directions were learnt by me from the ancient book *Primum Mobile* by Didacus Placidus de Titus, an Italian monk printed at Paris in 1657, and translated into English by John Cooper. Throughout this valuable treatise a certain humility of the author is apparent, as for instance when he observes : "And shall we with our confined powers of understanding presume to comprehend in any shape whatever the prodigious extent of the heavens, in any shape whatever, from an idea of the immensity of the surrounding space. The utmost stretch of human thought cannot attain the least notion of it."

Then we have the secondary directions, which, according to some, are not at all effective unless considered along with primary directions. According to the secondary directions planetary positions on the 2nd day after birth indicate the events to happen in the 2nd year and on the 50th day to the 50th year and so on. Secondary directions in a sense are no more than transits. The *Primum Mobile* was my source book and gave me enough material to comparatively study the western and Hindu systems.

Tacitus gives the horoscope of Phillip III of Spain and justifies his death on the basis of primary directions. He was born on 14–4–1578 (latitude of birthplace being 41° N). The Ascendant is given as 343° 9' (Sayana). Phillip died on 31–3–1621, aged 42 years 11 months. According to the primary directions the arc of direction of the medium coeli to Saturn is 42° 14', which means Saturn projects the square to the Ascendant. According to secondary directions, to use the words

Venus	Sun					Merc.	Ascdt. Jupit.
Rahu Ascdt. Merc.			Moon	Sat. Rahu			
	RASI				NAVAMSA		
Mars Sat.			Ketu				Mars
			Jupit.	Moon		Venus	Sun

of Placidus, "the Sun on the day he died was posited upon Mercury of the nativity, Saturn in the square". After elaborating some more directions he feels that they justified the event of the death of the king.

Consider the chart according to the Hindu system. Lord of the Ascendant Saturn is in the 12th in association with a malefic Mars. Lord of the 8th is in the Ascendant and a benefic is placed in the 8th. From the Moon, the 8th lord is again in the 7th with a malefic Mars, but the 8th from the Moon and Ayushkaraka are not aspected by Jupiter. This is therefore a *madhyayu* chart.

The Sun is a *maraka* both from the Ascendant and the Moon. Mars is in a *maraka* place from the Moon and in the 12th from the Ascendant. The king died in the sub–period of Mars in the major period of the Sun. The whole deduction is so simple.

After making a comparative study of the Hindu and western systems I came to the conclusion that the western system lacked depth and substance, the methods employed for timing events were not quite reliable and that the Hindu system alone could be considered the system *par excellence*. My fascination for western Astrology gradually waned until I rejected it in 1941 entirely in favour of the Hindu system.

The conflict in my mind whether I should concentrate entirely on the study of Astrology or I should also go deeply into other methods of divination could not be easily reconciled. Grandfather left the decision to my own discretion, emphasising at the same time, that specialization in Astrology was alone preferable, as it was not only a science based on mathematics but I had — this was his view — "a knack for analysing horoscopes".

Undaunted I pursued my studies of palmistry, numerology and card–reading in such a manner that sleepless nights were spent making comparative experiments in all the three subjects.

The year 1930 was highly significant in my life because of three important events. The first was of course, my marriage. The second was my re–starting as publisher THE ASTROLOGICAL MAGAZINE which had ceased publication in 1924. And the third was establishing some sort of contact with the then astrological savants in foreign countries.

The urge to master palmistry and numerology was so intense that I became thorough in Cheiro's *Language of the Hand* and *Book of Numbers*.

In October 1930 or so a lawyer from Tamil Nadu visited grandfather for some astrological advice. Before grandfather gave any predictions it was my responsibility to cast the horoscope, work out the Dasa and Bhukti ruling at the time of consultation and note down the presence of any important Yogas. The lawyer's case was no exception. He was then about 65 or 66 and wanted to retire from active practice and lead "a quiet religious life'. Curiosity made me study his hand. While western books on palmistry emphasise a close examination of the Mount of Venus, etc., for studying marriage and marital happiness, I had been taught to look to the line or lines sprouting from the base of the little finger and running parallel to the *Heart Line*. When this line is deeply and well set, one will have a happy marriage, If the line is crossed by another tiny line one will have extra-marital relations. If the Marriage Line is slightly bent towards the Heart Line the wife will have some serious health problem. If the bend is towards the little finger, one will renounce the world and takes no interest in marriage. The nearness or distance of the Marriage Line to the base of the little finger indicates early or late marriage. if there is a fork at the end of the Marriage Line, the couple may separate. In this manner results due to the different permutations and combinations of Marriage Line with Mount of Venus, Heart Line, Head Line etc., had been explained to me by Rama Sastry.

What struck me in the lawyer's palm was a whorl at the end of the marriage line. I must confess that compared to my "attainments" in Astrology then, my knowledge of palmistry was elementary. But still I thought that the Marriage Line had some peculiar disposition. I then examined the horoscope of the gentleman and found that Rahu was in the 7th from Lagna (Virgo) in association with Mars and Venus aspected by Saturn from Gemini. Affliction of the 7th house, and Venus equally afflicted in a common sign, are no factors for happiness in married life. I told the lawyer, "Sir, if you do not mistake me, your wife is not living with you and you have a concubine." He became furious and said, "What non-sense are you talking ? I am 66 years old and am thinking of retiring from mundane activity and taking to a purely spiritual life. Don't defame elders like me by such misinterpretation".

"But, Sir, your palm cannot lie," I persisted. He ruled me out saying, "You are pretending to be a great palmist which you are not". I objected to his remark and again told him that his horoscope corroborated the palm. He was much displeased. After consulting his horoscope with grandfather,and taking his advice, the lawyer departed. I narrated this incident to my grandfather. While broadly endorsing my inference he remarked that I should not give such categorical interpretations and that such predictions should be sugar–coated. Imagine my surprise when after a few days I received a letter from the lawyer marked "confidential" confessing that he had a concubine and that he had determined to get rid of her and divert his mind to religious studies. When I showed this letter to grandfather, he expressed his happiness with my predictive ability ; but in this case, he cautioned that "it might be due to chance also". This experience gave a boost to my desire to master palmistry.

One fine evening grandfather was relaxing on an easy chair in the compound of our bungalow. I was standing nearby trying to elicit from him answers to some astrological problems that were then agitating my mind. I again told him of my view that palmistry could be more reliable than Astrology because the basis was more correct unlike in Astrology where, in the absence of correct time of birth, predictions were bound to go off the mark. I could guess that he did not like the idea of my giving undue importance to palmistry. The matter was therefore dropped.

As grandfather was about to get up — he had to be helped to get up due to his trouble with his right foot— a Tamilian, dark in complexion, well–built and wearing a *dhoti* and upper cloth with *vibhuti* (Sacred ash) prominently smeared on his forehead made his appearance. He stood at a distance and bowed his head to grandfather and introduced himself saying "I am an *adi dravida* (Harijan) coming from Cuddalore side and well–versed in *rekhasastra* (palmistry). I have come seeking your blessings and financial help as I am poor and have to perform my daughter's marriage".

Fifty years ago we had in our house 2 or 3 *adi karnataka* (Harijan) servants who had access to all parts of the house except the kitchen and the pooja–room. Grandfather did not attach much importance to the then prevailing practice of keeping Harijans at a distance. In fact, the occasion of the palmist's visit was used by my grandfather to explain to me the evils of some of the social practices that had somehow found their way in the name of Sastras into the fabric of the Hindu way of life and how it was neither *Sastraic* nor human to call a set of people untouchables simply because they did a certain type of work. Quoting *slokas* purporting to be from Manu and Yagnavalkya he said that in ancient times robbers, thieves, criminals and those who had dishonoured their parents or gods and committed certain types of crimes and anti–social elements were considered outcastes and allotted separate residential areas for their living and that they were allowed to enter the town or village only with the permission of the authority. They were the real untouchables.

I do not remember the palmist's name. He stayed with us for over three weeks. He was a vegetarian and was simple in his habits. He knew only Tamil and Malayalam and could speak no other language. This was a handicap for me to enter into any discussion with him as I did not know Tamil. The problem was solved by a teacher in the middle school in our village. Though domiciled in Karnataka for generations, he spoke Tamil at home. He acted as our interpreter during his leisure time. Grandfather knew Tamil well. He and the palmist used to spend at least an hour or two every morning holding discussions. The evenings were of course taken by me.

Rama Sastry's coaching and my study of Cheiro's books had given me a fairly good knowledge of palmistry. But I wanted to make good use of this Tamilian palmist's knowledge. I feigned my ignorance of palmistry and requested the palmist to explain to me the *Rekha Sastra*. He said that it was a very difficult art and unless I under–went apprenticeship under him for a couple of years I would not be able to learn much. His answer was discouraging and disappointing. But I persisted. One evening he examined my palm and stunned me by saying that I had lost my mother in my 2nd year, that my Lagna was

Aquarius and that I had Saturn and the Moon in the 4th house. I asked him, "How did you find out from my palm my Lagna and positions of the Moon and Saturn ? Is it by mathematics or intuition ?"

"Partly it is the art of palmistry and partly *mantrasiddhi* . The *rekhas* emanating from your Saturn Mount have given me the details." But how ?" I queried. He retorted, "You can never learn this art. Your grandfather will not permit you."

"But why? Does it involve the practice of any *Kshudra mantras*?" I asked him. He replied : "Precisely so, one has to practise certain rituals and chant certain types of *mantras* to enable one to get control of a *kshudra devata* who will enable one to discover from the palm the details of the horoscope."

I felt dejected and disappointed but pressed him to teach me any methods which had nothing to do with *Kshudra mantras* but purely based on palmistic rules. Perhaps moved by my sincerity, he gave me certain methods on the strict understanding that under no circumstances I should make them public. But I gave him no such promise.

One of the methods is : Take the total number of lines on the third phalange from the four fingers of the right hand. Call this x. Then you get the constant c with the aid of the formula $c=x \times 2$. The other formulae worked out by me on the basis of the information given by him were the age of the person could be given with the formula $c \times 32 + 24$ if the approximate age is between 35 and 55. Similarly in the case of younger and older persons the divisor changes. For instance in the case of children the divisor employed is 75. Similarly the solar month of birth is to be found by the formula $c \times 8$ (+) 12 ; the remainder indicates the sign the Sun is in $4c \times 3$ (+) 2 gives the phase of the Moon. Somehow I felt that the palmist did not reveal to me the "secrets" even though what he gave was subsequently found to be more or less the same as given by my esteemed friend the late Mr. Fakir Chandra Dutt whom I met at Calcutta in 1938. The palmist also explained to me what he called the Line of Sukra (girdle of Venus?).

He dreaded the presence of a star on the girdle of Venus as indicating severe forms of sexual diseases. His remedy : One who has the star should never get married. This advice was alright when emphasis on restraints was heeded by the vast majority of people. But today when permissiveness is so rampant in our own country, the word "restraint" has lost all meaning. Some of the hints given by him could not be dismissed as imaginary. For example he held that a star at the junction of *ravi–rekha* (Apollo line) and Head Line would spell severe eye troubles.

The palmist had the remarkable capacity of reading hands. One day he recounted some tragic happenings in his own family : His only son suffering from lunacy — this he attributed to the presence of a mole on his *ayushyarekha* ; his daughter having become a widow at 18 — a mole on the *vivaha–rekha*, and the extreme poverty he was experiencing. His parting advice was : "On your palm *ravi–rekha* is well marked. *Ayushya–rekha* (life–line) is deeply etched. Velan (Jupiter) is strong because of his mount. Never practise any low–type (*Kshudra*) *mantras* which I know are the main cause of my miserable life."

I must confess that his advice was compatible with the advice of my own grandfather and was instrumental in making me avoid dabbling in *kshudra mantras*.

10

Lt. Col. Skipwith, a British military officer stationed in Bangalore Cantonment, was an occasional visitor to our place. His interest was mainly in astronomy and to some extent, Astrology too. He used to often discuss these subjects with grandfather. On a certain Sunday I was asked by grandfather to deliver a message to him. Those days only one bus connected Bangalore and Chickballapur. Our village was 12 miles from Bangalore and the bus charge was 6 annas the equivalent 36 paise today. In view of the financial stringency we were experiencing. I went to Bangalore on cycle and reached the Colonel's place at about 10 a.m. Gandhi's Civil Disobedience Movement had just then started and I had become "a nationalist" wearing a khaddar *jubba* and a khaddar *lungi*. When I appeared before the Colonel in this national dress with sandals on, the military officer scanned me from head to toe and remarked rather disparagingly : "You have come into my drawing room with your chappals on. Don't you know that you should leave your footwear outside before entering the house ?" This touched me to the quick. I felt somewhat insulted and shot back : "Leaving footwear outside is a custom observed in Indian homes. Europeans do not have such practices as they strut about inside their houses with shoes on." The Colonel was angered by my defiant attitude towards a member of the ruling race. He again taunted me saying, "Your dress is not quite decent ". I could not stand his remarks and firmly told him, "Sir, I am wearing national dress and I am proud of it. Please mind your business. I have a message for you from my grandfather that you are welcome to visit him the next Sunday." When I was about to leave, he smiled, asked me to sit and offered tea which

I declined saying that I would not take anything in the house of a European.

Mr. Skipwith said : "Do you know anything about Varahamihira, the astronomer ? I think that he was indebted to the Greeks for most of his astronomical knowledge. I want to discuss this subject with your grandfather." My knowledge of Varahamihira or his alleged indebtedness to Greek astronomers was meagre. I had only studied *Brihat Jataka*. But I did not want to swallow the Colonel's remarks. I told him : "Europeans are prejudiced against Hindus. I think the fact is the other way —Europeans got all their knowledge from the Hindus." The Colonel continued : "I have studied Chidambara Iyer's English translation of *Brihat Samhita*. Can you explain the movement of the Saptarishis, which to me makes no sense as no European astronomer refers to such a movement ?"

I had not studied *Brihat Samhita* nor had I seen the *Panchasiddhantika*. Believing that discretion was the better part of valour I told him, "The Europeans can understand the Saptarishis' movements if they studied Varahamihira in the original. Grandfather will perhaps be able to throw some light on this subject. But so far as I am concerned, I am concentrating my studies on Mihira's *Brihat Jataka*." He appeared to be cantankerous and persisted, "Look here, even in Astrology, Varahamihira has copied from the Greeks. In Sloka 19, Chapter 1, he says 'the measure of the Rasis from Mesha to Kanya is 5–6–7–8–9 and 10, multiplied by 4'. These are the figures employed by the Greeks. What do you say now ?"

I reiterated, "I now say what I have already said, that the Greeks borrowed what is given in the *sloka* from ancient Indian sources." With this discussion our meeting ended and I cycled back to the village and narrated to grandfather all the details of my discussion with Skipwith, including his remarks on my dress. He did not feel quite satisfied with my performance and scolded me for what he called my "ill–mannered behaviour". The Colonel could not visit us on the appointed day due to "some inconvenience".

In 1959, when I was travelling from New York to Southampton by the luxury liner S.S. "Queen Mary" I met on board one Mr. John with whom I crossed swords about the origins of Hindu Astrology. He was a confirmed believer in the theory that Astrology originated in Chaldea. He had a copy of *Greek Horoscopes*, edited by O. Neugebauer and H.B. Van Hoesen. After returning to India I secured a copy of this book and went through it thoroughly. The authors refer to a number of horoscopes taken from *Vetius Valens* in which terms like "Apoklima" occur. Merely on the basis of this, one cannot say that the Hindus were indebted to Greeks for some of their knowledge. I have discussed this in my book *Hindu Astrology and the West*.

When the Civil Disobedience movement by Gandhi was launched grandfather felt very perturbed and he publicly condemned what he called "Gandhi's law–breaking" activities. He felt — and I now feel he was right — that law–breaking by Gandhi and his followers would have a very serious repercussion on the future of law and order in the country and that there would be chaos in India when people lost respect for law and order. Not that he lacked patriotism. He was an ardent patriot and a nationalist to the core. As a historian — he was the author of the great book *The History of Vijayanagar or The Never to be Forgotten Empire* — it was his conviction that freedom could be won only by *danda* or arms. He differed from the then fashionable Congress brand of nationalism.

I was not only his secretary but a clerk and an attender, all rolled into one, getting the mail daily from a village post–office 2 miles away from our place and taking down letters dictated by him, carrying messages to his friends etc. One day he dictated a letter to Lord Linlithgow, the then Viceroy of India, in which while making it clear that the British must concede political independence to India he also said they should deal with the "law–breaking movement" with a firm hand. Of course Linlithgow sent a polite acknowledgement.

In those days I was emotional and impulsive, thanks to the situation of Rahu in the 2nd in my horoscope aspected by Mars. I would also cool down quickly perhaps because of Jupiter's aspect on Rahu. Jealousy, bitterness, hatred, vindictiveness have never found a place in my mental make–up. I became uneasy at grandfather's attitude towards Gandhi's movement. With due deference to his age and experience, I would firmly tell him that if we opposed Gandhi's movement, we would be doing an unpatriotic act. But he continued to be a harsh critic of Gandhi and the Congress. At this distance of time, I feel that some of his views were correct. Is not the present want of respect for law and order, a concomitant of Gandhi's encouragement for law–breaking and disrespect for authority ? Grandfather had the firm conviction that India's independence would come not because of the Congress movement but because of international developments. And he was perhaps right. But at that time I began to nurse a subtle hostility towards my grandfather because of the clash of opinions. But I never transgressed the limits of decency or restraint and our mutual affection was never in doubt.

It looked as if Col. Skipwith had a fairly good knowledge of western Astrology. I had another meeting with him when I had again to call on him to deliver a letter addressed to him by grandfather. This time he was more friendly. He said that Hindu Astrology was a mass of confused ideas and had not been as systematically developed as the western system. This remark was like adding insult to injury. He was a military officer and the British in those days, with very few exceptions, were generally arrogant. But I felt that I should defend Hindu Astrology and told him bluntly, "Sir, you are an Englishman. You do not know Sanskrit. You have not studied Hindu Astrology. Therefore I think your views are all based on imagination. Do you have Yogas, Dasas, Arishtas etc., to enable you to analyse horoscopes ? I am not impressed by your views".

He gave me his chart to be handed over to grandfather. There were rumours that he would be shifted to Lucknow or some other Cantonment.

Even without his asking, I made a rough study of the chart (which had been cast by some local astrologer) as I was sitting before the Colonel and said, "Sir, in this horoscope lord of the 7th Venus is in the Ascendant with Mars and aspected by Saturn who is in association with Rahu. This not only gives you stubbornness but your private life will be miserable." He patiently listened to what I said and queried "Can you tell me of any significant event that has happened in the past ?" This was embarrassing and my "reputation", if I had any then, was at stake. But I did not want to beat a hasty retreat. Had not my grandfather told me often that Jupiter in my 10th house would always act as a protective shield and that I would never come out scathed. I worked out the Dasas and found that the Colonel's Saturn's major period started about June 1916 and Saturn's own sub–period lasted till about June 1919. Saturn is in the 4th with Rahu and aspected by

				Merc. Jupiter	Rahu	
Sat. Rahu	**RASI**		Venus	**NAVAMSA**		
Merc.		Ketu	Sat.			Moon Mars
Sun Jupit.	Ascdt. Mars Venus		Moon		Ascdt. Sun Ketu	

Mars, lord of the 1st and the 6th. It could be a serious illness, I reflected within myself. But Mars who aspects Saturn is the lord of the 3rd and 8th from the Moon and Saturn is in the 6th. Therefore I thought it could be an accident.

And to my good fortune I found that about the same time the First World War was going on. Therefore taking all the courage into my hands I said : "Sir, in your 39th or 40th year — he was born in 1877 — you must have sustained a grievous injury by a firearm as Mars ruling weapons is aspecting Saturn, the major lord who is in the 4th house, which happens to be the 11th from Aries, ruling the knees. A bullet could have hit your knees." Flabbergasted, he said, I was perfectly right. It seems he was a cavalry–man in the First World War and when he was riding a horse, a bullet fired from the enemy ranks hit him near the knee–joint. He was operated and could walk freely only after 3 months.

I congratulated myself on this "distinguished performance" pinpointing an event that took place 13 years earlier for a European who was a critic of Hindu Astrology. I recovered my normal thinking remembering grandfather's remark made earlier in respect of some other predictions given by me, that my correct hit could have been due to chance. Col. Skipwith conveyed to grandfather how accurate I was in my judgement but grandfather — he would never compliment or praise budding astrologers like me, lest our heads might become dizzy — only smiled at me.

The joy of making such a successful prediction did not last long. I was again confronted with a situation in which I had a chance to show my astrological ability. The occasion was a gathering of a few astrologers hailing from nearby places, on the occasion of grandfather's 74th birthday. His birthdays used to be always celebrated in a fitting manner. All the state officers including the Dewan and members of Council would personally congratulate him. The mornings were set apart for the recitation of Vedas. The gathering would consist of all sorts of people — pandits, musicians and even jesters. The then leading musicians of the state like Veena Seshanna, Veena Venkatagiriappa, Vasudevachar, Bidaram Krishnappa and others would sing with accompaniments and seek his blessings.

There were about half a dozen astrologers, and they were asked to consider the marriage prospects of a girl whose father, a great friend of grandfather, was very worried because his daughter could not get married even though she was about to complete her 12th year! Today, things have changed and girls aged 30 or even 35 remain unmarried.

I think the girl's Ascendant was Capricorn and Saturn was situated in the 7th; Mars in Lagna and Venus in Sagittarius with Rahu and the Moon in Gemini. Opinions varied. One astrologer said that she would remain a spinster, another predicted a miserable married life and the third one, widowhood and the fourth one said that her character would be questionable etc. It was my turn. Of course I was not asked to give my opinion because I was still a *persona non grata*. But I volunteered on my own as I felt confident that I would hit the bull's eye. I said that Mars in Lagna aspecting the 7th where another malefic was situated spelled disaster in marriage. The consensus was in favour of unhappiness so far as marriage was concerned. The last one, an elderly person hailing from Mysore, contradicted every one of us. He predicted that the girl would get a good husband and good children and would lead a happy married life ! The father of the girl was pleased that at least there was one astrologer who gave a prediction that could bring him joy. But my restlessness again asserted itself and at the risk of being considered impertinent I said in a challenging tone that the Pandit from Mysore was betraying his ignorance, when in the light of the worst malefic combinations in the girl's chart he dared predict a happy married life. Warming up I said : "Sastriar, can you quote some authority for predicting a successful marriage when Mars in Lagna aspects the 7th, the 7th lord is in the 6th and Venus is in a common sign with Rahu ?" Humility was still not my forte. I quoted a *sloka* which said that Venus in a common sign with malefic could confer three marriages. The Mysore Pandit did not expect such a question from an inexperienced youth. The Pandit replied calmly : "Look here, *slokas* cannot be quoted for each and every prediction made. If you want I will give the *sloka*. But I go more by experience and God's guidance." Then he quoted a *sloka*, the meaning of which is : "If the lord of the 7th is in the 6th and Venus is in conjunction with Rahu, the wife will be beautiful and beget children."

Grandfather's role was that of a passive observer. But he nodded assent at this *sloka* which meant his own opinion favoured the Pandit's judgement. On the face of it the combination appeared to me to be absurd. How could Venus in a common sign with Rahu and the lord of the 7th in the 6th confer a good wife ? The combination specifying a happy marriage for a boy, it seems, was being applied to a girl"s horoscope. There was no further discussion and the matter ended there. A decade later, I was informed by the father of the girl that she was married into a good family and was living happily with a loving husband and beautiful children.

Here is an instance of an apparently malefic combination as viewed from common–sense, giving rise to exactly opposite results. I have come across several such exceptional rules and found them practically correct, especially if the Ascendant happened to be Capricorn. But in case of Cancer, the benefic effects do no happen and the marriages in the majority of cases have proved unfortunate.

On a fine day in June or July 1930, there was a surprise visit from a highly placed person in the then Mysore State. He had faced, it seems, a very difficult and tough problem in life and wanted astrological guidance from grandfather. I cast the horoscope and gave

RASI

Rahu Jupit.			Sat.
	RASI		
Ascdt.			Sun
	Moon Mars	Venus Merc. Ketu	

NAVAMSA

Mars		Mercury	Ascdt. Sat.
Venus Rahu	**NAVAMSA**		
Moon			Ketu
	Jupiter	Sun	

it to him with some of my observations. What was the problem ? I tried to discover it from the birth horoscope :

At the time of consultation the native was at the fag end of Venus sub–period in the major period of Rahu. My analysis was : The major lord Venus was in the 9th debilitated and aspected by Rahu and *putrakaraka* Jupiter. The sub–lord Rahu had conjoined Jupiter, Karaka for children and was in the 7th from the major lord and aspected by Saturn, lord of Lagna. He was undergoing *sade–sathi*. The problem could be a domestic one involving either the wife or the children.

How to clinch the issue ? I therefore noted that the problem could relate to serious illness of the wife. Grandfather went through my notes and felt that my interpretation was fairly accurate. But he went on to add that I had omitted a very salient factor, *viz.*, consideration of the horoscope with reference to the Moon. He said that from the Moon the 5th house was afflicted. Since Rahu was one of the mischief-makers and he was aspecting the major lord, the problem could relate to a matter pertaining to the marriage of children. He was correct. The native who had been conferred a knighthood by the then British Government, was holding a high position. He was restless by nature. His private life was not above board. But his distress then was, one of his daughters was stubborn in wanting to marry a son of a leading Muslim gentleman. The native was a high caste Hindu (not a Brahmin). His community strongly opposed the alliance. And he himself was unable to reconcile to the situation of his son–in–law being a non–Hindu. Grandfather advised him to do his best to dissuade his daughter, as the planetary influences were very bad. One evening the girl disappeared from her parents' place, got herself converted and married her lover. Throughout the remaining part of his life — he was then about 74 — his distress was indescribable. It was only after this incident that I realised how important Chandra Lagna could be in assessing a horoscope correctly.

11

THE ASTROLOGICAL MAGAZINE had always had a very checkered career until it was handed over to me in 1936 when it was re-started as a quarterly. In its palmiest days the circulation did not exceed 4 to 5 hundred copies per issue. Though the Magazine was started in 1895 at Bellary, it suffered severe strokes of *balarishta*, thanks to the fact that grandfather used to be busy with his book-writing and lecturing activities aimed at spreading the message of Astrology. The Magazine would come out say for 2 years or so and then suddenly stop and after a lapse of time again appear, sometimes 2 to 3 issues being combined together. I believe, some regularity in publication had been maintained from 1895 to 1912. It was in the year 1924 or so that its publication ceased in a final sense.

In January 1930, I suggested to grandfather that the Magazine be rivived. At first he was not quite enthusiastic. Our financial position was so bad that we could hardly make both ends meet. But persistence on my part paid off. A *prasna* chart was cast by me on 5-1-1930.

My knowledge of horary Astrology then was confined only to one book, *viz* ., *Chappanna or Prasna Sastra.* Taurus rising with Jupiter, and Mercury the planet of journalism and lord of the 2nd and 5th in the 9th and the Moon in the 10th were — at least I felt so then — ideal combinations to start the work. When I showed the chart to grandfather, he was not quite happy with it. Though he did not spell out his misgivings, I could glean that he did not like the situation of Saturn Yogakaraka and Venus, lord of the ascendant in the 8th in association with the Sun.

In my younger days, enthusiasm would often take the better of common-sense. I tried to convince grandfather that I felt confident of reviving the Magazine successfully. But what about the money for it ? There was no satisfactory answer. Grandfather took up his own horoscope to see whether the new venture would be successful. He was then having the sub–period of Mercury in the major period of Saturn lasting till 2–2–1931, to be followed by Ketu's sub–period. It was only after Saturn Dasa commenced that he, and naturally the family, started experiencing straitened financial circumstances. Grandfather had always felt that Saturn was a *maraka* and being lord of the 7th and a *naidhana star,* he would cause much trouble besides causing death. But I was not to be put off easily. I butted in and said : "Saturn is a Yogakaraka for you and he is in the 2nd house. In the Navamsa he is well placed. How could he cause all these troubles ? I do not feel convinced by the reasoning given by you." He appreciated my remarks saying : "According to Vimshottari Dasa the planets become constellational lords in the order of the Sun as lord of Uttara, Krittika and Uttarashadha, and so on. Saturn in my case is no doubt Yogakaraka and will continue to give Yoga in the shape of name, fame and respect. But being placed in the 2nd or house of wealth in the constellation of Mars, who owns the 7th a *maraka,* financially favourable results cannot be given. Likewise Mercury, though lord of the 2nd and 5th, has caused a Rajayoga being associated with the Sun,

	Rahu	Jupiter Ascdt.		Moon Ketu	Mercury	Jupiter
Moon						Sat.
		RASI			NAVAMSA	Mars Venus
Merc.						
Mars Sun Venus Sat.	Ketu				Sun	Rahu

to the extent of reputation, name and fame. But as lord of the 2nd occupying again the star of Mars a Maraka, he is not beneficially disposed as far as giving money is concerned."

This was the first time I learnt about the lord of a constellation in which a Dasa lord is placed influencing the results of a Dasa. Not being quite satisfied, I wanted grandfather to give me the source of this theory as no text that I had studied so far viz., *Brihat Jataka* and *Jataka Chadrika* had ever hinted at such a theory. This was construed as impertinence on the part of an upstart like me and grandfather almost shouted saying, "You demand authority for what I have said. Don't be foolish in asking for authority. My own experience is the authority. Satyacharya's statement in his *Dhruvanadi* is the authority." Not still satisfied, and risking my being dubbed impertinent I said, "But in your own books there is no reference to such lordship." This was too much for him and he dismissed me with the remark, "Arrogance and knowledge are poles apart." I became uneasy that I had wounded his feelings. The next day I apologised for my seeming discourtesy. But he had already forgotten the incident and was his normal self approving of my quest for astrological knowledge.

Since I was to be the publisher of the Magazine he took up my horoscope. He explained that I was then running the sub–period of Ketu in the major period of Rahu, that *ashtama sani* (Saturn transiting the 8th from my radical Moon) had started and that Venus in his sub–period might even give a change. He said that the time was not quite propitious for me then. "But," I protested, "Rahu is in the constellation of Mercury who had caused Rajayoga." Grandfather's reaction was as expected. Interpretation of Dasa results should be related to age, environment and the existing circumstances. "But nevertheless." he remarked, "Mercury being the planet of journalism may do some good. Human effort and Divine Grace can offset adverse planetary indications. It all depends on how sincerely one tries to face planetary threats. Go ahead if you are confident that you can bring out the Magazine regularly."

The result was I found myself in a very embarrassing situation, not knowing what to do. Within a week I went to Bangalore, met

V.B. Sreekantiah, Proprietor of the then well known printers V.B. Soobbiah & Sons situated in Avenue Road. He wanted an advance of Rs. 200 to be paid. I tried to convince him that he should print the first issue without any advance and that there would be no difficulty in paying the bill as there was a lot of demand for the Magazine. I knew I was lying but that was the tactics I had to employ. Reluctantly he undertook the printing and the first issue of Volume 19 was brought out in the first week of May 1930 in Demy 1/8 size. Grandfather was, of course, the editor and I, the publisher, The joy I felt then to see my name in print could not be adequately described. The article written by me for the first time ever concluded thus : "We have fixed the annual subscription at the low sum of rupees five only, with a view to place the Magazine even in the hands of any persons whose incomes are very moderate but whose thirst for knowledge is great".

Real trouble started for me. Day in and day out I had to visit teachers, lawyers, doctors, businessmen, etc. to enlist subscribers. Somehow I would collect the money needed to pay the bill amount of about Rs. 80 for the first issue. Making part–payment and persuading Sreekantiah, we could somehow bring out the Magazine. Cycling to Bangalore almost every day to visit the printer, examining the proofs and then canvassing subscribers affected my health and I became bed–ridden for about 10 days. In the meanwhile I persuaded the printers not to stop the work. Grandfather again studied my horoscope and said that the sub–period of Ketu and the major period of Rahu— Ketu in the 8th and Rahu in the 2nd — and Saturn transiting the 8th were unfavourable and that I would recover soon. I looked into *Krishna Misreeya* a classical work on directional Astrology and the results given for Ketu in Rahu "Increase of enemies, danger from thieves and weapons, poverty, hatred of relatives, change of place, loss of life, obstruction from rulers and loss of money" were frightening and almost unnerved me. Ketu was not conjoined with or aspected by any planet But major lord Rahu was aspected by Mars —epilepsy and difficulties" and by Jupiter "affliction to wife and children, ill–health and trouble from Brahmins". Had I looked into these predictions before reviving the Magazine I would perhaps never have decided to take the risk I had done.

Would Ketu in Rahu kill me? Ketu the sub–lord, occupying the 8th could give the results of Mercury, placed in a Maraka house and Rahu was in a Maraka place. Saturn was transiting the 8th, I figured out that my death was inevitable during Ketu's sub–period. The fear of death gripped me once again. But this was again allayed by grandfather. He said : "Don't be foolish, you have a long lease of life. Jupiter in your 10th house coupled with a number of other Yogas will lift you up to considerable name and fame far surpassing mine.How can you die now ?" This acted as a tonic and I recovered fully and resumed my difficult job of visits to the printers, enlisting subscribers etc. Grandfather had the uncanny power of prediction and his analysis of horoscopes was superb. My appreciation of this gift of his grew as I made advances in my own studies.

It is impossible to describe the agony, the suffering and the stress I had to pass through to carry out my decision of bringing out the Magazine.I would often ruminate why in a moment of enthusiasm or weakness I had undertaken this job. Though the printer Sreekantiah was kind and obliging, one day he told me bluntly after printing nine issues : "My dear young man, I admire your enthusiasm but that is matched neither by experience nor financial resources. I am sorry to say, only one more issue will be printed and if you want to bring out the Magazine – I would advice you not to pursue this foolish venture — get the work done somewhere else". This was a bolt from the blue. The printers were due about Rs. 500 which we could not pay. In fact the printers filed a suit against us for recovery of this sum. I could settle the account only in 1939 after the passing away of grandfather and after I had shifted to Bangalore. Some how the Magazine was continued somewhat irregularly for 3 years until 1933, when it had to cease publication again landing us in heavy debts.

I shall have more to say about the vicissitudes of the Magazine, the opposition I had to face, not from the public, but from some step–relatives who had been helped by me attributing mean motives to me and indulging in character assassination — and this is kept up even today.

Jupit.	Rahu			Mars		
Ascdt.	RASI		Ketu	NAVAMSA		
		Moon	Sat.			Rahu Moon Jupit.
Sun Mars Merc.	Saturn Venus Ketu		Ascdt. Sun Merc.	Venus		

One day, an ailing child's horoscope was brought to us by a relative of the owner of the new press, to which we had shifted the printing of the Magazine, for examining its longevity. I cast the horoscope and made some notes about he longevity of the child and placed the papers before grandfather.

My conclusion was that the child had good longevity for the following reasons : Lord of the Ascendant is in the 10th in conjunction with Venus, a Yogakaraka, and aspected by Jupiter. Three malefic were in the 11th. Lords of the 8th and the 3rd were in the 11th. The 8th from Chandra Lagna was occupied by Jupiter. At the time of consultation, the child was having the sub-period of Rahu in the major period of Venus. I was delighted that the combinations for good longevity had been so clearly marked that any astrologer could come to the same conclusion as I did. I explained to the father of the child who had come to meet grandfather that he should not worry about the longevity. But the gentleman did not appear satisfied with my explanation. When grandfather took up the chart he went on giving arguments as I had done and I was congratulating myself on how accurate I was and how I had mastered Astrology; but he stopped suddenly and said : "Though one could say theoretically that the child has a long life, there is a combination which spells disaster. Rahu Bhukti in Venus Dasa could prove critical unless suitable remedial measures are undertaken". All the castles I had built in the air about my ability to analyse horoscopes and about my astrological scholarship collapsed and I felt most miserable. There was not a combination I knew of which indicated death in the Dasa of Yogakaraka Venus. How could grandfather predict a period of crisis ?. What if his prediction failed ? Would it not affect the reputation of so great a man in the field of Astrology ? All my fears were found to be baseless when within two weeks news came that the child had died due to broncho–pneumonia.

I lost no time to again press grandfather to tel me how he could predict the death in the Dasa of a Yogakaraka and that too when the lords of the 8th and the 3rd were all well placed. He said : "Look here, there is a certain combination of a fatalistic nature which could negate the strength of the horoscope judged according to the usual canons of Astrology. When such special *arishtas* are present, they must be given precedence."

I went on ruminating as to what could be the special combination that had neutralised all the other strong dispositions in the horoscope. I dared not ask grandfather again about this, lest he thought I was arrogant. One day all of a sudden at the instance of grandfather I traced an old notebook written by his father. B. Gopala Rao which had been mixed up with other papers. In beautiful Kannada script he had noted a few important combinations which would prevail over all other combinations. And one sloka–*randhreshe labha rasisthe bhoume soorya samanvite, janmadaaye rahu bhuktou paralokam prayaasyuti* meaning that "If the lord of the 8th is in the 11th and the Sun conjoins Mars one departs to the other world in the Dasa ruling at birth and the sub–period of Rahu" caught my attention. This was the combination I was looking for. When I showed this to grandfather he just smiled. In the same manner certain other combinations affecting marriage, children etc., which could predominate over the general combinations were found in the notebook. These were gems of Astrology not found in the extant astrological texts nor available to the aspiring student.

My grandfather's grandfather Venkataramanayya, who was born in 1747 A.D. and died in 1828 A.D., had served as an Amildar (Tahsildar) of Devanahally Taluk in Bangalore District. He was said to have been a very principled and honest officer helping those in trouble. Grandfather, therefore, gave me, after my birth, this name *viz*, B. Venkataramanayya, as he thought that just as his grandfather lived till his 82nd year and had earned a good reputation, I too should live long and get name and fame My uncle's son, born on 6th August of the same year as me, was named Gopala Rao but he was always sickly and died in his 3rd year.

Somehow I felt that the name I bore looked redundant and out of fashion. A numerologist by name Subbiah, who was a frequent visitor to *Suryalaya* came to my rescue. He figured out on the basis of numerology that B. Venkataramanayya, when totalled, gave 1, a very unlucky number according to him and that I should change it. Though not much impressed by his arguments, I felt that I must have a fashionable name. The numerologist quipped : "B. V. RAMAN. The total comes to 8 which is in harmony with your date and month of birth." "But," I told him, "the name suggested by you may be misleading. I may be mistaken for a Tamilian." "No", he said, "It is B.V. RAMAN." (बि.बि.रमण) Anyway it appealed to me and I changed my name. But in actual practice it became B.V. RAMAN (बि.बि. रामन्).

According to the texts on Numerology 1 had read, a No. 1 person is a dynamic personality, an introvert, lacking in confidence, lazy and indecisive. How could I allow my name to be equated with No. 1 ? I was no doubt an "introvert" but never indecisive, lazy or lacking in confidence. But Cheiro whom I have earlier referred to had written to me that my zodiacal sign "being Leo, ruled by the Sun in its positive aspect, 1 and 4", were my numbers. My birth date was the 8th and the total of the day, month and year of birth was 2. Why not opt for a name which could harmonious with 2 and 4 ? These were of course my reflection at that time. Finally I liked the idea of Subbiah and consented to change my name.

I have already given my views on Numerology in which I have

developed certain reservations in the light of experiences extending over 5 decades. Numerology is no doubt a fascinating subject but why it should be based only on the English alphabets and not on *aksharas* or Sanskrit alphabets which are more scientific, is a matter I have yet to reconcile with.

To be fair to Numerology, I must confess that numbers 2, 4, 5 and 8 have always played a significant role for good in my life while No. 1 stands associated with losses, difficulties, and misfortunes.

To publish my name as B.V RAMAN in the Magazine was a bit embarrassing to grandfather. He did not want I should reject his grandfather's name but I was quite against It.

It may be felt by some readers that these matters may not be relevant to the present narration but sometimes even small details assume relevance, because readers then will be able to judge better the travails of one who has had to face obstacles at every single step of his life to reach his cherished goals.

12

SIR MIRZA M. ISMAIL, the then Dewan of Mysore, and grandfather were close friends. Sir Mirza first called at out place when he was ADC to the Maharaja perhaps in 1917 or 1918 A.D. to convey an invitation on behalf of Sri Krishnaraja Wodeyar, the then Maharaja of Mysore, to meet His Highness. At that time Mr. Mirza—he was knighted by the British after he became the Dewan — who was serving in the Mysore Civil Service, never dreamt that he would occupy he highest position in the State. But grandfather had given him the prediction that he would become the Dewan. In 1925, we were living in Visweswarapuram, a suburb of Bangalore; for here, facilities for grandfather's medical treatment were available. The house we lived in had a fairly large compound, the rent being Rs. 35 per month. One fine morning as grandfather was strolling in the compound, Sir Mirza came on horseback, got down at the gate and congratulated grandfather on the fulfillment of his prediction. Mysore had already been known as a model state and Sir Mirza said that as Dewan he would make it a better model. Though a Muslim, Sir Mirza was not a fanatic. He exhibited his loyalty to the Mysore throne and the Maharaja unflinchingly. He carried with him the dignity of a statesman and the culture of a trained mind.

One day in January or February 1931 Sir Mirza made an unscheduled visit to our place and looked somewhat worried. I seated him in our drawing room. Grand father was then in his Puja and he could not be disturbed. Sir Mirza knew this. He waited patiently for an hour. When grandfather came out of the Puja he was closeted with the Dewan for nearly 2 hours. Sir Mirza had a problem. His only son was not faring well in his education. Should he be sent to England ?

In those days children of Indian V.I.Ps. could, it seems, easily acquire some standard educational qualifications in England without much effort. His wife was ailing. Unfortunately the birth particulars of the boy were not known. Therefore the advice had to be based on Sir Mirza's own chart. After Sir Mirza left, grandfather asked me to work out the current directional and transit influences and also note down my opinion on Mirza's question.

Sir Mirza, according to details furnished by him was born at Mysore on 23rd/24th October 1883 at about 1h. 15m a.m.

			Ascdt. Venus		Sat.
Ketu	Saturn				
		Ascdt. Moon Mars Jupit.			Mars Ketu
	RASI			NAVAMSA	
			Rahu		
	Venus Sun Rahu	Merc.	Merc. Sun Moon	Jupiter	

Prima facie the horoscope did not reveal to me any Yogas worth mentioning. How did he then become the Dewan? What made grandfather predict Dewanship in the Sun's period? These doubts weighed heavily on my mind, but I could not discuss them with grandfather as I had been only commissioned to give my opinion about his son. Sir Mirza at that time was under the major period of the Moon and the sub-period of Mars. I was happy I had found the clue. Mars, lord of the 5th, is debilitated in the Ascendant. He is associated with the Lagna lord Moon and Jupiter, lord of the 9th (and 6th) and aspected by Saturn. I tried to dissect the combinations with a view to identifying the results, beneficial and harmful, such a cluster of planets would confer. My arguments were somewhat thus : The association of the debilitated lord of the 5th with the Ascendant indicated the source of unhappiness, *viz.*, the son (of Sir Mirza). *Putrakaraka* Jupiter also owns the 6th. This is bad so far as happiness from the issue was concerned. Saturn's aspect only intensified the affliction. But Mars, lord of the 5th, is *neechabhanga*. Jupiter, the Karaka is exalted. The 4th from the 5th is afflicted. Obviously while a good formal education was not possible, the son would shine well. For occupying a good position, the native's son must somehow become educated which meant —I concluded — he should be sent abroad to England to get a qualification. I stretched my astrological imagination to this extent and placed my opinion before grandfather. He carefully went through what all I had written and nodded his head in approval of my assessment. Naturally I felt elated that I could tackle such a tough problem in a manner that secured the acceptance of grandfather. The ego in me asserted and I must say that my head almost reeled. But all my round about reasoning was felt unnecessary in the light of a dictum of Satyacharya which grandfather quoted

पञ्चमे शुभ योगेतु पुत्रप्रबल्यमादिशेत् ।
प्रभुर्वा स्विप्रसिद्धिस्यातिसिध्दमन्त्रो प्रायया भवेत् ॥

meaning that if the 5th house is subject to favourable combinations or aspects, the son will become prominent and the native himself would either secure authority by dint of effort or secure *mantra siddhi*. Therefore, grandfather said, that if the son were to become prominent, he should somehow get a qualification which under the then existing conditions was possible only by being sent to U.K.

"But," I protested, "do you mean to suggest that my analysis is defective and my conclusion, incorrect ?" Grandfather said, "To some extent. You have beaten about the bush. All your reasoning is superfluous." Not being satisfied, I persisted, "The dictum given by you lacks clarity and is a bit confusing as it combines the son's prosperity and the native's own rise to power.The combination is ambiguous." Grandfather retorted, "Look here, your knowledge of Astrology is still in the process of assimilation. My knowledge of Astrology as of today is based on wide experience and intuitional perception. While theoretically your reasoning is a acceptable and the inference is also not bad, you must be able to *feel* the event by just looking at the chart".

This was too much for me to digest at that time. Though my ego was punctured. I had my own reservation about *feeling* a chart. There was no point in trying to argue with a master, as in spite of my "attainments" in Astrology, I was considered only an upstart.

What were the combinations in Sir Mirza's horoscope which conferred on him the highest position in the state? Dewans of those days, unlike the "popular ministers" of today, commanded respect. They were not corrupt and the administration was efficient and with all the limitations imposed by British suzerainty, worked for the weal of the common man. Of course there were no platform orations of politicians, in the name of serving the "weaker sections", while in reality enriching themselves, as we have today. The Mysore Government had one Dewan and 2 or 3 Members in Council carrying on the affairs of the state. The Maharaja was not an autocrat. He seldom interfered with the administration. Compared to the present "democratic" system of the government run by the "representatives of the people", the Maharaja's "authoritarian" rule was really a golden era almost approximating to the ideal of Rama Rajya.

Linguistic and sectional chauvinism was conspicuous by its absence. It was simply impossible to cash in on people's suffering to serve one's own selfish ends. The head of the government of such a model state was indeed held in esteem. But what were the astrological factors which made Mirza the Dewan for more than a decade?

After carefully studying the horoscope in the light of the astrological works I was then familiar with,*viz.,Jataka Chandrika, Brihat Jataka* and the Telugu edition of *Uttarakalamrita* — I figured out thus : Mars is Yogakaraka because of the ownership of both a *kendra* and a *trikona*. He is debilitated but has obtained *neechabhanga* and hence is very powerful. His Yoga strength is further fortified because, as a Yogakaraka he is in association with the lord of he Ascendant and Jupiter, lord of the 9th. The 10th house is occupied by no planet but is aspected by the political planet Sun who has secured cancellation of debility because Venus is in a Kendra from the Ascendant and the Moon. The Sun though associated with Venus, an enemy, cannot be deprived of his Rajayoga powers and Rahu, because he occupies a kendra is not malefic and indicates a powerful Rajayoga; the Dewanship being conferred on him after the commencement of the Sun's period was fully justified.

Suryanarayana Siddhanti was a frequent visitor to our place. When I explained to him Mirza's chart and why he became the Dewan in the Sun's Dasa, he was fully satisfied with my reasoning. He quoted some *sutras* from Jaimini bearing on Rajayogas. Since the Jaimini system was then Greek and Latin to me I could not follow anything. I was waiting for an opportunity to discuss Mirza's horoscope with grandfather so that I could get a certificate from him that my assessment was correct. Somehow he did not show much interest in this matter.

I continued to keep in touch with Sir Mirza until his death. In fact, he attended my son's Upanayanam in 1956 and daughter's wedding in 1961. He continued to be the Dewan throughout the Dasas of the Moon and Mars.

In December 1930, I visited Balehonnur, a small town in Chickmagalur District, about 180 miles from Bangalore, where my father–in–law Dr. M.C Srikanta Pandit was a Government doctor. Bu his sympathetic and helpful nature, he had endeared himself to the local people with whom he was very popular. The object of my visit was to spend some days with my wife Rajeswari, who was then in her 13th year. One day when I and Rajeswari were going for a walk, I chanced to meet a European "father"of the local church, who invited me to his house. After a few meetings, he started giving sermons on Christianity and how Christ alone was the real saviour. In those days, my knowledge of Christianity or Christ's teachings was superficial, though as a Hindu tolerance marked my attitude towards other faiths. But from my younger days I had been somewhat allergic to any downgrading of Hindu beliefs. When the Bishop, as he later turned out to be, made some offensive remarks on Hinduism, I retorted, "Look here, you have no business to come here to convert poor people by holding out all sorts of temptations. Do you know anything of Sankara's philosophy?" In fact I myself did not know anything. He was stunned by my bold reply, and changing the subject quickly he smilingly said, "You say you are an astrologer. Of course serious Christians do not believe in Astrology. For the sake of curiosity can you tell me something about me ?" I said, "Europe is full of serious Christians shamefully setting at naught the fundamental precepts of Christianity. Example is better than precept. If you have studied the Bible carefully then you would not say that no 'serious Christian' would nod belief in Astrology." He was just an ordinary missionary interested in prosetylizing 'low caste' Hindus, and there was no point in talking with him any further. When I was about to take leave he again said, "Tell me something about me." He had no birth details. I asked him to name a number of three digits, manipulated it and got as remainder, a number which represented Rahu. There were some rumours in the village about this priest having a keep. Cashing in on these rumours, and the number revealing Rahu, I said, "You character is questionable. You have relations with a woman." He was dumb-founded and dismissed me with a smile. We parted company never to see each other again. A number of such episodes has taken place in my long life. After I went through carefully both the old and new Testaments, my respect for Christ increased in inverse proportion to my dislike for the fraternity which controls the church. There might be exceptions and my remarks do not apply to them.

The 75th birthday of grandfather was celebrated, as usual, on a grand scale on 28th January 1931. A large number of friends, relatives and admirers had gathered on the occasion. The day after the celebrations, I found my father–in–law closeted with grandfather for more than two hours. It looked as if they were engaged in some serious discussions. In the evening, my father–in–law told me that he had discussed with grandfather about my future, and that the latter had consented, though reluctantly, to the prosecution of my studies. My father–in–law painted a grim picture of my future if I did not continue my studies. He said, "Who will care for you after your grandfather's death ? You have no education, financial resources or any qualification to enable you to chalk out an independent career or do private business. The burden of looking after your father and his family falls on you. Therefore you must enter college without any second thoughts and take up medicine so that you could have a lucrative practice or get into service." These arguments did not really convince me. I said, "I am hopeful of a bright future as I feel I can make a successful career, because Jupiter in the 10th house in my horoscope will give me fame, name, finances etc. I have confidence." My father–in–law just laughed at what he called my "impractical ideas".

The next morning grandfather broached the same subject and said, "I and your father–in–law have decided that you should prosecute your studies further." "But," I remonstrated, "if I continue my studies who will take care of the family ? You are advancing in age and father has no means of livelihood. As I do not wish to fail in my duty towards you and father, I do not want study further." My remonstrances cut no ice. It was finally decided that I should stay at Bangalore for further studies, visit our village after college hours every Friday evening, assist grandfather in his work during the weekend and return to Bangalore every Monday morning. Thus after a break of 30 months, I was reluctantly obliged to resume my studies. This was when I was undergoing the sub–period of Venus in the major period of Rahu which grandfather felt was propitious. Jupiter who should give the results of the major lord Rahu was aspecting the 4th and the sun–lord Venus owned the 4th house. I had my own misgivings about any beneficial results being given by Rahu. My father–in–law died in 1965. He had keenly watched the progress I had made in Astrology and the laurels I had won both in India and abroad. And he used to often express his happiness.

It has been within my experience spread over nearly 60 years, that Rahu as sub–lord, whether in his own period, or the period of other planets, would always create problems of a serious nature, affecting family and personal matters, which would test the mental and physical stamina of an individual whatever be his social, educational or financial attainments. It is also found, contrary to general belief, that planets like the Sun and Mercury, occupying Rahu's constellations are capable of conferring happy results financially and career–wise but would create situations in domestic life, which could shatter a person's self–confidence and make him experience results which he would ordinarily never expect to happen. There are, of course, exceptions which I will discuss in due course.

13

In July 1931, I joined Inter Science at the Intermediate College (now Government Science and Arts College), Bangalore, selecting Chemistry, Botany and Zoology as my optional subjects. As our village was 12 miles from Bangalore, it was decided that I should stay at Bangalore. The college would remain closed on Saturdays and Sundays. I would reach Bangalore every Monday morning and get back to the village every Friday evening so that during the weekends I could attend to family matters. At Bangalore I rented a room at Rs. 6/- per month at Sankaradevara Mutt, Manavarthapet, and became friendly with the head of the Mutt, who had close connections with the Mutt at our village. There were only two rooms in the front one of which was occupied by me and the other by two students — one studying engineering and the other, printing. The rooms had no attached baths and the Mutt had a number of a families living there so that the only toilet available had to be shared by all. This was a bit embarrassing for me having been used to spacious accommodation in the village. I became a boarder at the Udipi Hotel in Chickpet — it was for Brahmins only at that time — the proprietor of which Janardhanayya was the son of one Parameswarayya who was serving as a cook in grandfather's household at Madras between the years 1906 and 1911 or so. My father–in–law and grandfather had decided that they would share my expenses as a student — about Rs. 40/- per month.

These details may no doubt be considered irrelevant to my experiments in Astrology. But I would like modern young men and women to have an idea of how things were in my student days. The break–up figures for Rs. 40/- were — Rs. 6/- room rent, Re. 1/-

light charge, Rs. 11/– boarding , Rs. 2.50 morning coffee, Rs. 4.50 afternoon tiffin and coffee, Rs. 2/– laundry, Rs. 11/– college fees. This would still leave Rs. 2/– which was spent in buying fruits for grandfather. Once in a blue moon I would go to a movie — to the eight anna (paise 50) class. Otherwise the only relaxation was walking from college to my room, about 4 km. each way. Student life was peaceful as politicians dared not interfere in the working of the University, which for all practical purposes could be said to have ben autonomous. Examinations could be passed only by hard work and not by being pushed up on the basis of caste, community or favouritism. Merit counted, though backward classes were given certain concessions in the matter of fees etc. Student–teacher relations were cordial and due respect was shown to the teachers. Goondaism so pronounced today amongst a certain section of students by way of threatening the teachers with dire consequences if they are not allowed to copy in examinations, or are not made to pass, was unheard of. But there were student unions, which concerned themselves with the interests of students, sports etc., and elections held were peaceful and really democratic. On the whole the atmosphere in the campus was dignified, peaceful and befitting a temple of learning.

I did not take part in any of the college union activities. Instead I started the "Lotus Club" in my room. It consisted of about 8 to 9 members — mostly my classmates. We would meet every Friday and discuss matters of topical interest, *viz.*, Civil Disobedience Movement in British India, untouchability etc., besides having talks delivered once in 10 or 15 days by one of the members on Astrology, religion, etc. The object of actively associating with this Club was to press the cause of Astrology and make my student colleagues take some real interest. At least once in a fortnight I would take the horoscope of a member and discuss it and give some forecasts. One of the members H.R. Varadarajan considered himself a nationalist, donned *khaddar* cloth and often harangued on nationalism and Gandhi's movement. But I never agreed with his views that law–breaking would make India free. Moreover, I thought that as Mysore State was ruled by a Maharaja who acted as a constitutional monarch, there was no need for any freedom movement in our state. My forecast given to him in the course of a fortnightly discussion that he would occupy a high position as a medical man did not impress the members who thought I was saying something to please him. As luck would have it after graduation from Mysore Medical College, he joined the I.M.S. and retired a couple of years ago from a high position. This way the Club did some useful work. It functioned for about eight months and then it had to be wound up. Brief reports of our activities would appear in some local Kannada dailies and seeing our names in print would thrill us.

Once it so happened that one of my teachers, B.S. Bhimachar, lecturer in Zoology, got scent of our activities and paid a surprise visit to our club when we were discussing Astrology. He showed keen interest and spoke favourably about our ancient culture and Astrology. I became friendly with Bhimachar and tried to impress upon him how keen a student of Astrology I was and how I would like my teachers also to take real interest in its study.

The first practical class in Zoology was a nightmare to me. I saw specimens of earthworms, dead and half–dead, brought before us for dissection. When Mr. Bhimachar came to my table and started explaining how the specimen was to be pinned and dissected, I cursed my stars for having chosen Zoology. Providence came to my rescue. I vomited and left the class. The next day Bhimachar invited me to his house and enquired about my health. When I said that my indisposition was due to my having witnessed earthworms lingering between life and death and my being asked to do the dissection, he just laughed and said that I must condition my mind to do such experiments. I remonstrated : "You do not expect me to kill them for experimentation. What use will all this killing be?" My teacher explained that as I was to study medicine, dissection of animals would give me a first hand knowledge of their anatomy, morphology, physiology etc., and then after completion of my course I could study the evolution theory in depth and try to correlate the various evolutionary processes to astronomical factors. Somehow I did not feel satisfied with my teacher's sermon with the result I decided once and for all that I would not take to the study of medicine. Bhimachar considered himself a Gandhian and subscribed to the Gandhian way of life — wearing *khaddar*, practising *ahimsa* (non violence) and spurning foreign articles. In fact, of all the teachers in the college he was the only one using *khaddar* and soft–spoken. I tried to argue with him that killing animals for the sake of conducting experiments was against Ahimsa which he claimed he was practising. Perhaps my arguments did not impress him and he had his own logic to justify the experiments on animals.

One fine morning my teacher invited me to his room in the laboratory and after coffee and some light refreshment handed over to me a horoscope —only Rasi — and wanted to know some detail about the chart. My remonstrance that unless all the calculations were made, and birth time checked in the light of some past events, analysis of a chart was not desirable, he said : "Try and say something about the wife of the native." I was in a dilemma but I did not want to give my teacher the impression that I was trying to wriggle out. I could guess that the horoscope was his though he did not say so.

In the Rasi chart presented by him, Mercury lord of the 7th was exalted but in conjunction with Rahu and the 7th was aspected by Mars. Venus was in an inimical place. I therefore said : "The native's wife is not normal in her thinking. She may behave hysterically and

Ketu			
Jupiter			
Saturn	RASI		Venus
Ascdt.	Mars	Sun Moon	Mercury Rahu

violently as if she were a lunatic. The native's married life is not happy." My teacher was almost flabbergasted and exclaimed. "Wonderful. You have made a correct analysis. She is suffering from lunacy. Tell me something more if you can." I excused myself saying that any further light could be thrown only after detailed calculations of his wife's horoscope. I must say that I had not made known to any of my teachers my antecedents, lest they should flock to me and pester me for predictions. Bhimachar also was not aware that I was the grandson of a famous astrologer.

I and Bhimachar became good friends. He was anxious to help me in my predicament about dissection. As he was the Head of the Department, he instructed the attender — one Nair to see that the specimens given to me for dissection were all completely dead. I also told Nair that I would pay him four annas (25 paise) each week for his coffee and tiffin. I had no other alternative than to dissect dead animals with great reluctance, once every week in practical Zoology classes.

After a few weeks Bhimachar called on me one day to get further — what he called "enlightenment" on his wife's ill–health and he said he was convinced about my predictive ability.

	Moon		Sat.			Rahu
Rahu Ascdt.			Sun Merc.			Sun Merc.
Jupit.	RASI		Venus Mars Ketu		NAVAMSA	
				Moon	Jupiter Ketu Ascdt. Mars	Venus Jupit.

The chart given was incomplete but I recast it. The lady was born on 17th July 1914 at Bangalore at about 8–20 p.m.

I tried to find out whether there were any combinations in the lady's chart to corroborate my finding in the husband's chart that the lady was insane. Of course in those days I was not quite conversant with the different shades of mental ill–health such as insanity, obsessional neurosis, depressive mania, schizophrenia etc. What struck me in this chart—readers will note that I am giving expression to in these pages my thoughts as they flashed in my mind about 60 years ago — was the affliction of the Ascendant, the 7th, the 5th and *Kalatrakaraka* Venus.

I told my teacher, "Sir, Venus, Mars and Ketu are together in the 7th which happens to be the 5th from the Moon. Lord of the 5th (from the Moon) is in the 12th therefrom in association with Mercury. This indicates either 'possession' by an evil spirit or some sort of hysteria making her behave violently." My teacher nodded his head in approval and remarked : "Doctors say it is a case of schizophrenia bordering on lunacy and they have prescribed some drugs. My home life is hell. Is there any remedy to counteract this possession ?" I just could not answer these questions. My views then about "possession' were conditioned by what I had sen in our own and neighbouring villages as cases of possession by evil spirits. I advised him to consult some good *mantrik* which he said he would do. After a week I was again invited for coffee to the teacher's house. Mrs. Bhimachar received me courteously. She was fair looking and of pleasing manners. It was difficult for me to believe that I had before me an insane lady capable of violent behaviour. The teacher's anxiety was so pronounced that he would consult with me off and on about his wife who had by then a child also.

I think it was about March–April 1932, when I was again asked to examine her horoscope more carefully. Since my knowledge was confined mostly to *Jataka Chandrika* and *Brihat Jataka* and to some rare *slokas* given to me by grandfather, I tried very hard to search for combinations that indicated lunacy. However when I looked into my notes, I found the required combination — malefics aspecting the

Lagna (पापग्रहेशिक्षतम् लग्नं), Saturn aspecting the 7th (यूनं रविज बीक्षितं) and lord of the 8th weak (रंध्रेशो विबलो) — cause *Unmada* or aberration of mind. In the chart under consideration the Ascendant was aspected by malefics, Saturn aspected the 7th and the lord of the 8th Mercury was weak in the 6th as he was in combustion. Armed with this *yoga* I told my teacher that his wife was suffering from mental aberration and that since the Dasa current then was that of Mars (till 1936) to be followed by that of Rahu (till 1957), it was a difficult case. The Ascendant ruling the head was afflicted and aspected by Mars, whose affliction was pronounced because of his association with Ketu and the aspect of Saturn. I added, "therefore I feel she may have to undergo surgery."

Grandfather had always cautioned me not to interpret horoscopes fatalistically as Astrology was a science of tendencies. I advised my teacher to have remedies performed to alleviate the affliction. Bhimachar developed some sort of a faith in my predictions and started consulting me regularly. In Saturn's sub– period and the Dasa of Mars, the lady underwent surgery in the head and showed slight improvement. Practically throughout the Dasa of Rahu the lady had to be frequently admitted to the mental hospital and could not lead a normal life.

In the sixties, Mr. Bhimachar became the Director of Fisheries and our friendship lasted till he passed away some years ago.

One day a lecturer of English, a literature M.A., made certain disparaging references to Astrology in the class–room. He read some extracts from Scott's *Quentin Durward* and *Guy Mannering* and made the ridiculous remark that an astrologer was once proceeding somewhere looking at the heavens and making some calculations, but fell into a pit and died not knowing what his own immediate future was. I could not tolerate this insulting reference and I at once retorted that it was none of the business of Keats (that was the nick– name given to him) to talk ill of a subject he had not studied. The result was my expulsion from the class. But before leaving the class–room, I told the teacher in a challenging tone that he would meet with a great misfortune before the end of the year. That had a psychological effect on him.

The next day I was sent for, shown his horoscope and was asked to explain as to what made me come to this conclusion about the misfortune he was to meet with shortly. His horoscope*, as I could see then , was a fairly strong one. But the prediction made by me in the classroom was not based upon any astrological consideration for I had not seen his horoscope before. It was made on the spur of the moment under excitement. But when he gave me the horoscope, I just glanced through the positions of the planets and found that Saturn was in the 9th house and transit Saturn would be passing through the 9th from the Moon by the end of that year. I explained to him these two astrological factors, which, in my opinion, indicated the death of his father. Our interview ended. But strangely enough the lecturer pursued the matter further.He insisted that I visit his house the next day, which I gladly did, for he being the class teacher, we were expected to be in his good books.

When I reached his house, I was surprised to see before me a venerable Pandit whose face beamed with a smile and who I could feel was a man of great learning. He was, of course, a family astrologer and it seems he had contradicted my prediction. According to him, the teacher had no misfortune to pass through during that year or the coming two or three years. The Pandit insisted that I explain to him the reasons which led me to the conclusion about the probable misfortune. My knowledge of Astrology did not, and could not enable me to explain anything more than what I already had said—transit Saturn passing through the 9th house from the radical Moon. The learned Pandit gave quite a number of quotations from standard astrological books to show that there was no ghost of a chance for the fulfillment of my prediction and admonished me for being too hasty in conveying my judgment "without knowing anything of Astrology." But I did not feel very impressed with his explanation. This incident was forgotten. One day after eight months had passed, a young man of 25 summers entered my room and said : "I must

---

* Pisces — Ascendant ; Taurus — the Moon ; Gemini — Ketu ; Cancer — Mars ; Virgo— Mercury ; Libra — the Sun and Jupiter ; and Scorpio —Saturn and Venus.

congratulate you on the fulfillment of the prediction you had given 'Keats'. His father died about the period indicated by you. I hope he will no more make insulting references to Astrology in his discourses." "I hope so" said I. "But I am only sorry that I should have delivered a prediction of this type in the open class."

My friend, who came to congratulate me, handed me another horoscope. I was asked to say whether there was any chance of the native passing a certain examination then. It must be noted that these incidents happened nearly sixty years ago, when my knowledge of Astrology was almost nil or so meagre that with that knowledge I would now hesitate even to look at any horoscope. But I was seized with tremendous enthusiasm for making correct predictions that I never hesitated to study horoscopes. My friend called on me the next day again for knowing the result. "The person is going to fail", I said. My friend retorted, "What are the astrological combinations which make you come to this conclusion?"

"There are two reasons for that" I said. "The first is due to the fact that the lord of the house of education is debilitated and the second is due to the fact the person is having the Dasa of the debilitated lord." For some reason at this stage my friend sarcastically remarked: "But you forget that Jupiter occupies the 4th house. Moreover, at present, Jupiter is passing through his radical place." "Whatever it is," I continued, "my conclusion appears to be sound. There is no chance of his passing the examination." With these words I abruptly tore off from the conversation. After a couple of months, the same visitor called on me and said that the person, whose horoscope was the subject of discussion between us, had taken to some business, as he felt he could not continue his education and that my conclusion was correct.

These two events, in which I scored success, encouraged me to make further predictions with regard to the horoscopes of my friends and teachers. Moreover, these initial successes made me intoxicated and I overestimated my 'capabilities' with the result I had to pay a price. It was in the following circumstances.

Our Botany lecturer was a young man of great ambitions. He came to know of my astrological abilities from Bhimachar. One day he suggested that I tell him when he would be going to foreign countries for higher studies, when he would be the head of the department and when he would marry and so on. It must be fairly clear to any student of Astrology that in order to make such predictions one should not only have great proficiency in the subject but also enough experience of having handled a number of horoscopes. But my qualifications were of a peculiar type. I no doubt knew a good number of stanzas from classical works. But I was still unable to apply the various combinations appropriately. I must confess that most of my deductions in those days were either lucky hits or due to over–confidence born out of sheer enthusiasm. But whenever an opportunity arose to look into horoscopes I would never back out. I felt that I must somehow impress my consultors — then mostly my teachers and classmates. I started keeping a record of horoscopes studied and forecasts made so that I could keep track in case any predictions failed.

Mars Ketu Jupit.						Sun	
Sun Merc.	RASI			Rahu	NAVAMSA		Venus
Sat. Venus				Moon			Sat. Ketu
	Ascdt.	Moon	Rahu	Ascdt.	Mars Mercury		Jupit.

My Botany lecturer's pressure was so great that one day I was obliged to read his chart. When we met in his house for this purpose, the lecturer sprang a surprise by presenting before me an analysis of his horoscope made some years ago by a "famous astrologer". After examining the chart with some trepidation, I said that there was no chance of his getting married at all. My reasoning was : Venus, lord of the 7th and indicator of wife, was in conjunction with Saturn. Therefore I inferred that he would not get married. The now simple fact that the lord of the 9th the Moon in the 12th would give foreign travel escaped my thinking and I gave the prediction that he would not have any foreign travel.

After listening to my predictions the gentleman retorted with a vehemence which shook my nerves terribly. He said : "Are you an astrologer? You pretend to be an expert, but your performance can only earn for you the appellation of a quack. In your own interests I advise you not to dabble in Astrology any more and bring disgrace to the subject, but to concentrate on your studies." Placing the reading in my hands the Botany teacher almost shouted, "Look, here is the reading of my horoscope done by an expert astrologer. Go through it and convince yourself that you are no longer fit to be called an astrologer." I went through the whole reading, and the arguments advanced by the famous astrologer for the two conclusions he had arrived at regarding the marriage and foreign travel of the person concerned were as follows : "Marriage has to be judged from three factors, viz., Kalatrakaraka (Venus), the 7th house and the 7th lord. The 7th lord Venus is in a friendly sign in conjunction with Saturn. From the Moon the 7th lord is associated with Jupiter and Ketu in a benefic sign. Therefore the wife's physical appearance will be similar to the characteristics of Mars and Venus. She will be pretty, youngish in looks, fair in complexion, of phlegmatic constitution but of somewhat weak health as lord of the 7th both from Lagna and Chandra Lagna have joined malefics. Jupiter being the lord of the 2nd and Mars that of Lagna indicates that she will come from a respectable family. Mars–Jupiter association will make you less passionate while the association of Venus with Saturn cannot make married life very happy. Venus, who is also lord of the 7th, occupies the 3rd from Lagna. This means marriage is most likely to take place in Saturn Dasa and his own sub-period when Jupiter transits Taurus."

"Saturn being Yogakaraka for Libra sign and his being situated in the 4th in his own house, a moveable sign and in conjunction with Venus is favourable for higher studies in foreign countries under the same Dasa and Bhukti."

The marriage had taken place as predicted and arrangements had been completed for the person to go to Europe for higher studies.

For a time this incident shattered my confidence in my ability to predict and I spent restless days and nights pondering over the ignominy that had happened to me and why I gave out predictions on such a superficial study of the horoscope. I narrated this incident to grandfather. He said he knew the person through his own friend Mr. N.T. Gopala Iyengar, a District and Sessions Judge and he also knew the astrologer who had given the prediction. I was counselled not to be hasty or over–zealous in giving predictions to gratify people's curiosity but to stick to certain procedures — calculating the horoscope, studying it carefully and avoiding making predictions for the mere asking.

After a few weeks I was sent for by the Botany lecturer who expressed regret for his "blunt criticism" of my astrological knowledge and advised me to pursue with my studies. As the annual examinations were approaching, my astrological activities were kept in cold storage for the next three months.

Many years later thanks to the communal policy of the Mysore University, the lecturer wanted to resign his job which held no prospects. On a fine day in 1956, he called on me and said : "You have become a famous man and your reputation not only as a great astrologer but as a great exponent of Astrology is world–wide. My happiness knows no bounds that a former student of mine has become so well–known. I want you to advise me about my career as I am not happy with the present job." I studied his horoscope again and indicated that very soon he would relinquish his job and enter the Central Government service. Thanks to the kindness of prof. M.S. Thacker — and I had the privilege of his close friendship from 1948 until his death in 1982 — I was able to fix my former teacher in a good position. The teacher Dr. K.V. Srinath attended my special lectures delivered at Mysore University in 1963 under the chairmanship of the Maharaja of Mysore and he was all praise for what he called my "unparalleled achievements in the field of Astrology."

14

Immediately after the Junior Inter examination was over in February 1932, I went back to our village. The colleges were to reopen on Ist July. I had nearly four months of summer holidays, and they were spent in enriching my astrological and allied knowledge, in studying horoscopes and giving predictions.

During the vacation, some of my teachers used to consult with me about their problems. In many cases, they said, that my astrological delineations were not only accurate but were of considerable help to them to sort out their problems.

From the age of 14, I had cultivated the habit of maintaining a diary or at least noting down important points and this has stood me in good stead in writing these memoirs.

A lecturer of mine, one Gundu Rao, visited me with a request that I study the Kalatrabhava (7th house) in his horoscope as he said he "wanted to get married". He was already 36 years old and I felt somewhat curious whether he wanted to play a joke on me or whether he was really serious in his approach. I noticed that anxiety was writ large on his face and so I thought his intention could be genuine. Under such doubtful situations I had been advised to cast a Prasna chart, study the indications and then predict from the birth horoscope. He came to my place on 30-5-1932 at about 1-30 p.m.

I found that in the Prasna chart (No. 1) both the Ascendant and the Moon were afflicted. Venus, Kalatrakaraka, was in the 10th fairly well placed. Lord of the 7th Jupiter was exalted. These combinations, I thought then, not only confirmed the genuineness of the question but were also favourable indications for marriage. But in the Prasna chart the 7th house was occupied by the Moon and Rahu and aspected

by Saturn and Jupiter. The lord of the 7th was again subject to the
aspects of Mars lord of the 3rd and the 8th and Saturn lord of the 5th
and the 6th. I guessed there must be some peculiarity in regard to the
7th house.

Coming to the birth chart, Rahu was in the 2nd (family), the 7th
lord Moon was afflicted by his association with Saturn and the aspect
of Mars. Even Venus, the *karaka,* was afflicted. Had he been married
already? I figured out that Saturn Dasa and the sub-period of Venus
must have already given him marriage according to the dictum:

दायेशत्केन्द्रणेया दुश्चिक्ये लाभगेपि या ।
गृहे कल्याण शुभदां बन्धुवृद्धिस्तदा भवेत् ।

which means Venus and Saturn in mutual Kendras or trines would
give auspicious results. But Venus was in a common sign associated
with the Sun, a malefic. Therefore there would be intensification of
distress according to the dictum.

सूर्येण संयुते दृष्टै चिन्ता प्राबल्यमाप्नुयात् ।

Depending on all these various factors I made bold to declare,
"Sir, your question is not properly worded; it should have been, "Am

Rahu Moon	Mars	Sun Mercury	Venus		Mars	Merc.	Sun Venus
			Jupit.	Rahu			Jupit.
Sat.	RASI			Ascdt.	NAVAMSA		Ketu
		Ketu Ascdt.				Moon Saturn	

I going to get married again?" The teacher was so stunned that he began to gasp and said: "What do you mean by *married again?* Do you mean to say that I have already been married?" Trusting my "predictive ability", I shot back, "Yes Sir, you have been married twice and the two wives are dead. Am I right? Tell me the truth." The teacher became pacified, took me into his confidence and narrated his story. His first marriage, as I had inferred, had taken place in 1918 (in Venus in Saturn) when he was 22 years old. "After giving birth to a child in 1920, she died. I got married for the second time in 1925. She gave birth to a child and both the mother and child died in 1930. My domestic life is in a shambles. Can you advise me as to what I should do?" I pondered over the matter carefully and discovered that his second marriage took place in Rahu's sub-period in Saturn Dasa; and the wife died in Mercury's sub-period in his own Dasa. How does Mercury kill the native's wife? He is lord of the 9th and is situated in the 5th in a friendly sign having *parivartana* with Venus, the dispositor. Hence the only other flaw is his lordship of the 6th. I asked him to meet me after 2 or 3 days. In the meanwhile I racked by brain to find out as to how Mercury could have killed his wife, but could not identify any specific affliction. After a lot of cogitation I found the explanation in the following verse:

पञ्चमे सौम्य संयुक्ते तदीशेषष्ठ भावगे ।
स्वदशा स्वभुक्तौ च दारनाशं दृढं भवेत् ॥

meaning that if Mercury occupies the 5th and the dispositor is in the 6th, the wife dies in Mercury's own Dasa and Bhukti.

What about the next marriage? Mercury could confer marriage. What about the sub-period? I banked upon Venus, the Kalatrakaraka, as he occupied the 9th from the Moon and the 2nd from the major lord. I said that he would get married in 1934 in Venus sub-period in the major period of Mercury. Should I not pinpoint the event! I figured out, when Jupiter transited Libra, the event must take place. So I predicted the probable period would be the first quarter of 1934. His third marriage to which I was also invited did take place in April 1934. The teacher was all praise for my "infallible prediction". In fact he presented me with Rs. 25 which I accepted with thanks as I badly needed money to buy some books.

The fulfilment of the prediction and my discovery, solely on the basis of the horoscope, that he had already married twice heightened my own opinion about "my capabilities" and invested me with confidence that in future I could boldly venture predictions. After his marriage I lost contact with him for years. It was in 1948 or so that he again met me, "a great man" according to him, to have his daughter's horoscope compared with those of some boys he had in view.

My mind now turned towards writing a book on astrological mathematics. I discovered that most available books on Astrology dealt with the important question of casting horoscopes in a perfunctory manner on the basis of *panchangas* and that horoscopes were being cast taking into consideration *rasimanas* not applying to the place of birth. I had acquired sufficient proficiency in this branch of Astrology and my knowledge of English was not poor.

I had already specialised in *Sripathi Paddhati* and *Keshava Paddhati*, the two treatises which dealt with astrological mathematics fairly exhaustively. I had been wondering also why grandfather's writings had been confined only to predictive Astrology.

There were occasions when he used to caution me that indulging in too much of mathematics would atrophy my predictive abilities. Of course, I did not take serious not of this warning then. At that time my thinking was of a different type. Unless mathematical astrology was considered important why did the ancient writers emphasise on the need for calculating *bhavas*, planetary strengths, longevity etc.? Why did Varahamihira, the great exponent of predictive Astrology, write a purely astronomical treatise, the *Panchasiddhantika?* I spent restless days and nights cogitating whether or not I should write books on mathematical Astrology. There was no point, I felt then, in seeking the advice of grandfather in this matter as he would just dismiss my idea. Whom else to seek guidance from? At last I decided that I should meet V. Subramanya Sastry, the well-known translator of *Jataka Parijata, Phaladeepika* etc., into English.

Somehow grandfather and Sastry did not appear to be on friendly terms. It was not difficult for me to discover the cause. V.S. Sastry's English translation of *Jataka Parijata* first appeared in THE ASTROLOGICAL MAGAZINE of 1906 in instalments. It appears Sastry was desirous of running the book as a series of articles in our Magazine. But after publishing 2 or 3 instalments grandfather abruptly terminated the series. This was the main reason for Sastry's displeasure. I had heard from friends that Sastry was a bit rough, impulsive and did not suffer fools. One fine morning I met Sastry in his own house in Basavanagudi and introduced myself as an earnest student of Astrology. He was quite friendly and showed me all his library consisting of a number of books on Astrology, eastern and western. After meeting him 2 or 3 times, I revealed my identity as the grandson of Prof. Suryanarain Rao and he was surprised that I had kept my identity concealed. It was possible for me to remove the so-called misunderstanding between my grandfather and Sastry. In fact, I coaxed him to attend grandfather's birthday which used to be celebrated every year on a grand scale, and Sastry did attend the function. When I told Sastry about my idea to write a book on astrological mathematics, he said: "Go ahead. You have the knack and the ability."

I had still my own reservations. I wrote to Dr. V.V Ramana Sastri conveying my intention to write a book on astrological mathematics. Dr. Sastri was an eminent scholar not only in Astrology but also in Sanskrit, Latin, English and Tamil and had innumerable degrees and distinctions and held a high position in the Madras Government. He was an admirer of grandfather and had contributed some articles to THE ASTROLOGICAL MAGAZINE. He immediately wrote back that I should proceed with the work and that he would be glad to render any assistance I might require.

Having been fortified with the moral support of these two scholars, I turned my attention to the astrological factors.

Was the time propitious for me to write the book? I examined my own horoscope carefully and reasoned out thus:

I was then having the sub-period of Venus in the major period of Rahu, who should give the results of Jupiter as he is in Pisces. But still Rahu is aspected by Mars, lord of the 3rd (communication): hence writing of books would be beneficial. The sub-lord Venus is a Yogakaraka and he is bound to confer favourable results, but as the relationship between the major and sub-lords is *shashtashtaka* things might not move smoothly and uninterruptedly. According to *Krishna Misreeya* the results likely to happen are, "loss of money, misunderstanding with wife, loss of property, stomach trouble, eye disease". These were certainly not the ideal indications for my maiden attempt at writing an important book. I was determined that any book that I wrote should be the best and not just one of many. Again I was in a fix, my thoughts oscillating between the desire to write and the unfavourable astrological factors.

At an opportune moment, I broached the subject of interpreting Dasas with grandfather and put him a specific question : "What are the combinations in my horoscope that deprived me of my mother before I was 2 years old?" His reply was characteristic of his experience. "Look here," he said, "Saturn in the 4th denotes early death to mother," but before he completed the sentence I hastily butted in, "But Saturn in my case is lord of Lagna and hence a benefic?" This naturally upset the wizard and he retorted: "You seem to always presume that you know everything. You have not allowed me to complete my sentence. Your mother died in your Saturn sub-period in Mars Dasa. Both the planets are Marakas for the mother." Pressing another query I asked, "How can we predict whether and when one would become an author or artiste?" Grandfather's answer was to the point when he said, "the association of Mercury with the sub or major lord is enough." I got what I wanted. I started writing the book on 31-3-1932 and completed it by the end of August. We had no typewriter. I recopied the entire manuscript and one fine morning when grandfather was in a good mood, I presented it to him and requested him to write a foreword. It was an unexpected surprise for him to see a book written by his own grandson who was only 20 years old. He glanced through all the pages, congratulated me on my "achievement" and said that as I was to get three important Dasas — Jupiter, Saturn and Mercury—who were all well placed and endowed with powerful yogas "would enable you to win laurels." By nature, he was never emotional or demonstrative. But even he was moved to give vent to his happiness when he said, "To me the greatest joy is that you have already come up to my expectations and your name will reach the farthest corners of the globe, because of the powerful Gajakesari Yoga". I humbly acknowledged his blessings. In his—Foreword to this book (which could be published only in 1936), grandfather wrote:

I have been, during the last 60 years of my activities in the astrological line, dealing more or less with the judicial portion of Astrology, and have not given as much attention as the subject of mathematical calculations demands. Probably fate ordained, that, while I have fully treated in my own inimitable style the predictive portions, the mathematical portions should be reserved to be elaborated by my own grandson, adding a feather to the line of my succession.

There has been a very great demand for such a book and I am proud to say that my grandson B.V. RAMAN has supplied the want with credit to himself.

"To write a book on the mathematical portion requires patience, diligence and devotion, all of which my grandson has displayed in a commendable manner.

I pray God earnestly that he may live to a long age, as God has been pleased to give me longevity, and do as much service to the public as possible. I bless him with all my heart and pray God to make him successful and prosperous.

My astrological studies continued and I started devoting more attention to a deeper exploration of the Tajaka System. The only book available was *Laghu Tajaka* with which I was quite familiar. Whether it was a lucky hit or a prediction based on astrological factors, two important forecasts given to a local teacher Mr. Siddalingaiah made on the basis of Tajaka proved astonishingly accurate. The teacher's wife was ailing for some time. Medical facilities, such as we have now, were not available in our village. She was about 40 years old and the local Ayurvedic doctor had assured her that she would be alright. I calculated the *roga and mrityu sahams* and found that the lords of the two *sahams* were in hostile aspect. The same planets ruled the two *sahams* in the birth horoscope also. I told the teacher that the year might prove fatal to her health. She passed away within a month.

For a former class-mate of mine — his name was also Siddalingaiah—who belonged to the same village, I calculated the *vidya saham* and declared that he would not be successful in the examination. This also happened.

It was perhaps in June 1932, that one Narayana Sastry, a young astrologer, aged about 35 visited our place to seek some guidance from grandfather.

He said he had specialised in the Tajaka system and could predict successfully on the basis of Varshaphal charts. I had already made a thorough study of Neelakanta's *Laghu Tajaka*. The Sastry's stay in our village was availed of by me in increasing my own knowledge of Tajaka. He had a novel method of determining longevity. According to him, the moveable, fixed and common signs have 24, 28 and 30 years as constants. Treble these figures according to the nature of the Ascendant. Add to the product the years corresponding to the number of signs counted from Aries to the position of benefics. Deduct from the total the number of years corresponding to the number of signs intvervening between Aries and the situation of malefics. Deduct from the total the number of years corresponding to the number of signs counted from the sign occupied by the lord of the Ascendant to the sign the lord of the 8th is posited in. The total figure is the longevity. According to Sastry, the category of Ayurdaya, short, medium or long to which a horoscope belongs, should at first be ascertained. If it is short life, the constant is to be taken as it is; if middle life, double the constant; if long life treble it. What if a planet occupied a friendly, inimical or exalted sign? I tried this method for a long time.. In some cases the results were very accurate.

Sastry used to quote from rare books and I had the opportunity of noting several rare combinations, some of which I hope to give in due course for the information of the readers.

When I came in possession of *Sukra Nadi* in 1951, I discovered to my surprise that many of the combinations given by Sastry were found in this work, an English translation of which, God willing, I may present to the world of Astrology, before closing my mortal chapter.

In 1972 when this Sastriar was aged about 76 years or so, he met me at my office with the manuscript of a book on Tajaka written in Kannada, seeking my help for its publication by the Mysore Oriental Library. I not only recommended the book but also wrote a preface for it. I am not sure whether the Library has published the book and paid any honorarium to the author who badly needed financial help.

My contacts, established even during my college studies, with Dr. W.B. Crow, Head of the Department of Biology in Leeds University (England), Elizabeth Aldrich, Editor of *New York Astrologer* and E.H. Bailey, editor of the *British Journal of Astrology,* resulted in fruitful correspondence exchanged frequently with them. Dr. Crow invited me to write an article on Ayurveda for his quarterly journal *Proteus* devoted to occult sciences in general. While I accepted the invitation I found it rather difficult to prepare an article for a prestigious journal published in England. Undaunted I started gathering material from those who knew Ayurveda and I got the opportunity of studying such works as *Charaka Samhita* (English translation by Avinash Chandra Kaviratna) and *Surgical Instruments of the Hindus.* The editor of *Ayurveda* an English monthly published in Calcutta also gave me some assistance. Within two weeks I prepared the article and sent it to Dr. Crow. It was not only accepted for publication but Dr. Crow congratulated me on writing such an article. My joy knew no bounds when I saw my article in the *Proteus.*

The success of my first attempt to prepare an important article was considered by me as a stepping stone for my future career as a writer.

On Ist July 1932 I shifted back to Bangalore and resumed my studies.

15

I was never a rank student except in the first year Intermediate class; nor did I ever aspire to be one. There were two reasons for this. One, grandfather used to tell his friends that those who had passed their examinations with distinction generally did not shine well in their careers while many who never secured any distinction in their educational careers had become great and shone well in their careers. As examples he would cite the names of Sir Mirza Ismail, the Dewan of Mysore and Narayana Rao who retired as an Inspector General of Police in the erstwhile Mysore State. Sir Mirza was just a B.A. from Central College without any rank. But he not only reached the highest position in the State as the Dewan but was also known as a capable administrator. In those days, he had a charisma of his own and was known not only all over India but even outside. On the other hand Narayana Rao, who had a brilliant academic career and was a double graduate, no doubt reached a fairly high position. But he lacked tact, determination and ability required of a high state officer with the result he had to cut a sorry figure when as I.G. of Police he could not handle a tricky situation of communal riots that took place in 1926 or so at Bangalore resulting in the permanent installation of a Ganesa idol in the Sultanpet Middle School. The commission which inquired into the riots had no good words to say about him. And two, indifference towards studies and devoting most of my time to Astrology. Also, my abhorence at having to dissect animal specimens in the Zoology class made me decide once and for all that I would not study medicine. I was only aiming at an ordinary pass and completion of my collegiate education as early as possible.

When I was in the Senior Intermediate class I was able to collect a number of horoscopes of my class-mates and teachers. One of the horoscopes belonged to the son of the Organic Chemistry teacher. He used to handle the class with such skill that a dry subject like chemistry was made quite interesting. On a certain day, when he was explaining Kekuli's theory regarding the arrangement of hydrogen atoms round the carbon atom, and how the methane and ethane groups were formed, I nudged the boy sitting next to me and remarked that I felt, from the expression on the face of the teacher, that he must be very worried about some problems. Surprised, he said, "No, I have known him well. What do you mean by this? He is a very balanced person and he is always jolly." I told him ignoring the lesson going on in the class, "Look here, at the moment Mars is with the Moon. So the teacher must be restless." The boy did not reveal he was related to the teacher but was eager to know how I knew Astrology. The teacher noticed my inattentiveness and warned me that if I repeated my indifference to the lesson in the next class I would be asked to go out. I begged his pardon and assured him of proper behaviour and I thought the matter had been closed.

After 2 days he sent me a note asking me to meet him in the staff-room. I was a little apprehensive if my earlier misconduct in the classroom had annoyed him so badly as to make him send for me. But when I went there he was all smiles and he took me to the canteen where over a cup of coffee, he remarked,: "My relative, who is also your class-mate, said that you are a very good astrologer and that you remarked that I looked very worried in class. Yes, I am worried. Can you trace the cause of my worry?" This was a very ticklish question and I was at my wits' end. But I had cultivated the habit of maintaining my composure and not betraying any signs of embarrassment. Immediately I noted the time, mentally calculated the chart for it and started interpreting it. As a student I would everyday look into the *panchanga* and record in my memory the planetary positions for the day. This habit stood me in good stead now.

The date was 2nd September 1932 and the time around 2 p.m. Sagittarius was rising. In such cases I always looked for the positions of malefics and the Moon. In this case Saturn was in the 2nd (income) as lord of the 2nd, Rahu was in the 3rd (brothers) and Mars lord of the 5th(children) was in the 7th (wife). So *prima facie* his worry could be due to finance, brothers, son or wife. Lord of the 2nd in the 2nd was favourable. Finance was ruled out. Rahu was in the 3rd aspected by Jupiter and the Sun. Lord of the 3rd Saturn was in the 12th from the 3rd; lord of the 9th in the 9th was a good combination. Moreover, even according to common sense, a man of 50, if he had his father living would not worry much about him. It struck me that Mrs could be the culprit. As lord of the 5th he was in the 7th. The indicator of the mind was aspected by Mars. So I decided that his worry could be about his son. Suppose he had no son, what then? I relied on my good luck and the above combination and boldly declared "The 5th house is involved at the time you put me the query. Therefore, the problem is your son and his misbehaviour." Astonished, he said, "What! I am surprised at the accuracy of your answer. How could you say this? Is your conclusion based on mathematics?" I said, "Yes, mostly mathematics. I calculated in my mind the positions of planets and the Ascendant." He went on, "Could you also say how long this boy will have the mental aberration?" I explained, "Jupiter lord of the Ascendant is in the 9th aspecting the 5th. After Rahu leaves Aquarius there will be considerable improvement." He expressed satisfaction and complimented me saying, "this is remarkable. If Astrology could be so accurate in the hands of a young man like you then to what heights would its accuracy not reach in the hands of an experienced man?" I did not relish his concluding remark as I felt he had underrated my ability. However we became friends and he began consulting me regularly.

In those days my predictions were based on a combination of Astrology, common-sense and intuition. Somehow I had developed a confidence, may be a misplaced confidence, in my ability to hit at correct predictions. And this confidence, I attributed to my faith in *Gayatri mantra* which I was regularly practising

The teacher's son at the time of consultation was in the same class as I was, but in a different section. He was not only indifferent to his studies but somewhat waywardly also. He was more or less of my age but he was squandering money and had developed friendship with a neighbour's daughter.

Until I left college in 1935 after completing my B.Sc., the teacher was in frequent touch with me. When I met him in 1936, he said that my prediction about his son had been fulfilled, as he had passed his examination and had broken his friendship with his girl friend, but continued to be self-willed, nervous and high-strung when provoked.

Horary Astrology is perhaps the most reliable tool in dealing with on-the-spot questions. Except in a few cases, my predictions given to my lecturers, class-mates, and others were generally accurate.

Another important event that occurred in the latter part of 1932 was my coming into contact with a Kerala astrologer. He lived in a rented room in Balepet, a busy commercial centre in Bangalore. One day out of curiosity I went to him. There were already three clients waiting. To me time was important as I was to prepare for the public examination. When I told him I had come from a mofussil place he turned to me asking the other two to wait. I was then passing through the fag end of the sub-period of Venus in Rahu Dasa and wanted his interpretation. He spread the cowries in three places, made some manipulations and wanted me to come the next Friday before the commencement of Rahukala. On that day I did not attend the college as I was eager to know what he had to say about my future. He took my birth details, cast the horoscope and started explaining. When he said, "Your *atmakaraka* is the Moon", I immediately raised my hand and countered him by remarking, "For all persons, the *atmakaraka* is the Sun and never the Moon". He smiled and remarked, "I am following the Jaimini system according to which the Moon is the *atmakaraka* in your case. The *atmakaraka* changes for each individual and hence is variable." I was dumbfounded. I had not till then heard of Jaimini Astrology. I was wild with rage that grandfather who should no doubt be conversant with this system had not said a word about it. The Sastriar went on: "*Lagnarudha* is Simha. *Atmakaraka* exalted in the 10th is a very important combination. It makes you great." I told him that I was not interested in my future greatness.

"My present position is so bad I can hardly pay you even five rupees," I said. Quite unpreturbed by what I had said, he went on, "The *amatyakaraka* is the Sun. The Moon and the Sun, both *rajagrahas*, have reversed their roles. The Moon is in *parakrama* in the 3rd aspecting the *atmakaraka* and being aspected by him." Again I felt restless and firmly declared that I was not going to tolerate any tomfoolery. I asserted, "Even a beginner in Astrology knows that all planets aspect the 7th house though Mars, Jupiter and Saturn have special aspects. How could the Moon in my case aspect the Sun and *vice versa* ?" He quoted three *sutras* from Jaimini and justified his interpretation. Counselling patience he wanted me not to disturb him till his interpretation was over. After interpreting the *Karakamsa* chart in a manner that no one else had done before he declared, "You will achieve something unique in your life and enjoy Rajayoga without any political power because of Jupiter's aspect on the *amatyakaraka*. The end of Karkataka Dasa (age 24 to 27) will change the entire course of your life and beginning from Thula Dasa (age 27 to 37), you will have a prosperous period. You will die at the end of Niryana Sula Dasa of Kanya." In respect of "change" and "prosperity" there has been a time lag of a year which is permissible. The third prediction of my dying in Niryana Sula Dasa of Kanya of course, has not worked.

My meeting with this Kerala Pandit roused in me a desire to master the Jaimini system. After I told him that I was a college student and fairly well versed in Astrology and that he should teach me Jaimini, he hesitated for a moment but acquiesced in. He was also a scholar in what goes by the name of the Parasari system. In fact his forte was the immortal *Prasna Marga*, *Krishneeya* and Brihat Jataka. He would swear by these works and declare "The Sun may rise in the west but these works do not fail." He was a pious Brahmin not interested in making much money. He believed in simple living and high thinking. He examined my horoscope again and said that I would be a fitting pupil as "you have Jupiter in *Karmasthana* and would never be ungrateful". It was decided that I should take lessons in Jaimini every Thursday after sunset, as he said I was born on a Thursday after sunset. When I asked him whether these rules had any sanction in Muhurtha books he nodded his head but so far I have not come across any authority which says that the weekday and time of birth would be propitious for learning Astrology.

The Dasara holidays began and I returned to our village. I requested grandfather to teach me the Jaimini system. He said it was a tough subject and "you need not bother about it now. The best thing for you is to begin memorising the Jaimini Sutras — at least one *adhyaya* — and the meaning can be understood later on". When I told him that a Kerala Pandit in Bangalore had promised to teach me the Jaimini, he said that even for learning from him I should learn the *sutras*. In right earnest I started committing to memory the *sutras* beginning from *upadesam vyakhyassamaha* to *horadayaha siddha*.

Immediately after returning to Bangalore I saw the Pandit again and my studies started in right earnest on a Thursday after sunset

The lessons lasted for some weeks within which time I became familiar with *karakamsa*, aspects and *argalas*. I used to be given homework and on some days I would ask him to give me a gist of the Jaimini system. Despite the age disparity — he was about 60 we became friends and he was convinced of my sincerity. Just as I started learning the calculation of *chara dasa* my teacher left for Kerala because of some family problems. He never returned nor could I trace him again. Thus ended my adventures in Jaimini Astrology.

Of course I was not to be deterred. I secured a copy of *Jaimini Sutras* in Telugu script and was immersed in its study so deeply that in the class tests I got such poor marks in Botany and Zoology that Bhimachar and Srinath who were my good friends, apart from being my teachers, expressed disappointment at my performance. I assured them that I would pass the public examination to be held in March 1933. I passed the examination.

Coming back to Jaimini: After the Kerala astrologer left Bangalore I chanced to meet one day in my hotel B.N. Vijaya Deva, Bar-at-Law, an advocate. He was deeply interested in Astrology and knew quite a bit of the subject. When he learnt Suryanarain Rao was my grandfather, he invited me to his house in Basavanagudi and introduced me to his father, Nagappa, Bar-at-Law, who was then Legal

Rememberancer to the Government of Mysore. Deva had a good library and as he allowed me free access, I was able to lay my hands on two books on Jaimini, one in Kannada script and the other in Devanagari script. We would meet often and exchange notes.

In the meanwhile the college was closed for summer holidays for three months. I got back to the village and took to serious studies in Jaimini all by myself. Grandfather had just started translating the first part of the *sutras* but I found that the translation did not elucidate the methods of calculating the Dasas, longevity etc., except for giving some details. It was then that I decided that one day I should write a book on Jaimini making the system simple and easily understandable. Seventeen years later I wrote my *Studies in Jaimini Astrology* which is very popular today amongst the interested in Astrology.

According to the Kerala Pandit, the determining or deciding factor in Jaimini Astrology was the *atmakaraka* and his relationship with the other *karakas*. The *karakamsa* chart was to be primarily considered.

I shall deal with Jaimini Astrology in the appropriate place and also give some charts interpreted by me according to Jaimini. But Jaimini is tough and can be used successfully only for predicting longevity and certain important Rajayogas.

I joined the Junior B.Sc. class in the Central College in July 1933. This college had earned a reputation for having produced a number of great men. My grandfather, Sir M. Visvesvaraya, C. Rajagopalachari, Sir Mirza were all the products of this college. I liked the serene atmosphere and the active interest evinced by the teaching staff in the welfare and progress of the students.

It was in August 1933 that I started writing my second book *A Text-book of Hindu Astrology* which was later published in 1938 as *Hindu Predictive Astrology*. I completed the Text-Book before October and felt happy that I had produced such a comprehensive book in so short a time. During the period of writing this book, there could be nothing like relaxation after the college holidays. I used to get the Mss typed and tried to sell the type-script copy for Rs. 18.00. The cost of typing a copy would come to about Rs. 9.00, so that I could earn by the sale of this book an extra Rs. 18/- or so per month and this solved my financial problem to some extent. The book was dedicated to my grandfather and he felt very happy that two "outstanding books" had been written by me "at such an young age".

In the senior B.Sc. class I could not secure as much time for my astrological studies as I used to get in the Intermediate. The college atmosphere was more academic and our professors — Prof. C.R. Narayana Rao (Zoology). Dr. Sampathkumaran (Botany), Dr. Manjunath (Organic Chemistry), Prof. Sanjeeva Rao (Physical Chemistry), Prof. B.M. Srikantiah (English), Prof. A.R. Krishna Sastry (Kannada), were all men of calibre. They knew their subjects too well to be hoodwinked by any students. Whenever opportunity occurred I would meet these professors and broach my subject of Astrology. Some of them would be non-committal without making any adverse comments on Astrology though the bug of "scientific outlook" had not yet begun biting them. There were some others who were quite sympathetic to the claims of Astrology.

I recollect an important private meeting I had with Prof. B.M. Srikantiah. He was well known as a literateur in Kannada and his contribution to Kannada literateur was quite stupendous. When I was studying in Inter Arts in 1928, Prof. Srikantiah's book *Gadayuddha,* written in classical Kannada, had been prescribed to us as a textbook. I had made a thorough study of this book along with my then classmate A.N. Krishna Rao who later on became famous as a great writer in Kannada.·

I introduced myself to Prof. Srikantiah as an admirer of this book. Life was not kind to him because of domestic mishaps and he had almost become an agnostic. "Yes," he said, "Astrology is all right in the hands of persons like Suryanarain Rao, but what havoc horoscopes sometimes play?" He was in a pensive mood and I could sense his suffering. "I got my daughter married after consulting astrologers, but my son-in-law died soon. This is the harm that Astrology does." I did not want to be rude towards him as he was not only my professor but also was in mental distress. But I could not mouth his adverse remarks. "But Sir," I said, "a surgeon operates and the patient dies. Should we condemn surgery?" He said, "No I understand the point.

Study well. Let not your interest in Astrology come in the way of your studies." We used to meet now and then in his office room and he would make enquiries of grandfather's welfare. And once he was generaous enough to remark, "I know there are areas of knowledge which we do not know. Since you appear to persist in studying Astrology see if it could help and not harm others".

Prof. Frank R. Sell, a Scotchman, was our Principal. He was taking our English class. Once I dropped into his room introducing myself as a student in the senior B.Sc. class and as the grandson of the great author of "History of Vijayanagar" or "Never to be Forgotten Empire". At that time another Englishman — I think he was McIntosh, Inspector General of Eduction — entered the room and turning to me showed displeasure at my "shabby dress". I was wearing a white dhoti with a shirt and open collar coat and chappals. I resented his remarks and protested that he had no business to pass such remarks. Prof. Sell cautioned patience. When he learnt from Prof. Sell that I was a student in the B.Sc. class besides being a "budding astrologer" McIntosh Poohpoohed Astrology. I told him bluntly that he was a prejudiced Englishman and he had no business to decry Astrology of which he was ignorant. Had not Prof. Sell intervened, the situation would have turned unpleasant.

In one of our meetings when I explained to Prof. Sell the importance of Astrology he said he was reluctant to accept the fact that Astrology should be accepted, though it worked. I could sense he was an orthodox Christian and hence Astrology was taboo to him. I met Prof. Sell two or three times and he was surprised at what he called my "missionary zeal in preaching Astrology".

I had initiated into Astrology some of my class-mates — Maduranathan who later became an Inspector of Police, Ramanathan who retired as a Deputy Commissioner, Narappa, who became the Head of the Department of Botany in the same college and later changed his name to Dr. Narayan. We used to meet every week and I would teach them Astrology. This arrangement did not last long. But once in a way we would meet and take up a horoscope for interpretation. One such horoscope was that of the wife of a Zoology lecturer. The lecturer, who had heard about my "competence" in Astrology, was eager to get my opinion regarding his wife's health, but it seems he felt that a direct approach would not be in order. But I had my own reservations in such matters. If one wanted to consult me he should approach me direct.

Narappa, who was close to the lecturer, tried to play a trick. He brought the horoscope of the lady and pushed it into my hands stating that he was particular to know details about her health. I said, "Look here, it is none of your business to show interest in another lady. Let her come to me if she so desires." One day, Miss Kamala a lady class-mate—there were only three lady students in my section in Senior B.Sc.— handed over to me a note from the lecturer wishing to meet me. Miss Kamala was the daughter of the late T.P. Kailasam, the well-known Kannada writer. It is not clear whether this lady is the same Mrs Kamala Subrahmanyam whose books on *Mahabharata* and *Ramayana* have won laurels and who died recently.

When I met the lecturer in his room, he expressed his desire to have my opinion regarding the health of his wife. He did not reveal the nature of the problem. She was about 26 then.

			Jupit.
Saturn Ascdt.			Rahu Mercury
Moon Ketu	RASI		Sun Mars
		Venus	

In those days I was using only the *panchangas* and not the ephemerides. The Ascendant was Aquarius occupied by the lord and aspected by Jupiter. Lord of the Ascendant was in his own house aspected by the Sun and Mars. From the Moon, the 7th house was afflicted by the situation of Mercury (lord of the 6th) and Rahu. Kalatrakaraka Venus was well-placed being yogakaraka and aspected by Jupiter. I interpreted thus: "The Yoga caused by Venus could only benefit her husband as she was not educated and she was just a housewife. When the Lagna lord was so well disposed how could she have any health problem? Was the lecturer testing me out of curiosity? I cast a *prasna* chart and found that the 6th house was afflicted. I decided the lady had a problem. When the lecturer met me again I said, "Sir, the horoscope is a good one so far as finance is concerned. She must have brought a good dowry to you." The lecturer conceded saying, "You are correct. She hails from a well-to-do family and has benefited me financially. Please proceed further." After pausing for a while I continued, "Though the Ascendant and the lord are not afflicted, Chandra Lagna is considerably blemished. Mentally she must be unhappy. She is perhaps inclined towards harsh speech, is rash and sarcastic. The temper is quick and she is of a domineering nature. Rahu's aspect is not good for her mental health. She will be restless and depressive with peculiar changes in emotions. The domestic life is not quite happy. It is possible that she may even suspect your loyalty. Her physical health to which I shall come shortly is affected because of her mental attitudes." After saying this I stopped. Pausing for a moment, my teacher with tears in his eyes declared, "What all you have said is correct. She is suspicious by nature and hardly cares for me." I continued my analysis thus, "Lord of the 6th the Moon is in the 12th with Ketu. This once again fortifies my inference that her mind is the root cause of her disease. Two malefics are situated in the 6th which is aspected by the 6th lord. Of these Mercury owns the 5th but the 5th is occupied by Jupiter. Mars, lord of the 3rd ruling the lungs, also aspects the Ascendant. At the moment she is having the major period of Jupiter and the sub-period of Saturn. Her health problem could be tuberculosis, perhaps of the lungs. And the disease must have originated about 4 years ago when the sub-period of Mars in Rahu was operating.

I boldly gave this interpretation watching his facial expressions and trusting my "predictive ability". He broke down, "Everything you have said is correct. Four years ago the doctors suspected lung infection. But will she be cured?" At the time of consultation the native was passing through Saturn in Jupiter. The major lord, Lagnadhipati, was aspected by Mars. The sub-lord was in the 6th from the Moon. Saturn's transit of Capricorn could only indicate aggravation of the trouble. Lord of the 6th Mercury was no doubt afflicted. But Jupiter also aspected the Lagna. I figured out that she might survive the crisis and told the lecturer, "Her trouble will get worse for another two years and then continue till the end of Ketu's sub-period which means about 1935-36. She will survive the crisis provided adequate remedial and other remedial treatments are given." It looked as if my lecturer was completely satisfied. He referred in complimentary terms to my "predictive ability". I think the lady survived the crisis and lived almost through the entire period of Jupiter and a part of Saturn.

Of the various predictions given by me ever since I started interpreting horoscopes from 1929, this was perhaps the most amazing so far as the identification of the health problem was concerned. But how did I do it? Was it because of my own astrological ability?

I had not yet extricated myself from the weakness of patting on my own back whenever I succeeded in my forecasts but when my predictions failed I would accept my failure with some reluctance. This mental aberration of mine was perhaps due to my age and the high percentage of success that attended my predictions though I used to be cautioned now and then by grandfather that I should not think too much of myself as sometimes my own good luck and not my capacity was behind the success of my forecasts.

16

After completing my college education in March 1935, and vacating once for all my lodging in Bangalore, I returned to our village. Grandfather was already 78 and formidable problems started at the family. He was a practical philosopher and never allowed himself to be perturbed however difficult a situation might be. I feel I have inherited to some extent this trait and it has stood me in good stead whenever I have had to face difficult situations in the family or in my other activities.

I had made up my mind not to join any service but devote myself entirely to the mastery of Astrology and study of Hindu astronomy and the classics. Fortunately for me the Siddhanti whom I have already referred to before, again came to our village and stayed with us for a couple of weeks. He busied himself with calculating a *Panchanga* according to *Surya Siddhanta* .I availed of his stay with us to brush up my knowledge of Hindu astronomy especially the methods of · calculation of eclipses. He had a *Karana grantha* based on Surya Siddhanta and tables with Bija corrections had been prepared taking the year 1900 (12th April) as the epoch. The tables related to the mean positions of planets (*madhya grahas*), equation of centre (*mandajya*), aphelion (*mandochha*), parallax of the orbits (*makarajya*), etc. I had a lot of time at my disposal and was able to get a clear insight into the methods of calculating eclipses according to *Surya Siddhanta*.

I wanted to test the correctness of the time (given in the almanac in regard to the solar eclipse that occurred in 1935. We spent days together and calculated the time of commencement of the eclipse. I told grandfather that we were testing the accuracy of the timings given in the almanacs. He said : "How do you do this ? Have you calculated the time of the eclipse ?" I nodded my head. He became furious and remarked : "Probing into the secrets of the Sun and the Moon is not advisable. Anyone who indulges in such astronomical mathematics as calculating eclipses, planetary positions etc., independently will come to grief. I have already warned you about this." Though I had also been involved in the calculations, I said, "The Siddhanti has made the calculations and I have only assisted him." He was not satisfied.

On the eclipse day we had kept ready coloured water, coloured glass etc., so that we could observe the Sun being covered by the earth's shadow. The *panchanga* time arrived. But the Sun appeared to be clear. Exactly at the time calculated by us, the beginning of the eclipse was noticed. I told grandfather triumphantly that the *panchanga* was not dependable. His silence implied his acceptance of the correctness of our finding. The Siddhanti had taught me earlier the method of calculation of eclipses and I had burnt midnight oil to learn these "secrets". But I kept assuring grandfather all along that I would not "probe" into the secrets of the planets. I took some lessons in Bhaskara's *Siddhanta Siromani* and *Leelavati* and came to know for the first time that the ancient Hindus were quite familiar with the laws of gravitation, which we were taught in our classes, as having been discovered by Newton. I felt that I must equip myself with more details about ancient Hindu achievements in astronomy and other sciences and I availed of every opportunity to collect information from any available source.

Once grandfather presented me and the Siddhanti with the horoscope of a lady aged about 50 and wanted us to find out whether widowhood was indicated.

RASI

			Ascdt Sat.
Ketu	RASI		Moon Merc. Venus
			Sun Rahu
	Mars	Jupit.	Venus

NAVAMSA

		Jupit.	Ascdt Sat.
Merc. Ketu	NAVAMSA		Sun
Mars			Moon Rahu

Saturn's Dasa remained for about 17 years at birth.

I first tried to discover whether there were any Yogas for widowhood, banking on the dictum that a woman's widowhood is to be ascertained from the 8th house (सौमंगल्यमनिष्टमष्टमगृहात्). I said, "The Ascendant is occupied by Saturn, lord of the 8th, and lord of the Ascendant Mercury is in the 2nd subject to *papakartari yoga*. The situation of Mars in the 5th is also not desirable. From Chandra Lagna, the 2nd is afflicted and the 8th house is not only occupied by malefic Ketu but is also aspected by the Sun. The 8th house subject to malefic influences denotes, according to the dictum ; रंध्रे सपापे यघू वैधव्यं — clear widowhood. So the 8th house from the Moon is afflicted considerably. But Mars has the nothing to do with the 7th or 8th. He is well placed in a *trikona* (trine) from the Lagna and *kendra* (quadrant) from the Moon, being a *yogakaraka* from the Moon. *Kalatrakaraka* Venus who is as important as the lord of the 7th is afflicted in the sense that he is subject to *papakaratari yoga*. Lord of the 7th Jupiter is no doubt in a benefic sign, a *kendra*, but he is also subject to *papakartari yoga*. Apart from all this, if the lord of the Navamsa occupied by the lord of the 8th is Mercury 'widowhood is certain' रंध्रेशांश पतौसौम्ये विधवानि: संशयं भामिनीं This combination is also present.

Taking all these into consideration I concluded that the native is bound to become a widow. But when ? Ketu is the villain of the piece as he is in the 8th from the Moon and the dispositor Saturn is in the 12th. Therefore widowhood is indicated in Saturn's major period and Rahu's sub–period as Rahu aspects the 8th."

The Siddhanti also worked on the chart and came, more or less, to a similar conclusion. He said that the husband would die in the major period of Mercury and the sub–period of Rahu. After listening to both of us grandfather said, "Look here, both of you are partly correct. The finding given by you" he said turning to me, "is incorrect in regard to both the Dasa and the sub–Dasa. The finding of the Siddhanti is correct only so far as the Dasa is concerned. Actually the native became a widow in her 19th year, when Ketu in Mercury was operating." My performance was bad and I realised it. I took this also as a warning that calm and cool judgment should be the better of impulsive and hasty assessment.

Apart from studies and looking into horoscopes I was also interested in establishing contacts with European and American astrologers. Vivian E. Robson, a well–known author and admirer of Hindu Astrology, was in frequent correspondence with me. He presented me with five books he had written on western Astrology. He sought my assistance to prepare a few articles on *Ashtakavarga* for publication in the "British Journal of Astrology" edited by Mr. E.H. Bailey. In fact I contributed a series of articles on *Kalatrabhava* to this journal and they were, I was told, much appreciated. Mr. Bailey was not only a great scholar but an admirer of Hindu Astrology. He used to exchange many letters with me about the relative merits of the Hindu and Western systems. Mr. Bailey presented me with a copy of his book "Prenatal Epoch". It was indeed a pleasure for me to meet him in 1959 at London. He attended my lecture and appreciated what he called my "dedication to Astrology".

The other English astrologers with whom I maintained contact were Dr. W.J. Tucker and C.E.O. Carter. Dr. Tucker made a favourable review of my "A Manual of Hindu Astrology" in his now defunct "Science and Astrology". I was a staunch opponent of his thesis that the Hindus acquired their knowledge of Astrology from the Greeks and Babylonians. This difference of opinion persisted for nearly two decades until my meeting with him in London in 1959. In fact, he took a leading part in arranging my lectures in London. Introducing me to the London audience Dr. Tucker said, "We have gathered here this evening to listen to the address of India's most distinguished astrologer Prof. Bangalore Venkata Raman, Editor of one of the world's greatest astrological monthlies THE ASTROLOGICAL MAGAZINE and author of many astrological text-books. Before coming here Prof. Raman has been touring the United states of America lecturing to crowded audiences. He attended the International Congress of Astro-Science held in new York.

"Prof. Raman is, of course, one of the foremost of the world's astrologers and to my mind he must also be accounted as the greatest living authority on Hindu Astrology. Comparisons are invidious and I am not going to tell you that THE ASTROLOGICAL MAGAZINE is the world's finest and best astrological publication. But I can say that it is a remarkably strong challenger for that coveted honor and to my mind, and I speak completely objectively, judging against a very realistic standard of comparison, there are only three really outstanding astrological journals which are at one and the same time instructional-informative, entertaining, non-sensational, authoritative and progressive; these being *Horoscope* and *American Astrology* of U.S.A. and THE ASTROLOGICAL MAGAZINE of India. At present these periodicals are running neck to neck in the race; and the only thing which prevents Prof. Raman's magazine from taking the lead is the reason that so many western readers lack an elementary knowledge of the basis of Hindu Astrology and remain baffled by the relatively few Indian nouns which are naturally used by many of the writers. Yet despite this rather severe handicap, it does strike me that Prof. Raman's magazine bids fair to pass from the status of challenger to that of the winner, unless the American editors remain alert and become more discerning.

"This happens to be the first occasion on which I have had the great and enormous pleasure of meeting Prof. Raman personally. For this is the first time he has visited our country. By this time the audience must be impatient to hear our principal speaker of this evening whom I have had the honour of presenting to you and I will now vacate the rostrum in order that this great astrologer may address you."

I convinced Dr. Tucker about the originality and antiquity of Hindu Astrology and in his last days he appeared to have revised his earlier opinion.

Mr. Carter was a fair–minded astrologer. He said in his correspondence with me that there was no doubt that Hindu Astrology was great and unique, but his specialization being the western system he would confine his researches to the western system. My contact with Mr. Carter lasted until his death.

In 1931, the late Elizabeth Aldrich was considered to be a leading astrologer in America. She was editing a quarterly journal entitled "The New York Astrologer" and my first article published in its pages was on the "Development of Astrology". She was also a great admirer of the Hindu system and a dynamic lady.

My contact with Swami Yogananda began in a surprising manner. One Laurie Pratt, grand–daughter of Astronomer Pratt, was writing a series of articles in Swami Yogananda's journal on the Yuga theory. She had reduced the ages of the Yugas, given in ancient books in years to days. For instance she had been saying the duration of Kaliyuga was not 432,000 years but days which meant only 1,200 years. Thus a Mahayuga according to her was 12000 years. I wrote to Swami Yogananda refuting her theory and upholding the traditional ages. The Swamiji appreciated my article. Miss Pratt, the author of the article was also an astrologer. She sent me an analysis of my horoscope according to the western system and I must say that she did a really wonderful job.

I had also started correspondence with Marc Edmund Jones the well–known author of *Horary Astrology*. Mr Robert Deluce, an engineer by profession but deeply interested in Astrology, had adopted an Ayanamsa of about 26° or 27° and he had his own explanations to give.

It might interest readers to learn that the late Dr. V.V. Ramana Sastrin eminent scholar to whom I have earlier referred in these pages and who has contributed an introduction to my book "A Manual of Hindu Astrology", was also an advocate of 26° or 27° Ayanamsa. In 1937. Mr. Deluce stayed in Bangalore to learn Hindu Astrology, and he had several meetings with me and V. Subrahmanya Sastry.

The most important contact was with Herr Kraft referred to by European astrologers as "Hitler's personal astrologer". It was Kraft who sent me the correct birth details of Hitler. In his correspondence with me, Kraft had shown himself to be an expert n western Astrology. In fact he presented me with a copy of his latest book on Astrology written in German. Hitler was still a non–entity though his name was becoming popular. In 1940 or 1941 Kraft and other leading German astrologers were put in concentration camps by Hitler and all the published astrological literature including my own book in German *Indische Astrologie* were seized and several thousands of copies destroyed.

Another well–known German astrologer who merits attention and with whom I was in touch for a long time was A.M. Grimm who considered grandfather as his Guru.

But all these contacts and the articles I was writing were of no avail so far as the main problem of money was concerned. Adversity has its own advantages. It gives courage, determination and snubs one's ego. But too much adversity is also a curse when we see before our own eyes the sufferings of those near and dear to us. However these contacts were valuable and my name began to be gradually known amongst western astrological circles.

At the village, my time was fully occupied in domestic chores, astrological researches and studying horoscopes of people who visited grandfather for consultations. Financially, the family was passing through a crisis and I was at my wit's ends not knowing what to do.

Loans had to be raised even to meet the day–to–day expenses. To overcome this difficult situation grandfather secured a loan mortgaging our residence and land to the Apex Bank. After grandfather's death in 1937, the property was auctioned by the Bank authorities to collect their dues.

Father was helpless because of the disability Nature had imposed on him by way of loss of sight. Grandfather had an ulcer in his left foot preventing his free movement. All these made me depressed and distressed and I had to often spent sleepless nights worrying as to what should be done to retrieve the family from such adversity.

I wanted grandfather to look into my horoscope and suggest some means whereby I could do something to lessen the financial stringency. Of course, I could myself study my horoscope but the subjective factor was an obstacle in assessing the correct trend. I was having the sub-period of the Moon and the major period of Rahu. My analysis was on familiar lines. The major lord Rahu in the 2nd or house of finance could cause many problems. But because he is in the sign of Jupiter and Jupiter is the lord of the 2nd and 11th Rahu cannot come in the way of my earning money. The sub-lord Moon owns the 6th (ruling enemies, debts and disease). He is in conjunction with Saturn, lord of the Ascendant and the 12th, and aspected by Jupiter lord of the 2nd and 11th. This analysis was in accordance with text-book principles. But how to synthesis these various dispositions ? At this stage, subjective factors would creep in and leave me confused. But something had to be done to retrieve my family from a situation fraught with difficulties and uncertainties. As I struggled to resolve these confused thoughts, Suryanarayana Siddhanti came to my aid. After calculating the different charts including my *Ashtakavaraga* he said, "Look here, your own analysis upto a point is correct. Take the Ashtakavarga of Jupiter." I butted in, "The Dasa I am running is that of Rahu and not Jupiter's. Why should we take Jupiter's ?" The Siddhanti quipped, "Because Rahu is in Jupiter's sign and he could give the results of Jupiter." I was not satisfied. I said, "Rahu Dasa, by and large, has not been good to me. I have suffered break in education, ill-health, financial stress, mental worry and all sorts of bad things". The Siddhanti dismissing my doubts with a wave of his hand declared, "In Jupiter's Ashtakavarga, Pisces where Rahu is placed, has only 4 *bindus* which means good and bad are equally produced. The Dasa has been good because of the opportunity you got for training in Astrology under your grandfather. The Dasa has also not been good because of the happening of various unfavourable things you have just listed." I did not feel convinced but allowed him to carry on. "The sub–lord Moon is extremely strong because he is not only exalted in the 4th causing Gajakesari Yoga but also has 6 *bindus* in his Ashtakavarga. Rahu and the Moon are in mutual 3rd and 11th houses. Therefore your pessimism is not justified. Saturn the *yogakaraka* from the Moon and also the lord of Lagna is transiting Aquarius the 10th from the Moon and Aquarius has 5 *bindus*. Jupiter is transiting Libra having 6 *bindus* in the Ashtakavaraga of the Moon and 3 in his own. Hence he will give mixed results. Generally Saturn transiting the 10th gives not only travels but also a change of residence. I dare say that during the period of Saturn's transit of Aquarius and Jupiter's transit of Scorpio, you will not only travel and earn some money but may also change your residence."

I was simply dumb–founded at his interpretation. Travel and earning some money was alright because while in transit in Scorpio, his own radical position, he would aspect the 2nd. But change of residence ? Unthinkable. The object of my staying in the village was to remain with grandfather and father and be of some help to them. If I were to shift from the village I would not only be failing in my duty towards the family but would also be betraying its interests. I dismissed the Siddhanti's predictions with some contempt. But he firmly stuck to them, saying, "My dear young friend, Rahu in a common sign, the dispositor in the 10th, and the sub–lord in the 4th, and the transit position I have just mentioned, must change your residence. Take note of this principle.

After listening to the Siddhanti, I fell back on the well known work *Krishnamisreeya*, according to which when Rahu is in Pisces the results likely to occur would be "difficulties, fear from rulers (*nripadbhayam*), fear from thieves (*chorabheeti*), quarrels (*kalaha*), misunderstandings with kith and kin (*swajana virodha*) etc. Of course, all these results had been experienced by me in some form or other. What about the Moon's sub–period I was then having? According to the same text, the Moon in a quadrant or trine, or in the 3rd or 11th, and exalted, would give one during the Moon's sub–period "agreeable pleasure (*manollasa*), great happiness (*mahatasoukhyam*), acquisition of fame (*keertiprapti*), journey to the north (*uttaram disimasritya prayanam*). The Moon in the 3rd from the major lord indicated "Income from different sources (*naana mooladhanagamana*), and aspected by Saturn, "loss of money through various sources". By and large the indications seemed to be not quite favourable. But how was I to get income from different sources. The only means could be astrological consultations. But who would come to this village to consult with me about their horoscopes. THE ASTROLOGICAL MAGAZINE was in a shambles. Some stray orders were coming in for my "A Manual of Hindu Astrology" and the typed copies of "Hindu Predictive Astrology". There was darkness alround.

But the thought why I should not take a trip to Bombay and earn some money struck me all of a sudden. Trainfare, lodging and boarding in Bombay — all these involved expenses. I broached the subject with grandfather. He approved the idea without a second thought saying, "You know Astrology well. No one can beat you in mathematical Astrology. You are able to make predictions and they will prove correct as Jupiter lord of the 2nd or *vaksthana* is in the 10th aspecting the 2nd. Decide immediately." I decided that I must undertake a trip to Bombay and started making preparations.

17

I had already some admirers, those who had purchased the typescript copies of A MANUAL OF HINDU ASTROLOGY and A TEXT BOOK OF ASTROLOGY, in Bombay and other places. When I wrote to one such admirer Subbaraman, employed in a business firm in Bombay, he immediately responded inviting me to visit Bombay, and offering hospitality and assuring me of all cooperation.

I wrote to other friends in Davanagere, Hubli, Belgaum and Poona and their replies were not quite satisfactory. A sum of at least Rs. 50 was the minimum needed for me and an assistant to reach Bombay. This amount could not be secured.

The object of my trip to Bombay was five–fold, viz., (1) to earn enough money with a view to resolving the financial problems at home ; (2) to collect funds or at least secure promises of help for restarting THE ASTROLOGICAL MAGAZINE which was already dead after I tried resuscitating it in 1930 ; (3) to meet astrologers and astrological scholars and convince them about the need for specialization in astrological mathematics ; (4) to find some publisher to bring out grandfather's books like ASTROLOGICAL SELF–INSTRUCTOR, JATAKA–CHANDRIKA etc. which had gone out of print ; and finally (5) to "expose" quacks and montebonks who were misleading the public by offering cheep sun–sign readings etc. Here I must make it clear that I never wanted to become a professional astrologer and in fact I have never been one. Hence no rates were fixed for consultation and I decided to accept whatever was voluntarily offered.

On 10th July 1935 with a capital of Rs. 5/- only I and my assistant Sastri left for Madhugiri where my father-in-law was a well-known

Government doctor. My wife Rajeswari was a staying with her parents and I wanted to spend a day or two with her before embarking on my journey to Bombay.

At Madhugiri, a small town of about 5000 people, I became acquainted with Nanjundappa a lawyer locally well-known. He was also a bit of an astrologer. In my discussions with him I discovered that he was not only well versed in the subject but had made some research also. We became good friends. He said that a Pandit who knew Astrology well and who was capable of timing events accurately lived in a nearby village and that we should meet him. Accordingly we went to the village and met the astrologer. He revealed an important principle, *viz.*, Ashtakavarga prepared for each sub-chart (Navamsa, Dwadasamsa, etc.) could be used for timing events. For instance transits applied to Venus Ashtakavarga derived from Navamsa, would indicate the time of marriage etc. I found this method simple and fairly reliable. According to him the Ashtakavarga system was self-contained and could be used for analysing the entire horoscope. In the absence of classical authority endorsing his stance, applying Ashtakavarga to divisional charts cannot be considered as authoritative. But sometimes in the absence of authoritative dicta one's experience could be taken as a criterion. I shall have more to say on this subject in a subsequent chapter.

Nanjundappa promised to become a subscriber to THE ASTROLOGICAL MAGAZINE when I started it. In fact he not only became a subscriber but continued as on as long as he lived.

From Madhugiri, we went to Gubbi, a Taluk headquarters. After dumping my baggage at the Travellers' Bungalow — the rent for a room was eight annas (50 paise) per day — I sent my assistant Sastri to go round the town, meet the Amildar, the Government doctor, the assistant engineer, the Inspector of Police etc., and tell them that I would be in Gubbi for 24 hours and they were welcome to have their horoscopes examined by me. The response was poor. No one turned up till sunset. Feeling that discretion was the better part of valour, I went to the residence of the local doctor and introduced myself to him. He had just finished performing his father's annual ceremony and was relaxing, engaged in playing cards. I was made to wait till he completed the game and he invited me and my assistant Sastri to join him for supper. "Mr. Raman, since you are an astrologer I want you to solve a problem. A month ago some property was stolen. Do I get it back and if so, when ? Can you answer this question ?", he said. I had a ready–reckoner prepared to give snap–shot answers for such questions on the basis of the star of the day. The query was put on a day ruled by the constellation Pushya. Banking on the dictum that when a question put on a Pushyami day pertains to loss of property the answer should be, the property should be recovered (नष्टद्रव्य विषयकु प्रश्ने अपघात पदार्थ सिद्धिर्भवेत्). The rising Lagna at the moment was *chara* or moveable and I said : "Yes, you will get the property back within a week." He was both surprised and satisfied with my specific answer. The bonanza or reward for this service I gave him, was food for me and my assistant, six rupees as fee and an introductory letter to a colleague of his at Davanagere. The next morning just before leaving Gubbi, a local trader paid Rs. 5 for a consultation about his brother's marriage. The first lap of my journey was auspicious.

The next halt for 2 days was at Davanagere, a fairly big town and a commercial centre. We had to stay at a *musafirkhana* as no accommodation was available at the T.B. The rent was four annas (25 paise) per day. As I was standing in front of the lodging, one Mr. E. Ponnuswamy Aiyer, a P.W.D. clerk — perhaps struck by my neat attire (I used to wear western dress — a suit, vest and a matching necktie) — enquired where I had come from. When I mentioned my name and said I could read his past, present and future, he became friendly, took me and my assistant to his residence where we had dinner. He also arranged for our shifting to the T.B. and arranged for free boarding at a good hotel in return for my studying the hotel proprietor's horoscope. Mr. Ponnuswamy Iyer's problem was "no issues". I studied his horoscope and indicated that his 5th house was much afflicted but he would have a child in 1937.

I called at the residence of the local engineer with the letter of introduction given to me by the Gubbi doctor. He showed interest in my activities and introduced me to a local mill–owner, who badly needed my astrological counsel as to whether he would have any children. I cast a *prasna* chart and found that the Lagna and the 5th were masculine signs and the lords were in conjunction in the 9th with Ketu. I also considered the village astrologer's simple method of totalling the number of the weekday, lunar day and the day's constellation, and declared that he would have a son after performing remedial measures. He paid me twenty–five rupees as fee. He was also advised to have his horoscope studied in detail by grandfather. In fact he sent his horoscope to grandfather for his scrutiny, paying him Rs. 100.

The mill–owner wrote to me after a year saying he had performed the remedial measures as prescribed and a son had been born to him.

As I reflect on these early years I sometimes wonder how simple methods, popular amongst village astrologers, and used by me to give snap–shot predictions clicked. I was bent on making as much money as possible, of course, by conscientious work. Though I had carried with me all the reference books, ephemerides, etc. sometimes I used to fall back on these good old simplistic methods for want of time.

At Davanagere, I think it was in the premises of the Jayadeva Press, I met a retired engineer, who showed nothing but contempt for Astrology. He said, "Astrology has ruined me. I have burnt the horoscopes of all the members of my family. No one ever predicted correctly and my disgust knows no bounds. Why do you waste your time in studying and practising a deceitful art ?". My blood began to boil and being impulsive by nature, I could no longer tolerate his denigration of astrology. I burst out, "Look here, you call yourself an engineer. Do you know how many bridges constructed under your supervision have collapsed ? Burn all the engineering books and hang yourself ? You are an elderly person and you are not expected to talk non–sense."

The others who were watching the verbal pyrotechniques taking place between us restrained both of us and tried to calm me. I did not want to beat a humilitating retreat mouthing his disparaging remarks about Astrology. Recovering my balance and risking my "reputation", I calmly said. "My dear Sir, at the movement Virgo is

rising and the 5th is occupied by Rahu and the lord of the 5th is in
the 6th. Jupiter is in the 3rd. The 5th is aspected by the Sun, Ketu
and Mars. Could it be that your condemnation of Astrology was due
to the fact that your daughter became a widow soon after marriage ?"
Tears rolled down his cheeks. "Yes, my dear young man, my only
daughter became a widow in her 14th year even though the horoscopes
had been matched and the marriage performed at an auspicious
Muhurtha. By the by how were you able to infer that my daughter
became a widow ?" I explained to him the *modus operandi* I had
employed and also the relevant combinations. I told him : "Rahu in
the 5th denoted his suffering due to a child. As lord of the 5th is
Saturn and the issue could be the daughter I inferred that the root
cause of your trouble could be her suffering." Whether or not he was
satisfied I had the satisfaction of upholding the truth of Astrology.
Luck seemed to favour me in all these adventures. The reasoning in
support of the predictions made was as I had analysed the chart 55
years ago.

On my way to Hubli, the next day, while travelling in the Inter
class I got acquainted with a ticket collector, one Nair. He showed
keen interest in Astrology and palmistry and wanted to know when
he would get married. Here again on the basis of the question time
and manipulation of the lunar date, constellation, weekday etc., I said
that he would get married within two months. He did marry within
two months and wrote to me a letter congratulating me on my
successful prediction. After I gave him the prediction, the ticket
collector transferred me at Byadagi station to a II–class compartment
without any extra charge !

I had expected an admirer of mine to meet us at the Hubli railway
station. But he did not turn up. I did not know what to do. Seeing
our dilemma, a young man of about 30 or 35 offered to find a place
for us to stay. He was a worker in a factory and gave us a room in
his small house. When he learnt that I was an astrologer, he was all
attention to me. His wife was in the family way and the delivery was
expected within a month. He wanted to know whether she would have
a safe delivery and if so, when. I asked him to give a number of

three digits which he did. When reduced to a single digit it was 3, which meant Jupiter. The Ascendant, a moveable sign, was aspected by a planet in a friendly sign. I told him his wife would safely deliver a son within 24 hours. According to village astrologers, the event happens in an hour, in a day, in a month or in a year according as the Lagna is influenced by a planet in exaltation, own house, friendly sign, or enemy's or debilitation sign.

Hubli was not very congenial, I could earn only about Rs. 10 The next morning I left for Dharwar where I and my assistant were comfortably lodged with one Jakar, editor of a local weekly. His parents bestowed on us much attention and looked after us well. My stay of two days in Dharwar yielded some dividend. Jakar introduced me to some of his friends and consultations fetched about Rs. 50.

One G.C. Nandi, a native of Dharwar but working as an Inspector of Police in Satara was of much help to me. He had a fairly good knowledge of Astrology. Two lawyers promised to subscribe to THE ASTROLOGICAL MAGAZINE when it was revived again.

On 19th July I left for Belgaum by bus. The fare was Rs. 1.25. There I met one Mr. K.G. Gokhale, a well–known pleader and stayed with him for a day. Mr. Gokhale was happy that I had taken to Astrology. He was himself a good astrologer and had much regard for grandfather. He said, "Just as Gandhi is respected in politics as occupying the highest position, Suryanarain Rao is respected for the high position he occupies in Astrology." He also gave some sage advice as to how I should tackle clients and why certain types of predictions involving one's character etc., should not be given. He had participated in the freedom movement and had been jailed three times. He had his own astrological explanation for his incarceration for political offences. He said, "Because Jupiter lord of the 12th, in my horoscope is aspected by Mars lord of the 1st and 8th and the Sun is in the 6th along with the 1st lord, I was put in jail." His Ascendant was Aries. Mars situated in the 2nd was aspecting the 5th where Jupiter, lord of the 12th , was placed in association with Ketu and the 8th lord. Mr. Gokhale was a well–known personality in his days and was born on 14–9–1896 at 10–00 p.m. at Belgaum.

We arrived at Poona on 21st July and were received at the railway station by the elderly P.L. Bhagavat, Director of Telegraphs in Bombay and an admirer of grandfather. We were comfortably lodged in his house and were well taken care of. Bhagavat had a good knowledge of Astrology, but had his own reservations in recognizing my attainments simply because he thought I was too young to be taken seriously.

I tried to impress Bhagavat about my astrological abilities and reeled out a few *slokas* from *Sripati* and *Brihat Jataka*. This seemed to have impressed him to some extent. He wanted me to clarify his doubts about Satyacharya's method of longevity determination.

He said, "Varahamihira holds Satyacharya in esteem. I am confused about the calculation of longevity according to his method. Could you explain it?" I had a ready reply. "Yes, Satyacharya's method of longevity reckoning is reliable and simplicity itself. I have calculated longevity of a number of dead persons and the results obtained are very encouraging." I then quoted the verse :

सत्योक्ते ग्रहमिष्ठं लिप्ती कुत्या शतद्धये नाप्तं ।
मण्डल भाग विशुद्धे अब्दा: स्यु: शेषानुमामाङघ: ॥

Explaining the meaning I said, "Convert the longitude of a planet into minutes and divide it by 200 (a Navamsa). If the quotient exceeds 12, expunge multiples of 12 and the remainder is the number of years, etc., given by the planet as its contribution of longevity." Bhagavat interrupted me, "What about the Haransas or reductions ?" Then I explained the usual *chakrapata harana* and reductions due to *satrukshetra, neechakshetra, astangata*, etc. "What about Mars ?" quipped Bhagavat. "All *haranas,* except *satrukshetra,* are applicable to Mars also." Bhagavat thought for a while and again questioned me about increase in the longevity term and whether all the corrections should be applied. I explained, "When a planet is in *swakshetra*, the increase is twice, in exaltation or retrogression, thrice, When several *haranas* , etc., are involved, only one, that is the highest is to be applied."

In 1936 Bhagavat visited our place and stayed with us in the village for a couple of days. He was in touch with me even after I had become "renowned" and until 1957 or 1958.

During my stay at Poona, Bhagavat introduced me to Pandits Raghunath Sastri and Gore Sastri, well–known astrologers. Mr. Gore Sastri was in frequent touch with me. In 1958 when I had been invited by S.K. Kelkar to preside over the anniversary celebrations of Graha Nakshatra Phaladesa Mandal, an astrological institution, run by him and his friends, Gore Sastry attended my lecture and appreciated what he called my "sustained efforts to defend and demonstrate the truth of Hindu Astrology and especially of the Vimshottari Dasa system. Bhagavat paid me Rs. 100/- for studying his horoscope.

After the usual periodical remittances to grandfather and making sure that I had enough money. I travelled to Bombay in the second–class by Deccan Queen on 22nd July 1935. The fare was Rs. 7.50 while that for my assistant's travel by third class was Rs.2.75.

K. Subbaraman was at the Victoria Terminus– to receive us. He took us immediately to Vile Parle where a neat and fairly big room had been arranged for our stay, a few yards away from the place of Subbaraman's brother's residence. Subbaraman was still not married and was staying with his brother Seshadri Iyer, employed in a big firm. No efforts were spared by Iyer and his family to attend to our needs and keep us happy.

While travelling in the train Subbaraman, himself a student of Astrology, asked me what would be the consequence if for a person born in Virgo, Rahu and Gulika were in the 2nd. I said, "Deafness". Surprised, he said, "How accurate is your answer ? The combination is present in my case and I am partially deaf. Unless you shout I won't be able to hear you at all."

I had no idea as to what to do in Bombay and whom to meet ? However the first thing I did was to provide myself with a monthly railway pass. After food I would travel to the Fort area and start calling on lawyers, businessmen etc, until 7 or 8 p.m. and then return to Vile Parle. The first two days were disappointing. Ramasubban met a number of well–to–do South Indians engaged in business and other avocations with a view to arranging my meetings with them. Another gentleman, Narain Rao, who was also very much interested in Astrology, took the initiative of meeting one or two South Indian "Rao Bahadurs". At last a meeting was arranged at Matunga and I was asked to explain my mission. I introduced myself as the grandson of Prof. Suryanarain Rao and as one deeply interested in making Astrology acceptable and in promoting Indian culture. I said that THE ASTROLOGICAL MAGAZINE had to be revived and some of grandfather's books were to be published. About a dozen leading south Indians who were present did not show any interest. It looked as if they were listening to the woes of a schoolboy. Nothing came out of this meeting. Only a few persons promised to become subscribers when the Magazine was started, and I took leave of them. Anyway my experience with these South Indians in Bombay, was not particularly flattering. One gentleman said that he would give me a job on Rs. 100 per months to enable me to tide over my difficulties. Subbaraman and Narain Rao felt very sorry for they could do nothing to help me. After this experience I decided to fend for myself, relying on the strength of my own horoscope.

Once while commuting in a local train, I met a Parsi gentleman, who I learnt later on, was the editor of *Bombay Samachar*, a leading Gujarati daily. He took me to his office, made enquiries about me, said some good words about grandfather and promised to do his best to help me. The next morning's paper carried news about my visit to Bombay and also an advertisement that I was available for consultations. This brought in a spate of requests for astrological counsel. Vile Parle was too far and we had to think of a place in the Fort area. As luck would have it, one of the enquiries was from one Bapu Hari Ganoo, a share broker and commission agent, who offered to secure orders for consultation on a commission basis. The next day I met Ganoo in his office in the Fort area, which had a table, 2 chairs and a telephone in the office room of another broker. It was decided that I should do the consultation work in his office and that he should be paid 15% on orders that come to me directly and 33 1/3% on orders secured by him.

Ganoo, a Maharashtrian Brahmin, was no doubt a good man, but was a heavy smoker and addicted to alcohol. Once he took me to his house — a one–room flat in a lane in Girgaum. He had no children. Apart from his second wife, his only other companion was a monkey. He also knew Astrology and everyday he used to spend some time with me discussing the subject. I would do the castings at Vile Parle during the nights and give readings, mostly oral, at the office, from 11 a.m. to 4 p.m. Then I would go out with Ganoo to meet lawyers, doctors and others to enlist support for bringing out THE ASTROLOGICAL MAGAZINE.

While in Bombay I must have studied at least fifty horoscopes, most of the consultors being interested in speculation and business and some about health and family matters.

One day, probably 26th July, there was a surprise visit at about 11 a.m. from one Yousuff I. Lalji. I found him in a disturbed condition. He was polite and appeared to me to be a man of culture. Announcing his name he said, "I am an admirer of your grandfather. I am in great difficulty and I want your astrological advice." Before I said anything, he continued, "Let us go to our place and discuss the whole thing."

By about 11–45 a.m. we were in his house on the Napean Sea Road. His daughter joined us and he opened his heart. "Your see we are Muslims, but follow many Hindu customs as we belong to the Bohra community. The financial distress we are in, unless overcome, will seriously affect our honour in the community. I know only the date of my birth. I have studied your grandfather's books and can follow your arguments." I was in a dilemma as to what to do in the absence of the time of birth. Trusting to my strong conviction that Jupiter in the 10th would never betray me, I cast a chart for the time of question and Rasi positions for the date of birth. The constellation on that day was Sravana. A formula given in *Jyothishasastra Payonidhi* says that if a query made in this constellation pertains to loss of wealth we can say it will be recovered soon (नष्टद्रव्य विषयक प्रश्ने पदार्थं शीघ्रमेव लभ्यं भवति). Really speaking, the query was about the native coming out of the financial liabilities he was facing and not the loss of property. But I felt that the dictum could also be applied for the problem on hand. I told Yousuff that since the time of birth was not known and I could not fix it then and there correctly, I would proceed on the basis of the Prasna chart. Since Yousuff knew a little bit of Astrology, he said, "But Chandra Lagna is equally important especially because I am now more than 50 years old."

I caught his point and proceeded thus, "The Chandra Lagna is fairly strong. Yogakaraka Mars is in the 3rd with exalted Mercury lord of the 3rd. The 4th is occupied by Venus, lord of the 4th and the 11th. In fact, Venus has caused Malavya Yoga, one of the Pancha Mahapurusha Yogas. Lord of the 7th Saturn is in the 11th while lord of the 9th Jupiter aspects Kalatrakaraka. Lord of the 2nd Sun is in the 2nd. Therefore your earnings have always been good. Your wife must have brought you much property. Your father could have been connected with religious institutions. Jupiter lord of the 6th, aspects the 6th. You may be suffering from diabetes but the disease is under control as lord of Chandra Lagna is strong. Ketu–Saturn association indicates that you are not quite loyal to your wife. The house of speculation is occupied by Rahu but the planet of speculation Mercury

	Ketu Saturn	Jupit.		Jupit.		Mars
		Moon	Ketu Sat.			Sun Venus Merc.
Birth Chart				Query Chart		
		Sun	Moon			Rahu
Rahu	Venus	Mars Merc.			Ascdt.	

is exalted but afflicted. You are now having *ashtama sani* all of which means" : and before, I could continue, he took over, "You are remarkably accurate in all matters. I wonder whether you think that my Lagna is also Cancer. My married life is not happy. We have serious difference and my wife has not come to my relief." I paused for a while and again proceeded. "Yes, your Lagna could be Cancer but we have to apply corroborative methods."

Then switching on to the Prasna chart I observed, "Lords of the 9th and 10th, *viz.*, Mercury and the Moon are associated with the 11th lord. Jupiter *karaka* for money, aspects Lagna while the Lagna lord himself is in the 10th. From the Moon again Venus Yogakaraka, is in the 7th with Mercury, lord of the 5th, and the Sun, lord of the 8th." Interrupting me Yousuff said, "But the Sun is lord of the 8th." I said the blemish of 8th lordship does not attach to the Sun. The Prasna chart is quite encouraging. Considering all these I venture the prediction that you will turn the corner and come out of the ordeal." Yousuff, apparently satisfied, queried, "But when ? That is important for me." I again went on, "Saturn will be leaving Aquarius by about May 1936. Rahu is about to enter Sagittarius. Therefore I am of the opinion that most of your troubles may end by the end of 1936." In my interpretation I had mixed up natal and horary principles and somehow came to the conclusion that he would be free from his troubles, Expressing his satisfaction Yousuff said, "I have consulted several astrologers but you alone are clear in your analysis. I am satisfied with what you have said and I have confidence that your prediction will turn out correct." So saying he paid me Rs. 200 — Rs. 100 as donation towards starting my journal and the rest as my fee. I did not grumble as I did not expect Yousuff to be so good. He dropped me back in his car at my so-called "office". He also assured me of any help I might need during my stay in Bombay.

The next day a pot-bellied Gujarati probably in his fifties, called on me. He placed a ten-rupee note on my table with a scroll of paper — his horoscope cast in Gujarati, and demanded "Look here, I have been advised by Ganoo to consult you. I do not want much. A general reading of my horoscope, the date of my daughter's marriage and the nature of her married life, a general idea of my son's career. And the most important, when my ailing wife will die and whether there is any prospect of my marrying my concubine?"

I felt angry at this man's arrogance and asked him how much he paid his scavenger ?'. When he said "Rs. 30 per month", I shot back with vehemence, "Do you think that an astrologer is so cheap that you offer only Rs. 10 for a job, which involves hours of labour and intellectual work : for your requirements I would charge Rs. 2000. I have no time to do this work. But I am prepared to answer only your last question." He asked "About my wife ?" Then I pretended to go through the scroll and firmly declared : "Your wife will recover her health and your concubine will die." He got up in a huff and walked away with his ten–rupee note. In my long life, I have had several such encounters with unscrupulous people but I have always refused to answer questions involving family break–up, husband–wife separation etc.

After doing consultations for about ten days I wound up my "office" and wanted Ganoo with whom I had developed friendly relations, despite the age difference of 23 years — he was then 46 years old — to introduce me to some book publishers and business magnets so that I could enlist some patrons for the Magazine and a publisher for grandfather's books and also for my own book "A Manual of Hindu Astrology". We met several publishers but to no avail. In a private meeting Jal Hirji Taraporewala, proprietor of D.B. Taraporewala Sons and Co., had with me he tried to evade the subject of undertaking our publications but wanted me to give him some predictions. Jal said, "The book market is very tight. There is no demand for astrological books. Therefore we shall consider your proposal next year. Tell me something about my horoscope as I am facing some tough problems. I shall pay your fees." For the sake of curiosity I asked him how much he would pay. "Twenty rupees" was his laconical reply. I told him firmly that I would not touch his chart even with a pair of tongs unless he discussed with me about the possibility of his publishing our books. After all my persuasions Jal offered to buy the copyright of "A Manual of Hindu Astrology" for Rs. 200 ! I found him cunning, very business–like and evasive. I took leave of him stating that I would examine his horoscope when I visited Bombay again. He was born on 19-2-1905 at about 42 ghatis after sunrise at Bombay. Libra was rising at birth with Mercury and Saturn in the 4th house aspected by Mars.

B.H. Mirza, proprietor, Indian Book Depot, Meadows Street and Bhatkal, proprietor, Popular Book Depot, Grant Road, were of much help to me, by way of placing orders for our available publications and effecting payments in advance which greatly helped us in bringing out some of grandfather's books.

One day I called on Hiralal Motilal Mehta, a leading advocate and perhaps a colleague of K.M. Munshi, founder of Bharatiya Vidya Bhavan. Mehta was a "chela" of grandfather. He had visited our village and had got much astrological work done by grandfather. But their relations became sour after Gandhi launched his civil disobedience movement. Grandfather — he was indeed a great nationalist — did not approve of law-breaking while Mehta was an ardent admirer of Gandhi. Anyway Mehta received me warmly and said that his political differences with grandfather did not come in the way of his holding grandfather in high esteem. When I broached the object of my visit he readily consented to become a patron when I started the Magazine.

Sun	Mars Venus		Rahu		Mars	Rahu	
Merc.		RASI	Sat.	Merc.	NAVAMSA		Lagna
				Sat.			Moon
Ketu Jupit. Lagna	Moon				Ketu	Venus	Sun Jupit.

Ganoo was much helpful throughout my stay at Bombay. He had some queer views about interpreting his own horoscope. He was born on 23rd March 1889 at about 12-30 a.m.

"How is it that in spite of my having Venus Dasa now, I am living had to mouth ? Venus is lord of the 11th and occupies the 5th with Mars, lord of the 5th. Moreover progressed Sun conjoins my radical Venus in my 47th year ?" queried Ganoo. I said, "You would have become equal to Hitler had only your Moon been in Sagittarius, the Sun and Mercury in Aries and the Ascendant Libra : for you were born 28 days before Hitler. But unfortunately your destiny is differently constituted. First of all planets are disposed in the 2nd and 12th from each other. Your life has been successful only in patches." Ganoo quipped, "Exactly so. The only boom period in my finances was in Mercury Dasa and Rahu sub-period." I asked him not to interrupt me and continued : "Ketu in Lagna in the constellation of Venus and Venus being the lord of the 12th from the Moon should have given foreign travel in Ketu Dasa." "Correct, I was in Europe from 1923 to 1925, started my own business and was fairly successful", Ganoo said. I told him, "As lord of Lagna Jupiter is in the Ascendant, the horoscope has some strength. But there are no good Yogas worth the name." And I spoke as if I was an authority on the subject. "Ketu in the 1st has spoiled your horoscope. Such a disposition indicates that the native will not be grateful, will be generally unhappy, carrying tales, but Jupiter in Lagan has lessened the affliction. Ketu in Lagna can also give some physical disability and make one generally miserable." Ganoo went on nodding his head and at one stage remarked, "Yes, in business sometimes the partner has to be outwitted and certain transactions concealed. If you think this constitutes cheating, I am guilty." I proceeded, "Ketu makes you cunning but as the Sun is in the 4th and the lord of the 4th happens to be Jupiter you are not deceitful. Ketu makes you mediumistic. You will have weird thoughts and experiences and sometimes an idealistic trend of mind. You will have great foresight. But Venus in the 5th with Mars, indicates a sensual nature and intimacy with other women." Ganoo asking me to stop clarified : "Yes, what all you have said is correct.

But I do not agree on one thing. Ever since I lost my first wife in 1918, I have led the life of a bachelor though I may have flirted with other women as I and my second wife are not on good terms." I continued my analysis, "At the moment you are having Venus Dasa and the Moon's sub–period. The Dasa lord Venus is in the 5th with Mars lord of the 5th and 12th from Lagna and the 8th from the major lord. In the Navamsa Venus is better placed. Therefore I do not think Venus Dasa will give you any financial prosperity. The *status–quo* may continue." Ganoo said, "I am quite satisfied with your interpretation. You have justified your being the grandson of Suryanarain Rao whom we all hold in great esteem. Tell me when I will die. I am practising certain *mantras* which have been giving me peace of mind. Do you suggest any particular *mantra* for my daily practice ?" I was not well acquainted with remedial Astrology, but to gratify him I said, "Venus, your Dasa lord, is in the 5th house with Mars. Venus is fairly strong being placed in his own star. You can get initiated into Lakshmi *mantra*. So far as longevity is concerned, the sub–period of Mars in the Dasa of the Moon should prove critical."

I consider 4th August 1935 as a significant day in my life. A few days earlier I had been taken to the Bombay Astrological Society and introduced to the office–bearers by Ganoo. The secretary said, "It will be a great honour if you could deliver a lecture at our society on the 4th August Sunday." I did not know what to do for I had never addressed a meeting before. To speak before a gathering of scholars well–versed in the subject and astrologers, so I thought then, would be almost impossible. But I did not want to say 'no' for that would affect my dignity. So I accepted the invitation and the subject was the "Art of Prediction". I spent a sleepless night reading all the texts and pondering over as to what to talk. An extempore speech was quite out of question. I prepared with great effort my talk for the next day. The venue was a school on Grant Road. I was received at the auditorium by the Secretary. There were about 60 persons, most of them members of the society. I was introduced as "A young man deeply learned in Astrology, an author and grandson of Prof. B.

Suryanarain Rao" and it was hoped "a stimulating．talk on Astrology will be delivered."

As I stood up to deliver my talk I was gripped by some sort of a fear and my legs began shaking. Standing firmly on the ground and calling into play all my courage, I read my talk slowly but dared not look at the audience. The talk was over within 25 minutes. I explained the basis of Astrology and said, "To analyse a horoscope, we have to consider the lord, the house, etc." At the conclusion of the talk, the chairman, a learned *Jyotishi* from Baroda, remarked : "We had expected a better performance from the grandson of Mr. B. Suryanarain Rao." I felt ashamed and crushed. Thus ended my first performance as a public speaker. And this was the stepping stone for my becoming later on "an orator who can hold vast audiences spellbound."

Mr. Y.K. Pradhan, an advocate of the Sayana zodiac, who was present at the talk, came to my rescue by saying that the talk was well conceived and that I exhibited signs of becoming in the future not only a good speaker but also a good astrologer. He invited me to his house and we had a free and frank exchange of astrological thought. I refuted his theory that originally Hindu Astrology was based on the Sayana zodiac and countered his view by quoting Satyacharya and Varahamihira that it was the zodiac of constellations that the ancient Hindu astrologers employed.

Decades later, after I had become "famous", Mr. Pradhan acknowledged "my contribution to Astrology and the courage of conviction displayed" by me "in upholding the dignity and scientific basis of Hindu Astrology".

Leaving Bombay on 9th August, I returned to Bangalore on the 11th and reported my experiences to grandfather. He was happy the trip had been fruitful.

18

The funds secured from my trip to Bombay gave us some relief but nothing could be retained for the purpose of reviving THE ASTROLOGICAL MAGAZINE. During August and September 1935 I studied and restudied Tajaka Astrology, worked out a number of horoscopes, collected information and started writing the book VARSHAPHAL or THE HINDU PROGRESSED HOROSCOPE. While at Bombay I had secured an old printed edition of *Tajaka NeelaKanteeyam* and I had already thoroughly studied *Laghu Thajaka* and had my doubts cleared by no less a scholar than Mahamahopadhyaya Sivasankara Sastri. I worked out my own Varshaphal chart and I tried to interpret it in the light of my radix, according to which I was to get, as soon as my 24th year commenced, the sub-period of Mars in the major period of Rahu. These directional influences seemed rather frightening what with the major lord Rahu occupying the 2nd, a *maraka* place, and the sub-lord placed in the 7th in another *maraka* house, the former being aspected by the latter. There were two possibilities. First, I would pass through a very difficult and trying period financially, mentally and even physically. Second, the house of family (2nd) being afflicted by these two lords would deprive me of family peace and could even cause the death of Rajeswari who was then in the family way. Did not *Krishnamisreeya* say "death of close relatives (*apta bandhu viyogascha*), quarrels with all (*sarvatra kalaho bhavet*), going to outside places (*sthanantharecha gamane*) ; and because of conjunction with Mercury, fear in public matters, (*budhena samyute drishte vyavahare bhayam chaiva*) and fighting with relatives (*bandhoonam vigrahasthatha*); and both the lords being situated in the 6th and the 8th from each other, misunderstandings and quarrels with cousins (*gnati virodhascha*) and disputes (*vivadas*). Then there would be loss of money (*dhana nasa*) and affliction to children (*putrapeeda*) etc. The horde of evil results indicated seemed indeed formidable ! Nevertheless my mental attitude had changed and my worries proportionately lessened because of the conviction that Jupiter in the 10th aspected Rahu and the Sun, the dispositor of Mars. But still there were misgivings. Why not I cast a yearly chart on the basis of Tajaka, in which I felt I had gained considerable proficiency.

My 24th year* commenced according to Tajaka on 9th August 1935 at about 6-15 p.m. or so.

			Ketu
Saturn	Chart for 24th year		Mercury Sun
Lagna Muntha			Venus
Rahu	Moon	Mars Jupiter	

The Lagna was Capricorn and the lord was strongly placed in the 2nd in his own sign. Saturn was the year lord as well as the lord of Muntha which was the same sign as Lagna. These were encouraging factors. What would be the state of our finances and my own fame, and would Rajeswari have a safe-delivery ? The point of finance (*artha saham*) was in the Ascendant and the Muntha sign. The point of

---

*The calculation was based on what I have designed as Method A in my book VARSHAPHAL. After years of experience this method was rejected in favour of Method B. For details see the book.

business (*vyaapaara saham*) was Aries. And the lord Mars was in the 10th from the Muntha. Mars was not disposed in the 6th, 8th or 12th house. These were all favourable indications. But about my "fame" and the safe delivery of my wife ? The lord of the point of fame (*yasas saham*), the Moon was debilitated but occupied the 11th from the Muntha and was in benefic aspect to the Sun, lord of the 8th and Mercury, lord of the 6th and 9th. I figured out that the effects being neutral there was nothing to worry, some financial benefits should accrue and that as Jupiter, lord of the point of foreign country (*paradesa saham*) was in the 10th, I might again go on a tour etc. Lord of the 5th Venus in the 8th is a neutral disposition. Lord of the 5th and Jupiter were mutually well disposed (3 and 11). The point of children (*putra saham*) was the same as Muntha and Lagna. These indicated the birth of a son.

But one thing I could not reconcile with was what the Siddhanti had said, *viz.*, that I would change the place of my residence. Perhaps I could not see this event happening either in my birth or annual chart and perhaps the conditioning of my mind that I would never live away from grandfather and father could have been the main subjective factor coloring my judgment.

I told grandfather that I would undertake another trip so that we could get money we were so badly in need of and he readily agreed. It was decided that I should, this time, visit Madras the same way as I did Bombay. Two of my "admirers" M Thiagarajan a relative of late C. G. Rajan and Thiruvenkatacharya, who had just started publishing "Kashyapa Astrological Journal" welcomed my visit to Madras promising to do their best.

Accompanied by a Brahmin servant Gopala I left Bangalore on 20th October, 1935. I broke my journey at Kolar Gold Fields as Mr. Ratnavelu Mudaliar, one of my admirers was particular that I stop with him as some of his friends wanted to show their horoscopes to me. Mudaliar had made arrangements for our stay in the house of a Brahmin engineer. This gentleman was worried that the marriage of his 13-year old daughter was getting unduly delayed because the astrologers of the bridegroom's party did not favour the match on the plea of Kuja Dosha in the girl's horoscope, while his own astrologer had said the Dosha did not exist. The engineer wanted me to convince the boy's parents, who were expected the next day, that there was no Kuja Dosha. In the girl's chart Aquarius was rising with the Sun and Mercury, Mars in the 2nd, Venus and Ketu in the 3rd, Jupiter in the 7th, Saturn in the 8th and the Moon in the 10th. The boy's Lagna was Virgo with Mrs in the 7th and Venus conjunct Saturn. The father of the boy also said that as I was the grandson of Suryanarain Rao, he would accept my verdict. I was placed in a dilemma. I began, "The position of Mars in the 2nd from the Ascendant and the 12th from Venus definitely constitutes Kuja Dosha." The father of the girl began to get frantic while the boy's father smiled simply believing I was about to endorse his astrologer's opinion. "But", I continued, "It is present only theoretically. The dispositor of Mars is Jupiter and he is placed in the 7th aspecting the 7th lord also". In the meanwhile, I heard the bridegroom's astrologer whisper to the boy's father in Tamil, "Oh ! he is only a *bachcha*, let us not take him seriously." This roused my emotions and in a raised voice I declared emphatically, "Kalatrakaraka Venus who also happens to be the lord of the 7th from the Moon is no doubt with Ketu. But he is aspected by Jupiter. Even assuming that there is Kuja Dosha, it is balanced by the presence of a similar Dosha in the horoscope of the boy. Moreover the girl will not get the Dasa of Mars." And in a challenging tone I said, "Let any astrologer refute me if he knows Astrology." It looked as if I had won, as the bridegroom's father nodded his head in approval. Months later, I was given to understand that the girl's marriage took place with the boy in question.

The Engineer was all praise for me. The consequence was, he placed the horoscopes of all his children before me along with fifty rupees. Of course, I took the money and asked him to send the horoscopes to Bangalore. The first lap of my second trip had also begun on an auspicious note.

I was preparing to leave K.G.F. the next morning but Mudaliar persisted that I should extend my stay for another day as he had arranged for my lecture to be presided over by one Dr. Seshadri, the local Health Officer, to be followed by a dinner at his house. My experience as a speaker at Bombay was still fresh in my mind. I could not say 'no' because Mudaliar had already issued printed notices announcing my "lecture at the King George Hall, Robertsonpet on 21st October 1935 at 6.00 p.m.". An extempore talk ? Impossible ! I worked on my talk the whole night. The lecture hall was full with the officers of the Government and the Gold Mines. My nervousness had partly disappeared. Slowly delivering my speech, I would now and then look at the audience. The lecture was over in 30 minutes. Dr. Seshadri, the President, was all praise "for the way Astrology was presented in such a scientific manner". It was a day of triumph for me, when compared to how I had fared at the Bombay lecture. I thanked my stars that I had stood the ordeal bravely.

At Madras I went straight to the residence of Thyagarajan's father who had just retired from the Madras Corporation. The house had been newly built in Bhimanna Gardens, Mylapore and the front room for my stay and a thatched hut in the back–yard for cooking food had been placed at my disposal. Thyagarajan's parents took particular care of me during our stay of nearly 12 days. Thyagarajan who had just then been married was working in the postal department. I think he retired as post master of Mylapore about 15 years ago.

I and Thiruvenkatacharya became good friends. He was well–versed in Astrology and had his own ambitions. He would come to my place at 10 in the morning and return by 7 or 8 p.m. As at Bombay, I would call on leading lawyers, businessmen etc. For the first two days Acharya took me round the city to acquaint me with the topography of the place.

My first catch was C. Radhakrishna Chetty. He was running a laundry at Mount Road. He was distantly related to the Vummidiar family and owned a house at Mambalam which was just then developing. Chetty placed his *riksha* at my disposal. At Bangalore City there were no *rikshas* and I did not like to ride in a vehicle pulled by a human being. Therefore, I declined his offer.

The Muhurtham for Chetty's daughter's marriage was fixed by me in Mithuna Lagna occupied by Mars and Venus aspected by

Jupiter. It seems, as usual, the bridegroom's astrologer took objection to the presence of Mars in Lagna. But I overruled his objection, declaring that Mats in the 8th was taboo and that as Venus was in Lagna and Jupiter aspected Lagna, all the *doshas* stood cancelled. Again as luck would have it Chetty's daughter's marriage took place on the date fixed by me and the marriage proved successful.

Grandfather had given me an idea of Nadigranthas and how a Nadi astrologer living near his residence (in 1905 or so) in Linghi Chetty Street had earned a lot of mney but had died in dire poverty! I was a bit anxious about Rajeswari's health as she was in an advanced stage of pregnancy. Acharya took me to two Nadi astrologers — one I think a Nadar on the Royapettah High Road, and the other, a Mudaliar at Egmore. Mudaliar's Nadi — Markandeya Nadi — impressed me. He took my Rasi chart and asked me to come the next day. It was said to be a dialogue in Tamil between Sages Vasishta and Viswamitra with Goddess Parvati as the moderator. Thiruvenkata- charya translated the reading. Of all the Nadis and Bhrigu Samhitas — more than 50 — I have seen and examined so far, it is only the Markendeya Nadi that had proved fairly accurate. For the information of my esteemed readers I give below the Nadi reading :

After describing the planetary positions, the Nadi proceeded thus: "Birth place is a city in Karnataka and birth in mother's place; house facing south; delivery attended by an old dark woman, another lady and a widow; native eldest. Lord of Ascendant Saturn in Venus sign aspected by Jupiter—fair complexion, lean body, ordinary height, polite, modest, sympathetic, business-like, attentive, no *kapatam*, has good longevity, acquires wide knowledge and will become an impressive speaker. He will have frequent travels. Helpful, he will become happy and surpasses his grandfather. Because Mercury is lord of the 5th, he becomes a mathematician and acquires high qualifications in Astrology. His father's case is different. The native is associated with his grandfather and will earn much reputation. The lord of the 2nd is strong aspecting the Moon and Saturn. He will have high education and will become a Pandit. Danger in Saturn Dasa will be overcome and he lives upto Ketu Dasa."

All of a sudden the tenth house was taken up by way of a dialogue between sages Vashishta and Viswamitra.

Viswamitra: "The lord of the 10th is in the 7th with the lord of the 8th. The lord of the 7th is in the sign of the Moon and the Moon is in the 4th with the lord of the 1st, aspecting the 10th. Lord of the 2nd and 11th is in the 10th. Therefore he will have no fixed profession. He will do agricultural operations and will get some profit from agriculture and printing. He will enter government service in education or banking line. He will face much opposition in business."

Vasishta: "Lord of the 10th Mars and Mercury, lord of the 5th, and Venus, lord of the 4th and 9th, well-placed and Jupiter in the 10th aspected by lord of Lagna suggests much success in Sastras. He will become learned in Astrology and mathematics and will take to grandfather's profession. He will study planets, become learned, helping mankind by knowing several Sastras. He will have a virtuous occupation. He will publish books, will own cash, will have a prosperous career and will become famous, will earn international reputation and will add to the family dignity. Saturn is strong. He may have rivals but will always hold his own. Jupiter aspects Saturn. He will edit books and will develop a profitable business. Jupiter Dasa will be good for business. He will break fresh grounds and will become an institution. In the latter half of Jupiter he will become widely respected. In Saturn Dasa he will head an organisation having many subordinates. He will secure a prominent place and uninterrupted prosperity. He will have *vaksiddhi.* He will not enter government service but will have association with kings. He will lead an independent life, brooking no subordination. Jupiter and Saturn are Yogakarakas."

The reading ended abruptly. Most of the future predictions given in 1935 have turned out to be correct. I feel this is the only *Nadi* which has proved satisfactory. Acharya said that he was very happy because the Nadi had predicted a bright future for me.

My next encounter was with a Nadar who claimed to be in possession of *Agastya Nadi.* When Acharya introduced me to the Nadi owner he examined a few **leaves and** said that the direction in the Nadi was that we should **come the next** day. When we went there at the appointed time, the Nadi man examined my right thumb carefully and noted what he called an important line on it. On the basis of this line he read from the palm leaves the planetary positions at my birth giving the *nakshatra* and the *tithi*, I was born in. This performance of his in tracing my horoscope on the basis of a line on the thumb almost stunned me. When I asked Nadar to explain the method which enabled him to find out the chart, Acharya said in English, "Don't ask him such questions. He will never give out the secret."

The next morning when we again went to meet him **he read out** the first Bhava giving a general delineation. One of the **specific** predictions made was that within a week my wife would give **birth** to a son who would have *madhyayu* or medium life. The first part of the prediction was fulfilled as a son was born within 10 days.

The Nadi leaves mystified me. What exactly was the basis of this? How were they able to reveal the past events with such astounding accuracy? Why were they kept secret? These questions agitated me for a long time until in 1953, a Nadi—to be specific Guru Nadi— gave me the answer. I shall have much to say about Nadi granthas in due course.

We met a number of local astrologers, well-known and not well-known, with a view to learning from those who knew the subject well and "teaching" those that had only a smattering of Astrology. In all these meetings Acharya was present. He was of course the interpreter as I did not know Tamil.

I had interesting discussions with Pandint Natesa Sastri, then living in Triplicane on Nabhasa Yogas. His scholarship was evident from the way he tackled the subject. One day Sastri casually remarked: "You are the grandson of Suryanarain Rao, a great *sanatani*. How is it you are wearing western dress?" I had a ready answer when I said, "I am also a *sanatani* at heart. The change is only on the surface." He laughed.

One evening I called on Pandit Kaliyur Srinivasachariar. I think he was then living in Mylapore. As I entered his room I saw a figure full of charm dressed in the typical South Indian style wearing a dhoti, long-black coat and a turban with the *namam* prominently itched on his face and wearing a number of rings. I had seen his advertisement offering to answer four questions for a rupee. Without revealing my identity, I placed a one rupee coin on his table and put only 2 questions. He surveyed me from head to toe and said, "You are much worried now. You will be alright after 3 months." I asked him on what basis he gave the prediction. His reply was terse. "On the basis of the time you entered my room. By the by where do you come from?" I said I was the grandson of Suryanarain Rao and had specialised in mathematical and predictive Astrology. Now it was his turn to ask me questions. "Then tell me how long I will live?" I made some mental calculations and said, "Over 80". He laughed and our meeting ended.

The next time I met him was at the seminar on astrology organised in 1982 by Vidwan Lakshamanan at the AVM Kalyana Mantapa at Mowbrays Road, where I presided. Pandit Srinivasachari was also a speaker at the seminar and he said that he was 82 or 83 and that my prediction had come true.

I spent a few hours discussing Astrology with Swamy, an astrologer and father-in-law of Prof. L.V.S. Mani. When I started showing how to analyse a horoscope, Swamy seemed pleased with my scholarship and said that he had no doubt that grandfather's work would be continued by me. We next visited Pandit Satagopalachariar or "Gandhi Astrologer" as he was also known and who was widely advertising his services. One day, we just walked into his house at Tiruttani and wanted to know what methods he employed to give astrological predictions. He was surprised at what he called my "audacity" in questioning an elderly astrologer of his eminence as to the methods he employed for predicting events. There was a reason for my putting the question to him. In 1933 I had sent three questions to this astrologer remitting one rupee. I had got answers for all the three questions. For the question whether I would be successful in the examination, his answer had been just one word "doubtful". There was no astrological explanation whatsoever. Eversince I had been waiting for an opportunity to accost the astrologer. "How would you answer questions when they are put to you ? I am myself a specialist in Astrology and I want to know more from you." He was not pleased with my question, but said, "On the basis of Aroodha." I told him about my having sent questions to him two years ago and how without giving any astrological reasoning he had said 'yes' or 'no'. I also explained to him—of course it was highly improper on my part to have spoken in this vein to an elderly person—the importance of shadbalas etc., and how mathematical Astrology was the basis for all predictions. Finally I revealed to him that I was the grandson of Suryanarain Rao. We parted as friends. He was no doubt a great scholar.

One of the most significant events of my visit to Madras was my meeting with the great doyen of journalism Kasturi Srinivasan, proprietor of The Hindu. I had a letter of introduction to him from grandfather. The first meeting was in the afternoon at his residence "Sabarmati" on Mowbrays Road. I found him friendly and frank. The first thing he said was, "Do you know my father (Mr. Kasturi Ranga Iyengar), while reviewing the first issue of THE ASTROLOGICAL MAGAZINE in The Hindu criticised[1] your grandfather for having taken to Astrology but later became an admirer consulting him now and then. In fact when my father was ailing, your grandfather was sent for and he predicted that my father's end was very near. He died within a few days." Of course grandfather gave a suitable reply[2] to the criticism of The Hindu in the May 1895 issue of THE ASTROLOGICAL

---

1. "We have received a copy of the 1st number of the THE ASTROLOGICAL MAGAZINE edited by Mr. B. Suryanarain Rao, B.A. After reading the first article in it on the necessity for THE ASTROLOGICAL MAGAZINE we still think that energy and time may be devoted to better purpose. India has been preeminently many things but so far as we known her 'being an astrological country's is rather to be regretted than rejoiced in. From the time of Prithvi who withdrew from his expeditions against Sebagtgin on the advice of his astrologers, the astrologers have been one of the many undesirable features of our society. A graduate of the Madras University should surely be able to find a more sensible way of employing his time than preaching Astrology to an already too credulous and superstitious people." — The Hindu dated 10th May 1895.

MAGAZINE.

I explained to Srinivasan briefly the purpose of my visit to Madras and how I was bent on pursuing Astrology and restoring it to its former importance and glory. I told him, "Sir, I want to revive THE ASTROLOGICAL MAGAZINE and make it the instrument for projecting a healthy image of Astrology. You must encourage my efforts." He smiled and said, "We shall meet tomorrow evening. You must have supper with me." The next evening I again called on Srinivasan. Probably he wanted to test my bonafides or to convince himself about my astrological knowledge. He remarked, " We find that birth times are never reckoned correctly. Many astrologers even today give them as so many *naligas* (ghatis) assuming the Sun to rise at 6 a.m. every day and in every place. For instance take my own case. I was born at Coimbatore on 7th August 1887 at about 1.30 p.m. Vivian Robson has taken it as 1.30 p.m. L.M.T. The late Dr. V.V. Ramana Sastrin has also taken it as 1.30 p.m. What would you say and how would you rectify it?" He gave me the castings of his and his father's charts made by Robson and Dr. Ramana Sastrin.

Dr. Ramana Sastrin's casting was in Latin while the one made by Robson gave the usual western type of the chart with a speculum marking the general aspects etc. I told Srinivasan that I would work out the chart and give my own finding. When I was about to take leave of him he said : "Yes, go on with your plan to restart your magazine. I shall give publicity in *The Hindu* ." With these words, he gave me Rs. 100 as donation. Later I was also introduced to his brother K. Gopalan and other members of his family.

---

2. "Our friendly Editor of *The Hindu* has apparently not gone beyond the first article in our Magazine and his difficulty may be easily guessed. To read a scientific work, to take a calm and unprejudiced view of a publication that does not fall in the line of daily newspaper, and to give credit where it really is due are not things which our friend could easily do. He ignores the existence of facts found in the land of his birth, and thinks that the style he adopts towards THE ASTROLOGICAL MAGAZINE is sure to mark him above the too credulous and supersitious (Hindu) class' to which he unfortunately belongs. Editorial vanity often jaundices our eyes and makes us see things in a different color. Surely, it requires a higher stretch of nobility to appreciate good work done by others." — THE ASTROLOGICAL MAGAZINE, May 1895.

At this distance of time I mut record my indebtedness to Kasturi Srinivasan for the way he extended cooperation. He gave wide publicity to my astrological and other activities. In fact, my presidential address delivered at the first Andhra Astrological Conference held at Nellore in 1952 was given such wide coverage — it was published in the editorial page and in those days the front page of *The Hindu* carried only advertisements, the editorial and the page facing it giving important news now carried on the front page — that it evoked wide response from the educated public and universities all over the country. Srinivasan kept up his promise till his death. He used to consult with me on all important matters affecting him and his family members. In 1959, he became ill and his secretary Narayanan wrote to me on his behalf as to how the planetary situations stood. Since Srinivasan knew Astrology fairly well, he appreciated my findings. He died in 1959.

Srinivasan intoduced me also to T.T. Krishnamachari, then a businessman, C.R. Srinivasan, editor *Swadesamitran*, S.S. Vasan of Gemini Studios and other leading citizens. Those contacts were all valuable.

Madras enabled me to make some money. After a stay of two weeks I and my assistant Gopala left for Gulbarga in response to an invitation from an admirer C.G. Rao, employed in a textile mill. Rao was a self–made man, polite, friendly and of helpful nature. His object in inviting me to visit Gulbarga was to consult with me on what he considered to be a very important matter, *viz.*, the longevity of his father. In 1930 or so his father had suddenly left his residence and his whereabouts were unknown. There were rumours that he had gone to the Himalayas where he had died. Some astrologers had advised Rao to perform the death ceremonies. Rao was in a dilemma. He himself knew some Astrology, but felt that he must take the opinion of a "well-known astrologer" like me. The time of question was about 7 p.m. on 4-8-1935. I also studied the birth horoscope.

---

* I rectified the time of birth as 1–21 p.m. (LMT). The methods employed will be explained later.

Radix

		Ketu	
Moon		Mars	Sat.
	Radix		
Rahu	Ascdt. Venus Saturn	Jupiter Sun Merc.	

Prasna

			Ketu
Sat.			Merc. Sun
			Venus Ascdt.
Rahu		Mars Jupit.	Moon

To fortify my judgment I also cast a chart for the time of question.

After going through the birth chart, I said, "Saturn Dasa commenced in September 1934. For the 9th house Saturn is a *maraka*. Mars occupies the 9th house. Transit Saturn was afflicting your Moon. So I feel that your father could have died in the latter half of 1934."

Then taking up the Prasna chart I said, "The Ascendant is Leo and the 9th signifying father, is Aries aspected by Mars and Jupiter. The 8th from the 9th ruling the father's longevity is Scorpio. Mars as the 8th lord is in the 7th, a *maraka*. The 9th is aspected by Saturn and the 3rd from the 9th is occupied by Ketu. Therefore I am of the opinion that your father is not alive at this moment." Rao apparently satisfied, questioned, "When do you think he died ?" This was too tough a question for me to answer. But how could I remain without answering it ? I said, "Saturn entered Aquarius in March 1934 afflicting your birth star. Saturn Dasa commenced in September 1934. Therefor I am of the opinion that your father might have died about this time. Since Mars is in the 9th house, the cause of death could not have been natural." Though Rao seemed satisfied he appeared to be reluctant to perform the obsequies when he said, "I respect your opinion but I would also seek your grandfather's view and then decide." Grandfather confirmed my opinion and the obsequies were performed. After 2 or 3 years Rao got the information that his father had died by being knocked down by a truck somewhere in north India.

Before leaving Madras for Gulbarga, I received the news that Rajeswari had given birth to a son on 2–11–1935. I rushed back reaching Bangalore on the 6th November.

Things went on in the usual manner. But my earnings at Bombay and Madras had only been sporadic. The same problems cropped up again and again. What about the Magazine ? It was dead. Money was still due to the printers who had printed it in 1931 and 1932, before it again collapsed. Grandfather had his own misgivings. One day he called me to his room and said, "My dear boy, I have great confidence in your ability to run the Magazine and carry on the work of propagating Astrology. I shall be having Moon in Saturn. This may prove fatal. Believe me you have a bright future. You have never given room for my displeasure and you have shown yourself to be a dutiful and loving grandson." Emotionally moved, when I said that I would abide by his decision, he made over THE ASTROLOGICAL MAGAZINE to me with no assets but all liabilities.

In January 1936, Rajeswari returned to our village with the baby. This was an added responsibility. Rajeswari was only 17 years then but she was very intelligent and had enough commonsense. She was also attached to my grand-parents and my father and she began worrying about the state of affairs here. No solution was visible. One day I casually asked Rajeswari how she would feel in case we shifted to Bangalore where we could earn some money and help the family, re-start the Magazine and tide over the difficulties. At first her reaction was not helpful as she felt that by our shifting to Bangalore we would not be serving our elders and it was our duty to be with them and look after their welfare. But after a lot of discussion she veered round to my point of view. I moved the matter with grandfather and he gave the green signal.

I moved down to Bangalore with Rajeswari and the baby and a servant in February 1936, rented a house in Seshadripuram and started practising Astrology. The Siddhanti's prediction had been fulfilled.

Without any capital, but full of confidence, I decided to restart THE ASTROLOGICAL MAGAZINE as a quarterly. S. Sivappa, proprietor of S.G.N. Press, an ordinarily equipped press in Bangalore, was a good friend of mine. I told him about my idea of re-starting the Magazine and wanted him to do the printing without any initial payment but that his bills would be paid only according to my convenience. He hesitated for a moment, but assured me that he would undertake the printing of the Magazine. Collecting about 40 or 50 subscribers I launched the publication.

When the first issue of the quarterly for July, August and September 1936 (400 copies) published on 5th June was presented to grandfather, his joy knew no bounds. I was the proprietor and publisher and the Magazine came out under the joint editorship of grandfather and myself.

The following is the reproduction of the editorial I wrote in the first issue:

"Every endeavour, like every human being, will have to pass through a series of strides, in its career, before it can successfully appear before the world. So also, THE ASTROLOGICAL MAGAZINE has had to pass through critical times and stem the tide of malignant attack which it was being subjected to by many of the so-called educated people who pursue the dual policy of encouraging quack-astrologers on the one side, while denouncing the real and scientific Astrology as an art of credulity and make-belief on the other.

"It is with feelings of justifiable pride that we present THE ASTROLOGICAL MAGAZINE, in this, in its new form, to connoisseurs of truth. Ours is the only journal that has really braved the onslaughts of the modern orthodox scientist, who, full of prepossessions, is extremely reluctant to say that Astrology is a science, even though Astrology can demonstrate its claims as such.

"In spite of the pronounced prejudices of the orthodox scientist, Astrological activity has now been, on the increase, throughout the world. It would certainly be absurd to be silent on this fact when we fully know that the study and practice of Astrology has had no mean share in influencing human affairs. Astrological rules regulate the daily conduct of millions and millions of people, all the world over; and this will be more so in India, when we realise that India is pre-eminently an astrological country. We have shown in our vigorous activities, in this line, all these days, that the various astrological rules, are not certainly the many obstacles thrown on our way of material and moral progress; but on the other hand, they have been conducing to the prosperity of the individuals and natios, which the ancients aimed at and achieved. Therefore, we have no justification to keep Astrology in a wretched condition and allow its sacred truths to be exploited by the mercenarily inclined quacks.

"THE ASTROLOGICAL MAGAZINE has been the only organ, throughout India and the foreign countries which has been successfully ventilating the grievances under which its professors are placed. It is the only journal, which deals with astrological matters in a scientific and popular style.

"We propose to continue the useful task of reviving Astrology and other ancient Indian sciences and place before the scientific and educated world, facts which would justify our claims as regards the utility of Astrology, as a practical and useful science.

"From this month and onwards, the Magazine will be issued as a quarterly, in July, October, January and April with a view to accommodate the wishes of many of our readers. THE ASTROLOGICAL MAGAZINE, in its present form, has been expressly designed to appeal to all.

"The section under 'Astrology for Beginners' will be a real and long-felt want for those who seek its study without going in for cumbersome and costly books. This section will be of particular help and advantage to our Western readers who have had no occasion to know before what Hindu Astrology is. They will now be enabled to compare their own methods of horoscope-casting and delineation with those of ours and appreciate how far the Hindu system is reliable.

"Discussion of eminent horoscopes under the caption 'Notable Horoscopes' will be a most welcome addition.

"Elements of Astronomy will be another interesting addition. Articles under this heading will give the readers a clear insight into the principles of Astronomy, a knowledge of which is absolutely essential to become a successful astrologer.

"Articles on Mundane Astrology will be like a search-light and give clear and definite information regarding the fates of different nations, every three months.

"Weather forecasts, Daily guide, Financial Astrology, etc., will become regular features of the journal.

"Finds from investigations into old and standard astrological books will form an extremely interesting material.

"Editorial comments, in the light of astrological reasoning, on latest developments, Political, Social, Religious and Economic, are sure to interest our readers.

"All sorts of controversial questions, appertaining to astrological problems, will be discussed without fear or favour, in our correspondence columns, and the fullest scope will be given to our readers to express their views.

"In spite of such variagated, useful and interesting material, the annual subscription is fixed as low as Rs. 3-6-0 (Sh. 6/6, foreign, Dol. 2.20 American) just to give the generous and educated public the benefits of our wide experience and to enlist their sympathies for the noble cause of expounding the sublime sciences of Indian culture.

"We trust that the public will come in larger numbers, become our subscribers and patrons and help us to realise our ambition of establishing the downtrodden subject of Astrology on a firm and definite basis. We wish all our readers a happy and prosperous New Year."

The Magazine had to face several hurdles all of which I could overcome due to the grace of God and blessings of grandfather coupled with my own determination, hard work and firm conviction that I was only an instrument of God to propagate *Jyotisha* and highlight its greatness and make it acceptable to the educated public.

19

Though I shifted to Bangalore with my wife Rajeswari and son Surya Prakash in February 1936 with grandfather's full consent and blessings – the main object being to earn some money - we could not easily reconcile ourselves to the change. The thought that we had left behind an aged grandfather, a disabled father and other family members hung heavily on our minds. The change of residence, which had been predicted by the Siddhanti, was unexpected since I had not been able to gauge it from my chart, probably because of subjective factors.

The residence was quite spacious. It contained a big hall, two bedrooms, front and rear verandahs, dining hall, kitchen and front and back yards, all for a monthly rent of only twenty-five rupees! The general manager of the Bank of Mysore, T. Subramanyam and its cashier C.R. Venkataramaiah were known to me. As officers of the bank they were respected for their sense of duty, straight-forwardness and integrity. When I casually told them that I was living in Bangalore they not only showed keen interest in consulting with me, but introduced me to some of their friends. The consultations covered such issues as job prospects, promotions, health, progeny, etc. Of course none wanted to know when he would become an M.L.A., M.P. or a Minister as the blessings of "democracy" had not yet descended on India!

A typical horoscope that was once brought to me by an elderly couple was somewhat intriguing. No details were given. But I wanted to demonstrate my "predictive capability" by revealing one or two past events. I considered only transits. I did not bother to study the horoscope because, not that I wanted to make my job easy, but my object was to test my "intuitive power".

Moon Rahu		Sat.		Sun	Venus	Mercury Mars	Ketu
	Birth 25-10-1912			Sat.	Gochara 19-5-1936		
	Jup Venus Ascdt.	Sun Mars Merc.	Ketu	Moon Rahu	Jupiter		

Grandfather had often said that too much reliance on mathematics would atrophy one's power of judgement. There were instances when by just looking at a horoscope he was able to say whether or not one was employed, married, etc. This ability, he attributed, not only to some combinations in his own horoscope but also to *vaksiddhi* which, he said, could be developed by leading an ethical and disciplined life and practising regularly certain types of *mantras*. I had of course been initiated into one such *mantra* which I was practising regularly and therefore wanted to test for myself how far my intuition had developed.

After glancing through the chart and discovering that transit Jupiter was passing through radical Jupiter and Venus, I said "in all likelihood your question relates to the marriage of the native". Surprised, the father remarked, "How did you know that we have come with this question in our mind?"I paused for a while and remarked, "Oh, that is simple! But there is another problem also which is quite serious". They became uneasy and looked at each other. I continued, "Look here, the 5th is the house of intelligence. It is occupied by the Moon, the indicator of the mind and Rahu, a shadowy planet. The dispositor Jupiter is in the sign of Mars aspected by Saturn. Jupiter aspects the 5th. It looks as if the native is a mental case. He will be impulsive, unsteady and restless, upsets in the digestive system cause mental disturbances of different kinds, sometimes religious, but often fanatical in observance. You may call him mad. He generally goes to extremes. Saturn at present in Aquarius causes the first phase of *elarata*. This is a further indication of aggravation of his mental troubles." The father was quiet, but the mother with tears in her eyes explained the case in detail. The boy, though 24, was behaving irresponsibly and indulging in temper tantrums. Parental advice was spurned with arrogance.

I advised them not to get him married until Saturn left Aries. They said they would go by my advice. Probably due to other factors, they had the marriage performed and within six months the girl returned to her parents' place and never joined her husband again. Of course, there was no divorce in those times!

Though the Gochara interpretation hit the bull's eye and for a moment I felt happy at my power of intuition, I also felt rather guilty of an ethical lapse in not studying the horoscope in details.

Sometimes I would also predict on the basis of primary directions with a view to getting confirmation of the conclusions arrived at according to Dasa influences.

Doctors, engineers, lawyers, university lecturers and government officials would come to me with their problems seeking my counselling. Since I was not interested in being a professional I had not fixed any fees for consultation. Many would simply thank me or present me with some fruits and flowers and go away. I was however able to earn enough to meet the family expenses. Twice a week I would go to the village with provisions and attend to the requirements of grandfather and father. Often grandfather would stay with me because he wanted "the company" of his great-grandson Surya Prakash.

Every day I would handle 3 to 4 horoscopes and the honorarium, which I never specified, varied from Rs. 5 to Rs. 20. On the whole my shifting to Bangalore was a blessing in disguise as it enabled us to overcome, to some extent, our financial problems.

Though scores of horoscopes were being examined by me, only typical cases are being dealt with in these "experiences" for the information of the readers. Dr. C. Ramanujam, a civil surgeon of Madras, called on me sometime in May 1936 wanting to know the nature of the disease a patient of his was suffering from, as medical tests had not revealed where the trouble lay. He said he was a firm believer in astrology and a friend of Dr. Guruswamy Midaliar, a noted surgeon and physician who would always look into the horoscopes of his patients before medical diagnosis and treatment. He said my diagnosis would enable him to treat his patient correctly. For a while I was in two minds, as I suspected that perhaps he wanted to test me. But the initial reluctance was overcome as this was a test case for me also involving my "reputation".

	Saturn	Jupiter Ketu	Mars
	RASI		
Ascdt.	Mars Mercury Rahu Moon	Sun	Venus

My analysis, which I now find was somewhat round about, was a follows: As the second Drekkana of Sagittarius was rising, the 6th refers to the chest, and the 5th to the heart and the 7th to the naval. The 4th lord Jupiter was much afflicted because of his association with Ketu. Lord of the 8th the Moon was debilitated in the 12th and aspecting Jupiter. The 6th house was subject to a *Papakartari Yoga,* planets involved being Saturn and Mars. Of all these houses, the 7th was most afflicted because of the presence of Mars and the aspect of Saturn. Mars was in the 7th house, a *maraka.* I said, "The heart will be the seat of the trouble. The native may be suffering from pain in the heart region and sometimes may find it difficult to breathe". The doctor remarked, "Your diagnosis confirms my suspicion. The patient has some coronary problems and I shall now be able to decide on the line of treatment."

I continued, "Mars Dasa for the patient will commence in July 1937. Mars as lord of the 12th (and the 5th) being placed in the 7th, a *maraka,* could cause the death of the patient, especially that the Moon, lord of the 8th, occupies the 12th with Mercury and Rahu. Your patient may not survive the year 1937. He does not have *poornayu* (full term)." The doctor again met me by the end of 1937 to "congratulate" me for what he called "a remarkable prediction".

My forays into political astrology had started with the collection of data of the founding of nations and horoscopes of world leaders. The Dutch astrologer Karl Kraft had supplied me with authoritative birth details of Hitler, Mussolini and other European leaders.

Italy had suffered defeat at the hands of the Abyssinians in 1896. To avenge this defeat, Mussolini invaded Abyssinia (Ethiopia) achieving the first "conquest" of Haile Selassie's empire. The flight of the Abyssinian Emperor, who was also called the Negus, after a strenuous resistance against poison gas and the collapse of the Ethiopian army for sheer want of modern equipments of warfare, had made the Italians masters of Abyssinia. Mussolini had already announced the annexation of Ethiopia and King Victor Emanuel had already become the "Emperor" of the conquered land. The Negus fled to the United Kingdom reposing complete faith in the League of Nations.

My first article on Mundane astrology, written after a careful consideration of the astrological and international factors, was on "The League and Ethiopia". Grandfather appreciated the article. But as usual his appreciation was hedged in with the remark, "it could have been better written". Of course this criticism was well meant. Had he showered unqualified appreciation, I would perhaps have felt that no improvement was needed. If some of the editorial articles written by me in the fifties and sixties were hailed as master-pieces, the credit must indirectly go to grandfather.

The following is an extract from the July-September 1936 issue of THE ASTROLOGICAL MAGAZINE:

"What will be the ultimate future of Abyssinia? Is it going to remain under the subjugation of an Imperialist Power?

"A survey of the planetary motions during the next few months will give us an idea of how things are going to shape with regard to the League, Italy and Ethiopia.

"Mars and Saturn have major influences over Italy and Ethiopia respectively. Till about March 1937, the position of Saturn will be excellent, because he will be in Aquarius, his own sign, without any malefic conjunctions or associations. The ingress of Mars into Gemini, where he comes in contact with the incendiary planet Ketu without any other favourable elements to relieve, will land Italy into further troubles. As soon as Mars enters Cancer, he becomes debilitated and casts his glance over Ethiopia (Saturn) powerfully. This will doubtless lead to the outbreak of hostilities between the various Abyssinian races and the Italians, whose pride will receive considerable check, because of Saturn's good position. On account of Mars in Cancer, Italy will not be saved of any troubles, incidental to subduing a powerful nation. The further movements of Mars in Leo will give a general signal for mistrust and war-activities in Europe, and Abyssinia may perhaps he benefited. The League will not adopt a policy that is worthy of its traditions, and thereby receives a rude shock, which might lead to its ultimate collapse.

"We trust, the various statesmen will preserve its strength and show that after all justice has its own reward."

In response to a letter I wrote to the Negus, then exiled in U.K., he sent me his birth details minus the time of birth. Haile Selessie was born on 23rd July 1890. By examining his life events and his physical and mental characteristics I fixed the time of birth as 8.39 a.m. with Leo as the Ascendant. I may not myself approve now, the reasoning given by me more than fifty years ago. But the following observations reproduced from the same issue will be of interest to my readers:

"It must be noted that in His Majesty's horoscope, the Ascendant, Saturn and Mars have obtained the special distinction of Vargottama. The lord of Ascendant and the lord of the house of wealth have fallen in the twelfth or house of loss. The Sun in addition to being Lagnadhipati (lord of Ascendant) represents political power and his unfavourable situation in Rasi and his conjunction with debilitated Venus and the incendiary planet Rahu in the Amsa are all unfavourable.

Jupiter in the Rasi is vitiated by being the lord of kendras, the 4th and the 7th from the Moon. The Negus is now passing through the end of Jupiter's major period. Jupiter is the lord of the 8th in both Rasi and Navamsa. He should have practically killed the Emperor, being a powerful *maraka;* but his exaltation in Amsa has saved him from death. His debilitated look on the Sun made him lose his empire. He will be generous and free from cupidity. Mars in his own sign, and in Vargottama, indicates an imperious nature and great skill in military operations. This combination will enable him to regain his forces and renew his fight. The Moon is not afflicted in any way.

RASI

		Rahu	
	Negus		Sun Merc.
Jup.	**RASI**		Venus Ascdt. Saturn
Mars Ketu		Moon	

NAVAMSA

Ketu		Moon	Jup
			Ascdt. Saturn
	NAVAMSA		Sun Venus Rahu
Mars	Merc.		

Therefore, he will be pure in heart, strictly continent and merciful to his vanquished enemies. Mercury, with the Sun, gives him shrewdness, high intelligence, education and natural talents for governing and gaining the esteem of others.

"The sub-period of Saturn in his own major period has just now commenced. In the Amsa, Saturn is the lord of the 9th and the 10th from the Moon and is a Yugakaraka. These 3 years and 3 days will be a period of uneasiness, distrust and disappointments, much mental anguish, much sufferings to family, fever, serious enmities, etc. The next sub-period is that of Mercury. This will last for 2 years, 5 months and 8 days from July 1939. This will enable him to gain wealth and some part of his territory, as Mercury is the lord of the 10th from the Moon and he is placed in the house of gains with the political planet Sun. He is also responsible, with the Moon, for causing what is called *parivartana yoga* or mutual exchange of houses. He is lord of the house of wealth from the Ascendant. He has also caused *Parivartana Yoga* in the Amsa. This period must prove profitable to the Negus, in many ways.

"The seventh house indicates foreign relations. In this horoscope the seventh lord Saturn is in the Ascendant. He will get the sympathies of the masses. European nations will wait for further opportunities to exploit his country. The aspect of debilitated Jupiter renders him trust in the integrity of other governments to help him who, in turn, betray him.

"Provided the Negus exerts his every nerve, he may be enabled to retain some independence at least of his vast country and Saturn's sub-period will surely be beneficial to the reorganisation of his forces and collection of funds to continue the war."

Other forecasts made by me about the Negus and his return to Abyssinia will be referred to at the appropriate places in this series.

In the same period, apart from writing most of the articles for the Magazine I completed two of my important books, *viz.*, VARSHAPHAL or THE HINDU PROGRESSED HOROSCOPE and GRAHA AND BHAVA BALAS. I have always been a hard worker, a trait largely inherited from grandfather and even today in my 80th year I keep to the same schedule of work, as I did some 25 or 30 years ago. My dedication to the cause of astrology has inspired me to face and overcome all sorts of odds.

Out of 400 copies of THE ASTROLOGICAL MAGAZINE generally printed 300 copies would be distributed free to likely subscribers. Yet, until the end of 1937 I could not get more than 75 subscribers though the annual subscription was as low as Rs. 3-6-0.

The first two issues of the Magazine brought in a lot of appreciations. According to Mr. Ramdhar Sinha, pleader and district courts member, Daltonganj, "the journal has no equals in India and stands the best of all. The contents are so interesting that one cannot stop in the middle without finishing the whole."

Running the Quarterly became a herculean task because of tightness of funds. My printer B. Sivappa had been told that he should not insist on payment of bills within a specified period and that payment would be made according to my convenience. He knew my plight and extended to me full co-operation. He was a great and good friend indeed. Now 94, he is hale and healthy.

The horoscope of my son Surya Prakash born on 2-11-1935 at 5.30 a.m.* always intrigued me. His longevity question troubled me considerably. It looked as if subjective factors were in the way of my correct assessment of the length of his life. Lord of Lagna (and the 8th) Venus was in the 12th with the 12th lord Mercury. From Chandra Lagna again, Lagna lord was in the 12th aspected by Saturn a *maraka*. As anticipated, throughout Venus Dasa he suffered from severe strokes of *balarishta* requiring extra parental care. Since we had no elders with us to advise us in these matters, there would be often clashes between me and Rajeswari as to what medical treatment should be given to him. Rajeswari was only 18 years old. As her father was an allopathic doctor, her thinking was perhaps conditioned to administering medicines even for small ailments. Since I was brought up in the village by my grand-father, who had never had a high opinion about allopathy, my thinking was perhaps conditioned to ignore medicine and allow nature to do the healing. In spire of her earlier protests as a mother, she would acquiesce into the view. This does

---
*Libra – Ascendant and the Sun; Scorpio – Jupiter; Sagittarius – The Moon, Mars and Rahu; Aquarius – Saturn; Gemini – Ketu; and Virgo – Mercury and Venus.

not mean that we never gave any medicines to our children when they were ill. We did administer medicines very sparingly. Today all my children are very healthy and there is hardly any need for medical consultation.

When Prakash cried much he would get fits. Then we had to call in Dr. Prahlad, who lived near us. An elderly person suggested that the fits could be stopped once and for all if the child was given the ancient treatment of branding with a red hot glass bangle. This was done and Prakash had no more fits thereafter.

I was then at the fag end of Rahu Dasa and it looked as if things were again going wrong. Rahu in the 2nd (family), dispite Jupiter's aspect, did not mend matters much. My attention had again to be diverted to family problems both at Bangalore and at the village. Grandfather had started insisting that I wound up the show at Bangalore and get back to the village. I doubted the wisdom of his insistence and tried to convince him how if I returned to the village, all the plans which I had in view for continuing the magazine and for giving relief to the family would go awry.

I would often relapse into bouts of despondency but would regain my equanimity in the hope things would clear with Jupiter Dasa which was to dawn shortly. For Mars in Rahu when both are *shashtashtaka*, *Krishna Misreeya* predicts "enmity of relatives, disputes, heavy expenditure, affliction to children, ill-fame and accidents". In some form or other all these happened in my case.

What about the Dasa and sub-period of Jupiter (18-8-1936 to 11-4-1938)? Would Jupiter occupying the 10th glorified by grandfather as the planet *par excellence* build up my life? Would all my difficulties vanish? Almost every classical work I was familiar with predicted nothing but good.

Jupiter is lord of the 2nd and the 11th from the Ascendant and occupies the 10th. He is aspected by Saturn, lord of the Ascendant (and the 12th), and the exalted Moon (lord of the 6th) having caused Rajayoga. Hence only good must happen during this sub-period, while after the commencement of Saturn's sub-period, I must become prosperous and get name and fame. These were the thoughts uppermost in my mind as I was looking into my own horoscope.

All of a sudden my old friend Siddhanti, who had successfully predicted my change of place, turned up. When I told him about my dilema in assessing the results of Jupiter in Jupiter he looked into my horoscope again and said, "I think you are at the fag end of your troubles, because Jupiter will take control of you. When I interrupted him saying "Yes, I know that Jupiter is so well placed that he can do only good", he silenced me remarking, "Look here, your assessment is again subjective, as you are harping only on the good points. There is the other side of the coin. For Kumbha Lagna, Jupiter is not a benefic. Moreover in *swa-bhukti* (own sub-period) a natural benefic can only give the darker side of his indications. Jupiter is a *maraka* for your grandfather because he owns the 7th from the 5th (9th from 9th). Jupiter is aspected by Saturn, lord of the 12th—ignore for the moment he is lord of Lagna. Jupiter is lord of the 8th from the Moon. So you think all these negative factors do not have any effects?" I paused for a while and confessed that I was still not capable of an objective assessment of my own horoscope. When I asked him whether Jupiter in his sub-period would cause the death of grandfather, he said, "Yes, that is exactly what will happen. Jupiter will also give the shock of your life! Saturn is transiting the 10th from the Moon. Jupiter and Rahu are in the 8th. Do you think these transits will have no adverse effects? But I assure you, my friend, beginning from Saturn's Bhukti, you will rise in life, earn well, get respect and achieve something in the field of astrology, which no one, including your grandfather, has done so far."

When I found that he was able to combine successfully the Dasa and transit results and give me certain hints, I began attaching significance to Siddhanti's views on the effects of transits, *vis-a-vis* Dasa indications.

I had been living in Bangalore for over a year now. Three issues of the magazine had been published. The fourth issue (April–May and June 1937) was to come out early in March. But there were certain sudden developments at home. My son Surya Prakash fell seriously ill with typhoid, and I had to give all attention to him. As I was the boss, editor, clerk and proof-reader all rolled into one, the press work got dislocated.

In response to an urgent summons on 10th March 1937 I had to rush to the village to meet grandfather. He seemed to have had a premonition of his impending death. For three hours he talked to me on various matters. It was like the Buddha's last Sermon. "Never underrate any person, big or small, deal with him politely. Help when you can but never cause harm to anybody. Always feel humble even when you reach a high position in your field. Don't interpret horoscopes deterministically. Never seek favours from others. Safeguard your self-respect, cultivate an attitude of non-attachment. Be patient whatever the provocative circumstances. Never underrate another person in a public assembly or in a private meeting. Do not listen to tale-bearers. Keep before you the mission in life and put forth efforts to achieve it. But the Karma you practise should be *nishkama* (desireless). God bless you".

I have tried to put into practice these guidelines in my long life, but I do not know how far I have succeeded.

When I returned to Bangalore and told Rajeswari about grandfather's "sermon", she said "I think the great man is expecting his end and we must immediately go to the village and live there." On the morning of 12th March 1937 a message was received that grandfather was ill, we rushed to the village with a qualified doctor who advised that grandfather be shifted to Bangalore immediately. But grandfather said, "Today is *amavasya* (new Moon). Let us think of it tomorrow." It was 12 noon and he wanted Ganga water to be given to him. He was restless and was complaining of intense pain in the head. At 1.10 p.m. he breathed his last. Thus ended the life of a great man, a staunch nationalist, historian, scholar, philosopher and a lover of all that is great in our ancient culture.

Under the caption "The Astrological Sun has Set", I wrote an editorial in the April-June 1937 issue of THE ASTROLOGICAL MAGAZINE, paying well-deserved tributes to my beloved grand-sire. From then on a new phase started in my life.

20

The death of grandfather left a void in my life. It took nearly one year for the wound to heal, though the scar continued for a long time. From my young age I was nurtured on a philosophy that would look at life realistically and not sentimentally.

"The best way to mourn the dead is to care for the living" was the advice tendered to me by some of my well-wishers.

A period of uncertainty stared me in the face. Rajeswari was in the family way and was to be sent to her father's place for confinement.

Within one year from the date of grand-father's death, several unexpected things happened. Our lands in the village were auctioned to recover the loan taken by grandfather, and as there were no bidders for the bungalow, which was our residence for 25 years, the Apex Bank held the bid in its name. As per father's desire, arrangements were made for him and my step-mother and her children to stay in Yalahanka. Every week I would visit the place with provisions so that he was not in any way inconvenienced. The financial situation continued to be tight. And the Magazine was becoming more and more of a burden, what with legal notices coming from the printers of the 1930-31 issues, to settle their bills.

Added to all this, pressure from father-in-law and some friends of grandfather that I should join government service kept mounting.

"My dear young man", said N.T. Gopala Iyengar, a retired district judge, "remember the adage discretion is the better part of valour and dispense with your idea of serving the cause of astrology and all that. Join government service so that you can eke out livelihood without difficulty. I shall take you to the Dewan who is my friend tomorrow morning."

Though I resented in the innermost recesses of my mind, the advice of this elderly man, out of respect for him I agreed to meet the Dewan with him. When Rajeswari was appraised of this, she did not say anything. She knew the situation was precarious. The next morning Gopala Iyengar took me to the residence of the then acting Dewan S.P. Rajagopalachari, told him about my family background and suggested that I be given a job in the Secretariat. The Dewan readily agreed. Looking at me he said: "You meet me tomorrow at the Secretariat. You will be taken into service as a clerk on a monthly salary of Rs. 35/- and by honest and hard work you can retire after 25 years service as an Assistant Secretary to the Government."

This was too much for me. After thanking both the Dewan and Gopala Iyengar, I raced back to my place, explained the details to Rajeswari and decided firmly that I would never join any service, least of all Government service. I was sure I was made for something great according to my horoscope and that with the dawn of Saturn Bhukti in Jupiter Dasa, prosperity would attend on me. I immediately wrote a letter to Gopala Iyengar telling him firmly but politely that I had made up my mind not to join any service but to pursue my favourite occupation, come what may. This put an end to a miserable episode in my life.

One night I had a dream in which Sri Ramana Maharshi appeared and asked me to visit his place. The next day I dashed to Tiruvannamlai and met the Maharshi's brother who was the *Sarvadhikari* or manager of the Ashram. I was asked to share a room - a small thatched hut - with another visitor. I think he was Swamy, Editor of "Sind Observer". In the evening as the meditation was going on, I entered the hall where the sage was reclining on a couch, introduced myself as the grandson of late B. Suryanarain Rao. The sage smiled and beckoned me to sit. Of medium height and fair-complexioned he had a dignified appearance. His eyes were emanating spiritual lustre. At the dinner I sat next to the Sage and we had a brief conversation in Telugu. I sought his blessings and he replied in

Telugu that everything would be alright.

The Sarvadhikari was also good to me though the general feeling in the Ashram was that he was dictatorial, rude and unsympathetic. When I was about to take leave of him, he quipped: "So you are an astrologer. How did you like your stay in the Ashram?" I said: "Yes, I deal with astrology and my Darshan of the Sage was highly rewarding." he smiled for a while, placed a Rasi chart in my hand and almost demanded "Look here, this is the horoscope of a person in whom I am interested. Spiritually how do you rate it?" I immediately guessed that it should be the Maharshi's and went on.

"The native appears to be spiritually advanced. The situation of Saturn, the Yogakaraka in the 6th, demonstrates the pitfalls and the struggles the native had to face before attaining the peak of spiritual bliss. Sublimation of the carnal instincts into spiritual channels is due not only to the presence of Mars in the 7th but also due to Venus occupying the 2nd with Mercury, lord of the 9th or *Dharma*. The mischief that Mars could do as occupying the 7th has been offset by his being stationed in the constellation of Ketu, the karaka for *Moksha*. Jupiter aspecting the Moon in the 9th weaned the mind of the subject away from any thought of sex. The Sun and the Moon representing

Sat.	Mars		Ketu Moon	Jup.		Ketu	Moon
Jup.	**RASI**			Merc.	**NAVAMSA**		Venus
Rahu Sun	Merc. Venus	Ascdt.		Sat.	Rahu Mars	Ascdt.	Sun

the soul and the mind respectively are in benefic signs and are fairly powerful indicating the high degree of development and strength of mind. The Sun is with Rahu. The native must have undergone an intense mental and spiritual struggle within himself before perceiving reality".

Years later my analysis of the Sage's horoscope was given in my book NOTABLE HOROSCOPES wherein I concluded that the chart revealed "that the Sage belonged to the galaxy of those great sages and saints who have kept the light of India eternally burning."

My brief stay at the Ashram and my meeting with the Sage gave me inner peace and confidence and strengthened the decision I had already taken to pursuing astrology with added zeal.

Securing a loan of Rs. 500/- by pledging some of Rajeswari's jewels, and clearing some previous debts, I started concentrating on THE ASTROLOGICAL MAGAZINE.

In the latter half of 1937, economic conditions forced me to shift to a smaller house in the second main road, Seshadripuram, for a rent of Rs. 12.50 per month. It was a two-room apartment with a kitchen and a bath. The front toom served as my office-cum-bed room. In June 1937 Rajeswari went to Madhugiri for confinement. Being alone enabled me to complete two of my important books. VARSHAPHAL and GRAHA AND BHAVA BALAS. I had no funds to get them printed and published, and I kept hoping to get a publisher.

Rajeswari joined me with the new child, a daughter, in February 1938. She was a sickly child and generally ailing so that except for bringing out the Magazine, I had no time for any other serious and sustained work for promoting its circulation. My consultation work was progressing fairly well. Most consultors were interested only in the marriages of their daughters and job prospects of their sons.

I think it was in September 1937, that a young man of my age came to consult me about his job. He seemed to be in great distress. All his attempts to secure a job had proved futile. He almost wept saying, "I am the eldest son in our family. My father is confined to bed with tuberculosis. There is no other bread winner except me. You must not only tell me when I would get employed but also help me

Rahu		Sat.		Sun	Sat.		Venus
Ascdt.	**RASI**		Sun Moon	Rahu	**NAVAMSA**		Merc, Ketu
			Mars Merc. Venus				
	Jup.		Ketu		Mars Jupiter	Ascdt.	Moon

with some money". Feeling sorry for him I gave him ten rupees and asked him to meet me after 3 days. He was born on 11th August 1912 at about 6 p.m.

When I cast the horoscope I was simply dumb-founded. It was more or less the same as mine, the only difference being the situation of the Moon in Cancer and the constellation being Pushyami. Should I interpret the horoscope keeping my own chart in the background? I just could not decide. Cogitating I said to myself, "The Rasi chart has all the yogas that my horoscope shows. Inspite of these yogas I am no entity and my life hitherto has been one of struggle and suffering though I may have a bright future. His father is ailing. My father has an eye defect. My mother is dead whereas his mother is alive."

With this sort of reasoning and argument I finally decided to cast a *prasna* chart and find out from it whether I could take Chandra Lagna in preference to Lagna. The *prasna* chart was revealing. I had no difficulty in concluding that I should study the birth chart from the Moon only. When he met me after 3 days I said, "You have just started Saturn in Mercury. The lord of the 10th, Mars, a yogakaraka is in the 2nd with the Dasa lord Mercury and the lord of the 4th and

11th. Mars lord of the 10th from the Moon is in Scorpio Navamsa. The 10th house is fairly well-disposed. Saturn's sub-period is about to commence. Saturn rules labour, factories etc. Therefore as soon as Saturn sub-period commences you will join some chemical factory as an accountant (Dasa lord Mercury), will continue the same job in Ketu Dasa, and that after the commencement of Venus Dasa in your 32nd year you will do building contract work and become a rich man" I took into consideration the *karaka* factors of all the three planets in the 2nd from the Moon. He was satisfied with my prediction. He came back to me after a week with the news that he had got a job in a brick kiln on Rs. 40/- a month and he was quite satisfied with it. Years later – 1964-66 – he met me when he had become a big contractor and had acquired much property and expressed his gratefulness for what he called "predictions of hope given when I was in great depression and distress."

With the exception of a single planet, the Rási charts of the native and myself are the same. But how could there be such a significant variation in the results. This question engaged my attention for a long time. Had I not made the predictions from Chandra Lagna, my interpretation would have gone wrong. It is in such a tricky situation, I felt then, that one must seek guidance from a *prasna* chart.

Hoping to secure some help for bringing out my books and to run the magazine, I was thinking of undertaking an all-India tour. This idea came to my mind early in 1938. In the October-December 1937 issue of THE ASTROLOGICAL MAGAZINE in my leading article, "Hitler, Mussolini and World Peace" in which, after analysing the charts and indicating that a European War was likely in 1939, I had said: "The nativities of Mussolini and Hitler will drift Europe towards a dangerous zone. It now remains for countries with wise statesmen, to set right the equilibrium in European politics. Note the Emperor of Japan's horoscope and see how Italy, Germany and Japan, with absolute impunity break the public law of the world". Harichand Kakar, a Delhi reader, doing export business in leather, perhaps impressed with my forecast, invited me to Delhi as he wished to know whether there would be a war in the near future so that he could regulate his future business activities.

In May 1938, I left for Bombay enroute to Delhi. At Bombay I stayed for a couple of days to earn some money for my onward journey. I had a letter of introduction from Kasturi Srinivasan to the industrialist G.D. Birla. N. Salivateeswaran, Bombay representative of THE HINDU was instructed to accommodate me at the Hindu flat at Ahmedabad House. Salivati was all kindness to me. One day he took me to Birla. Handing over to him K. Srinivasan's letter, I briefly explained to Birla my mission of serving the cause of astrology and Indian culture and said: "You are a well-known philanthropist and you should help the cause of astrology by a liberal donation." My belief that Srinivasan's letter of recommendation would find a solution to my financial troubles, was shattered when. Birla patronizingly asked me to meet him after 2 days when he would consider my request. This so hurt my feelings that I resolved then and there never again to seek any favours or help from anyone in my life. This incident happened 53 years ago and I must confess that I have never asked for any favour or help from any source. When I reported to Srinivasan the result of my meeting with Birla, he advised me to take it easy. Salivati also felt sorry for the attitude of this industrialist.

My desire to secure some advertisements for THE ASTROLOGICAL MAGAZINE led to my being introduced to one Rajan who was then the Bombay representative of the Mysore Government for advertisements. When I appraised Rajan about the Magazine and how I would appreciate if he could get some advertisements, he said he would do the needful. Rajan had his office-cum-residence in the building next to The Hindu office at Ballard Estate. The next day Rajan threw a big party to all the advertising agents and I and Salivati were also invited. The party was attended by many advertising agents. I got the shock of my life at the party. Wine flowed freely and it looked as if advertisements were being bartered for other kinds of immoral considerations. I retreated at once from the scene, disgusted with the whole thing. I decided that I would seek no advertisements for the magazine, come what may.

I was also introduced to the then leading advertising agents in Bombay such as L.A. Stronach & Co., Walter Thompsons, Lintas,

Sistas etc. When the heads of these agencies learnt that I knew astrology, most of them said that THE ASTROLOGICAL MAGAZINE would be included in their next advertisement budgets and that in the meanwhile they were interested in knowing something about their future. I realised the shallowness of their assurances and decided not to have any more contacts with them.

Those who are of my age will have seen advertisements published in the press by one "Pandit Tabore" who claimed to reveal "the past, present and future". I was a victim to this fraud as the reading sent to me was a stereo-typed one generally doled out on the basis of Sayana Sun-signs. When I tried to meet Tabore at Bombay, I was surprised to learn that no one by the name of Tabore existed and a Parsi gentleman was running the show under the trade mark of "Pandit Tabore". I think Stronachs was the advertisement agent for "Tabore". I was very angry at the exploitation going on in the name of astrology and wrote an article in THE ASTROLOGICAL MAGAZINE on "Rupee Astrologers" exposing the tactics employed by some to mislead the public.

Mention must be made of D.D. Deshpande, manager of the New Citizen Bank of India and Majumdar, manager of Hindustan Life Insurance Co., who were two of the clients secured by B.H. Ganoo. Both of them were keenly interested in astrology. I shall have occasion to refer to them in the future articles.

One day I called on Nanalal K. Shroff, Manager of A.H. Wheeler & Co., leading Railway Book Stall owners as I was interested in having THE ASTROLOGICAL MAGAZINE sold at their stalls. I was received with courtesy and Shroff wanted to know the object of my visit. I explained to him the importance of astrology and how by selling THE ASTROLOGICAL MAGAZINE, the only journal of its type, in their stalls, Wheelers could serve the cause of astrology and Indian culture. Shroff perused a copy of the Quarterly, shrugged his shoulders and said to my utter disappointment, "My dear young friend, who do you think would read the A.M.? Not at any rate the English educated persons. The craze today is for imported English journals, film magazines etc. We do not have enough space in our stalls. We are businessmen first and all talk of serving the cause of Indian culture etc. makes no sense to us. Please do not press me any more".

I changed my tactics. When I told him that I was myself an astrologer having made successful predictions, Shroff's tone suddenly changed. He took me to his private room, placed his horoscope in my hands and wanted to know something about his health. By now I had learnt the art of baiting fish. The very name 'Astrology' was tempting and one could not resist the temptation of consulting an astrologer. I simply said "a snapshot interpretation is not desirable and the office is not the place for astrological consultation" and I left, giving him my local address.

The next morning Shroff called on me, first to break the news that to start with Wheelers would take 100 copies of THE ASTROLOGICAL MAGAZINE to be sold at their stalls in Victoria Terminus, I and II, Churchgate and Dadar, B.B. & C.I and that I could arrange for sending the copies immediately. So astrology played the trick!

Shroff was born on 5-6-1891 at about 4-10 a.m. At the time of our meeting he was having Venus Dasa and the sub-period of Rahu. Venus the Dasa lord, was in the 2nd, sub-lord Rahu was in conjunction with the Sun, planet of health and Mercury, lord of the 6th (and 3rd) aspected by Saturn from the 5th house ruling the stomach. The major lord Venus occupied the constellation of the Sun and had *dwirdwadasa* disposition from the sub-lord. After explaining these details I said: "Venus in the ascendant gives much liking for rich food. Rahu with Mercury lord of the 6th makes the nerve cells weak and sluggish. Saturn in 5th can obstruct the flow of gastric juice in the stomach. This state of affairs will continue practically throughout the Dasas of Venus and the Sun. By regulating your diet, avoiding rich food and working less, the effects of the affliction can be considerably toned down. The gastric trouble will completely disappear in 1956, when the Moon Dasa commences.

Shroff was fully satisfied with my diagnosis. Later we became good friends. Our friendship developed and in fact I became 'great'. He would often say that the A.M. which at first he declined to sell, was one of the few journals which were sold by thousands in the Wheelers stalls.

Venus	Moon	Sat Sun Merc Mars	
Ketu Ascdt.	**RASI**		Rahu
			Sun
	Jup		

Jup Venus		Sun Ketu	Merc.
	NAVAMSA		Sat
			Mars
	Rahu	Moon Jupit.	

Shroff sought my astrological advice as to what occupation would suit his son Indravadan who had just completed high school.

I said: "Your son's horoscope is very good. He has a bright future. Yogakaraka Venus exalted, the ascendant lord Saturn aspecting the ascendent and lord of the 8th well-placed in a kendra confers long life. The 10th house is fortified by the combined aspect of four planets, viz., Saturn the Lagna lord, the Sun, lord of the 7th, Mars, lord of the 10th and Mercury lord of the 5th (and 8th) causing a powerful Rajayoga. Lord of the house of education is exalted. Mercury's position in the 4th indicates high education, Mercury rules communication of ideas, books, manuscripts and commerce. Venus, lord of the 4th denotes law and the principles of justice. Mercury tends to confer resourcefulness. Saturn the ascendant lord aspecting the 10th is also conducive for progress in law. Taking all these into consideration, I feel the law would be suitable for Indravadan and he will shine well as a big lawyer. As Rahu is in the 7th, it is likely he may have an unconventional marriage."

In accordance with my advise Indravadan joined the local Law College and secured a degree in law and became a successful lawyer. He was one of the leading solicitors in Delhi. Just before his death some years ago he called on me at Bangalore and recollected the predictions given about him to his father.

Shroff who saw the rise of his son before his eyes would often make appreciative references to astrological advice I used to give him at crucial moments. The last time I and Rajeswari Raman met him was in 1963. He told me then that as predicted by me he was completely free from his stomach troubles and that daily long walks and drinking water in the mornings from a copper vessel had helped him a lot to overcome his trouble.

No progress could be made in getting a publisher for my books. I met one Habibullah, a talisman maker and dealer who lived in Pali Hills, Bandra and who used to occasionally advertise in THE ASTROLOGICAL MAGAZINE. He had offered to publish my three books and deputed his secretary one Rao, to discuss terms. Our discussions went on for two whole days but Rao never gave out the mind of Habibullah as regards the financial aspect of the transaction. I was prepared to sell the copyrights of all the three books for a sum of Rs. 3,000/- Habibullah offered Rs. 1,000/- and I rejected his offer. He used to advertise in newspapers about the benefits conferred by his talismans on the wearers. I disuaded him from playing on the creduilty of the people, as I felt convinced that he had no spiritual powers. I stopped publishing his advertisement in THE ASTROLOGICAL MAGAZINE.

On the whole, this second trip of mine to Bombay could be said to be successful. On 5th February 1938, I left for Delhi responding to the invitation of Harichand Kakar.

21

On my way to Delhi, I broke my journey for a day at Jhansi. The Rani of Jhansi was a house-hold name for patriotism and sacrifice and as a student of history I was interested in visiting the place. Of course after the Rani's death Jhansi became a part of British India. I went round the historical places and felt proud of Indian womanhood.

During the journey between Jhansi and Gwalior, I found that about a dozen persons, apparently educated, had gathered round an elderly pandit, a palmist, showing their palms. The consultation was brief lasting for a couple of minutes, and each man was paying the palmist a rupee. Curiosity aroused, I paid a rupee to the pandit and stretched my palm awaiting his interpretation. Speaking in broken English interspersed with Hindi, he said, "your hand resembles that of Peshawa Madhavarao. Your fate-line is deceptive. It starts from the base of the line of Mars. Your longevity will be 32 and your death will be due to an accident. The Mount of Venus is not well developed. Just below Mercury line and above the head line, there are two small parallel lines, out of which one is pale, which means that you are thinking of a second marriage." Taken aback, I retorted: "It looks as if you do not know palmistry but are only interested in making money. Don't talk non-sense. I know astrology and palmisyry. My Jupiter mount is well formed. The heart line – *ayushya rekha* – is also clear. How can you say that I have a short life. Under cover of palmistry you have been lying. I guess you have Rahu in the 10th house in your horoscope". Ruminating for a while, the palmist said: "Yes, I have Rahu in the 10th house. How did you know?" I said, "Intuition". The palmist got down in the next station and all those passengers who had surrounded him flocked to me.

Some desired consultation on the spot. Some gave their birth particulars to be answered later on. Prasna always came to me handy in such cases. One of the questions pertained to the disappearance of the consultant's brother, whose whereabout were not known. I applied the following simple method. The consultor must give a number within 27. That represents the Prasna constellation. Count this from Krittika. Divide the number by 7. The remainder represents the result thus: 1 – the concerned person is staying nearby; 2 – returns soon; 3 – has gone away to a place other than the one he was expected to go to; 4 – returns the same day; 5 – his return is delayed; 6 – he is sick; and 7 – is trying to get back.

The number given was 25, which corresponded to Purvabhadra. Counting this from Krittika and dividing the figure by 7 (23/7) the remainder was 2, and my prediction was the missing person would return soon. The consultor was sceptical about my forecast. I had given him my Delhi address. Five days later he called on me at my Delhi residence and said that the missing person had returned. My consultation work in the train fetched me about Rs. 75/-.

I was received at the Delhi railway station by Harichand Kaker and taken to his residence in New Delhi. I was comfortably lodged in his outhouse. Since he was a non-vegetarian, he said that I could take my food at a hotel nearby owned by a south Indian Brahmin.

One day, when I was taking my food in the afternoon, the proprietor, quite-friendly, came to my table and said that he was a reader of the A.M. and that he was keen to have his horoscope interpreted by me. I offered my services in return for his taking care of my food and tiffin requirements, as long as I stayed in Delhi. He had, to mention in his own words, "a peculiar health problem". He did not reveal the details but wanted me to find out the nature of his illness. I asked him to mention a number of three digits, which he did. The number given was 2, 8, 6. According to Hindu numerology the lower, middle and upper parts of the body are signified respectively by the unit, the tenth and the hundredth digits. The eight planets in the order of the Sun, Mars, Jupiter, Mercury, Venus, Saturn, the Moon and Rahu correspond to numbers 1 to 8. Of the three individual numbers, ruled in this case by Mars, Rahu and Saturn 1 should consider Rahu as most malefic. And number 8 is the centre digit indicating the middle part of the body. 8 is ruled by Rahu signifying skin troubles in the secret parts etc. I boldly said that he must be suffering from some skin trouble in his private parts. Why I picked on the middle number, I did not know. It could have been intuition or just guesswork. It clicked. The hotelier, struck with surprise, remarked: "You are wonderful and your analysis is superb. What you have said is absolutely correct. But tell me whether I would ever get any relief from this dreadful disease". I opted for Prasna. The date was 11th February 1938 and the time, about noon.

Mars Sat		Ascdt Ketu	Moon	Sun Merc Venus	Mars	Ketu	
Sun Venus		**RASI**			**NAVAMSA**		
Merc Jup				Jup.			
	Rahu				Rahu	Moon Ascdt.	

The ascendant was Taurus occupied by Ketu and aspected by Rahu. The Moon was in Aridra ruled by Rahu. This confirmed my initial inference about the nature of the disease viz., blotches and eruptions in the skin. I explained to the hotelier: "The Prasna chart is not very encouraging. Venus, lord of the ascendant and the 6th is no doubt well-placed. But the Lagna itself is vitiated by the aspect of Mars–associated Saturn. Doctors themselves may not be able to diagnose the nature of your skin trouble. However, as Venus is in a friendly sign and the ascendant is aspected by Jupiter some relief is possible." He said that he was not interested in knowing how he got it, but would like to know when he would get relief.

I explained to him the significance of Venus as lord of the ascendant and his placement in the 10th and observed:

"In the Prasna chart Ketu's sub-period will terminate by the end of 1941 and you will get relief from 1942". He appeared quite satisfied. We became friends and we used to have astrological discussions whenever possible. He also introduced to me some of his friends.

My host Harichand Kakar was a businessman. My visit to Delhi had been sponsored by him and naturally he wanted to get from me as much information as possible on his horoscope. Except for sight seeing, an evening stroll in the Connaught Place and visit to the hotel for food, I would be mostly engaged by him either at his residence at New Delhi or in his shop in old Delhi. His cousin Vaishno Dutt, hailing from Peshawar had stayed with us in our village in 1935 or so when grandfather was alive. Vaishno Dutt was himself an astrologer and had cautioned his cousin that he might get into trouble when Saturn entered Aries. Hence Kakar was very particular to consult with me. He had business interests in London where he would often go. Would there be a war in the near future, involving European countries which could adversely affect his business interests? These were the problems agitating his mind.

Mars Jup.	Ascdt. Rahu				Venus	Mercury	
		RASI				Jup.	Rahu Sat
					NAVAMSA	Ketu	Ascdt. Moon
Sun Mercury	Venus	Ketu	Saturn				

Esteemed readers must note that analysis of horoscopes and Prasna charts given in these articles were as made by me then when often enthusiasm had the better of discretion. Kakar said: "How do you think my horoscope is constituted. Can you give me some past events to convince myself that your approach is correct".

I felt a bit hesitant for a while, but recovering my self-confidence, I said: "Your Lagna is Aries conjoined with Rahu. This makes you appear old, eccentric and indicates many changes in occupation. Lord of the ascendant Mars is in the 12th with Jupiter, lord of the 12th aspected by Saturn, lord of the 10th and 11th and Venus lord of the 2nd and 7th, is aspected by Saturn. These combinations indicate temptation, passionate approach to women, indolence and danger through deception. I am afraid you may not be quite loyal to your wife, who, because lord of the 7th is in Scorpio, a martian sign and is aspected by Saturn could be short-tempered and suspicious of you". Kakar, nodding his head in assent, said: "Look here, I am a self-made man. As you have mentioned I have been deceived by the very people whom I have trusted. What you have said about my personal life is correct. I go out of India for months together and do you think I could be a Rishyasrunga"?

I was not interested in tendering any advice to him in this matter. "But," I proceeded, "the situation of Venus is such that he may expose you to the risk of catching diseases which may destroy your health. You often allow your feelings to get the better of judgement. Unless this tendency to excitability, morbid imagination and strange appetites and acts of indiscretion is curbed, even your business may be affected".

I then switched on to the other aspects of his life. "Marriage could have taken place by the fag end of Venus Dasa. The first issue might have been born in the beginning of Moon's Dasa (1919 or 1920). Mars Dasa saw several ups and down in your business".

Kakar appeared to be quite satisfied with my analysis and said: "So far you have been correct in your interpretation. I am interested in the results of Rahu Dasa which I am told has just commenced and you must relate it to developments in the international field".

"Rahu", I proceeded, "who should give the results of Mars is in
the ascendant and Mars as the lord of the ascendant and the 8th is in
the 12th. Lord of the 10th Saturn is in Cancer Navamsa, which is
occupied by Rahu. Therefore your main business during Rahu Dasa
will be dealing with hides and skins and their export. The major lord
is free from afflictions but occupies the constellation of Aswini and
the fiery sign of Aries. By transit both Ketu and Saturn will be shortly
converging on Rahu. After Saturn enters Aries in May 1939 there will
be a conflagration in Europe affecting your export business".

After explaining the astrological factors in detail and how a war
might break out in 1939, I advised him to take such measures as he
deemed appropriate. I brought to Kakar's notice my prediction under
the caption "Saturn versus Fascism" published in the January 1938
issue of THE ASTROLOGICAL MAGAZINE wherein I had observed... "These
complications will plunge the world into an unhappy war. Saturn is
now in Pisces. He enters Aries by about May 1939. Saturn, the
representative of democratic thought, is under very adverse influences.
And his debilitation in Aries will have far reaching consequences on
democratic governments, while the Dictator countries will be further
allowed to pursue their methods un-checked. In the near future Fascism
gains further ground and Mars transiting Saturn gives rise to troubles
in democratic countries. The ingress of Saturn into Aries will be note-
worthy as Fascism will be at its height and that will be a moment
when the need for statesmen of foresight and farsight will be felt
imperative to save humanity from another world war". I explained in
detail the astrological configurations which would lead the world to
the brink of war in 1939. Kakar felt satisfied.

While I was in Delhi, one of my readers B.N. Mathur, an engineer
by profession, invited me to his residence in the area of Chandni
Chowk. I was introduced to his brothers and other family members.
The discussions centred mainly on astrology and *mantra sastra*. One
of his brothers, aged about 30 or 31 and a medical practitioner had
his own misgivings about the use of astrology. I explained to him
how on the basis of the allocation of different organs to different
zodiacal signs one can find out the area of trouble and the nature of

the ailment. He gave a piece of paper containing his Rasi chart with the remark: "Say something about my health".

I said, "The ascendant is Sagittarius and the lord is in the 6th in an inimical sign while the 5th is occupied by the lord of the 6th Venus is in conjunction with Mars and aspected by Saturn. The 5th house rules the stomach. Lord of the 6th also aspects the Moon. You are a victim of a serious stomach ailment brought about by tension and restlessness. There is a chance of your undergoing surgery when Mars transits Aries". He was "amazed" at my analysis and his somewhat arrogant attitude toned down. From then on the Mathur family was all praise for me. They took me round Delhi and invited me to dine with them several times. They were of course vegetarians.

One evening the senior most brother took me to a middle aged man, who was said to be a famous *tantric*, living in a small house in old Delhi. We were ushered into the *puja* room and the "tantric" was said to be, rather pretended to be, in deep meditation. When I was introduced as a budding astrologer from South India capable of reading one's past, present and future, he cast a patronizing smile at me and started listing his 'achievements'. "So you are an astrologer, I am a prophet. Without any calculations, I can forecast things to the very day" boasted the "tantric". Mathur was nodding his head as if in approval. I looked at him for a brief while and shot back: "I believe in *Tantra sastra* but not in *tantrics*. I do not think there is any prophet now who can prophecy the future. Astrology alone can do it". The "tantric" waved his hand declaring, "Don't have assumptions. Because of sustained *upasana*, I get a vision of things that have happened, that are happening and that will happen. It is all Her grace. Mathur became somewhat uneasy, gently tapped my back and whispered into my ear that I was going too far in suspecting the bonafides of the "*tantric*". According to Mathur, the "tantric" had much influence in higher circles and was even capable of casting spells. I would not be taken in. I had the Prasna chart ready (No. 3) in my mind.

The Lagna was Libra with the Moon aspected by Mars. Rahu was in the 2nd aspected by Mars. Ketu in the 8th was aspected by Saturn. Jupiter was no doubt in a Kendra, but his dipositor was not well placed. Exalted Venus was associated with malefic Saturn, the Sun and malefic Mercury. I simply said, "Sir, notwithstanding all the claims you make for your 'tantric' powers and foresight, my astrological knowledge tells me that you are an exhibitionist and cannot have any real spiritual power". His face turned red with anger. In a menacing tone he chided Mathur for having brought with him "a presumptuous youth" who dared question his powers. I apologised to Mathur for my indiscretion but stuck to my point that the "tantric" was only duping the innocent people. After two or three years I learnt that the "tantric" had fled without leaving any trace of his whereabouts.

I visited Hardwar and Rishikesh and had dips in the Ganga. At Hardwar I stayed with one Nanjunda Sastry, brother-in-law of the well-known Kannada literature V. Seetharamaiah. Nanjunda Sastry took me to Rishikesh, Lakshmana Jhoola and other places. It was the first time that I had a view of the magnificent Himalayas, said to be the abode of Lord Siva and great sages. At Hardwar I chanced to meet quite a number of sadhus, fake as well as genuine. Some of them claimed to be astrologers. In fact I had my horoscope read by a sadhu who was said to be spiritually evolved.

A brief discussion with this sadhu led me to the conclusion that he not only knew astrology well but had also the power of intuition. On the basis of my Rasi chart he revealed that my mother died early, that I was married at 18, I had two children, that I was passing through a very difficulty period and that I would have "a brilliant future". "When do you think some prosperity will dawn on me?" I queried. His answer was "in Saturn in Jupiter". Saturn's sub-period for me would last from October 1938 to April 1941. I again posed the question, "Saturn enters Aries in October 1939 when *sadesathi* will commence. How would you reconcile this with your prediction of prosperity dawning after the commencement of Saturn's sub-period". Trying to clear my doubt the sadhu said, "Saturn is a yogakaraka for you from the Moon. He is also your Lagna lord. Your good time actually starts after Saturn enters the 4th quarter of the constellation of Aswini. Sade sathi will affect you both positively and negatively – positively you will get reputation, fame an name and finance will improve. On the negative side your father will pass away before Saturn leaves Gemini, Jupiter and Saturn in mutual aspect involving *kendras* will raise you high in the field of astrology. Make note for your future guidance that *gochara* Saturn especially when his own Dasa is running will not cause any catastrophic events. He will create such conditions as will make one taste the bitter fruits of life but mellow him and pave the way for a bright future". He spoke in Hindi and it was translated into Kannada by Nanjunda Sastry. He declined to accept the five rupee note I offered him. On the other hand, he gave me a silver coin embossed on one side with the picture of Sri Rama saying "keep this in your pooja. It will be the harbinger of prosperity. You have Jupiter in the 10th and hence I have been divinely inspired to give you this". I was amazed at his simplicity, unassuming nature, indifference to physical comforts, his spirit of renunciation and his knowledge of astrology. What he told me about Saturn's *sade-sathi* has been found to be correct in the majority of horoscopes studied by me during the past five decades. The silver coin given by him is still kept in my pooja room.

February 24th saw me off to Jalandhar in response to a cordial invitation from Shivnath Khanna. He was living in the fashionable "Civil Lines" area and I stayed with him for 2 days. He was dealing with grains, wheat etc., and was getting my forecasts on market trends. He had been impressed by the articles on commercial forecasts I was then writing in THE ASTROLOGICAL MAGAZINE. Mr. Khanna wanted forecasts about cotton, wheat, gold and silver. In those days I would base my forecasts on the principles given by Varahamihira—Aries rules cotton etc. The movements of the Sun and the Moon, their declinations, and the adverse aspects formed with malefics would indicate rise in the prices of gold and silver. I must say that most of the market forecasts given by me turned out to be correct.

When I expressed a desire to see the Golden Temple at Amritsar and also visit Lahore, Mr. Khanna readily placed his car at my disposal.

Amritsar is notable as the centre of Sikh faith and the site of the Golden Temple. Ramdas, the fourth Guru, laid the foundation of the city upon a site granted by Akbar. He also excavated the holy tank – Amrita Sarovara or the "Lake of Immortality".

The temple is on a small island in the middle of the tank. Amritsar was under the rule of Ranjit Singh and passed with the rest of the Punjab into British hands after the second Sikh war.

After a day's halt at Amritsar, visiting the Golden Temple and partaking the *prasad*, I reached Lahore on 27th February and was received by G.M. Chawla one of my "admirers". He was an accountant in the automobile firm owned by one Rai Saheb Narain Das. I stayed with Chawla and my comforts were well attended to.

Lahore, situated on the left bank of the river Ravi fascinated me. Tradition traces the origin of the city to Lava, the son of Sri Rama. The name of the city is mentioned even by Hiuan Tsang, the Chinese traveller. Originally it was governed by Chauhan Rajputs. The Sultans of Ghori and Ghazni made destructive assaults on this city. The city owes much of its architecture to the Mughal rulers. Lahore became the capital of Ranjit Singh until it came under the British after the second Sikh war.

I visited the Mall, and the mosque of Wazir Khan and the Samadhi of the great Ranjit Singh. The Shalimar Gardens, said to have been laid by Shajehan, were beautiful. I also visited the tomb of Jehangir. The streets of the old city were narrow and tortuous. The Mall is the main street. Anarkali bazar situated south of the city wall brought to my memory the story of Jehangir. Lahore was also an important educational center. I went round the Punjab University and also Atchison Chief's College for the "sons of noble men". Now of course Lahore has become part of Pakistan.

Chawla was himself a keen student of astrology. He showed me his library containing all my grandfather's books and some astrological literature written in Urdu. He was doubtful about his time of birth, which was said to be at 1.25 p.m. on 26-5-1894 at Lahore. Applying Parasara's *Pranapada* theory I rectified the time of birth to 12th. 55m. and 36s. p.m.

Rahu Venus		Sun Merc. Jup.					
Mars				Ascdt Mars Rahu Saturn			
Moon							Ketu
			Ascdt. Sat. Ketu	Venus Jup		Sun Moon Merc.	

I told Chawla, "Lord of the 7th Jupiter is in the 9th with the Sun, lord of the 12th and Mercury, lord of the 10th. But you will get Jupiter Dasa only when you are about 23 years. Rahu is also capable of giving the results of Jupiter especially that he is in the 11th from Jupiter. Venus *kalatrakaraka* is exalted in the 7th and occupies the 11th from Mercury lord of the 10th. Therefore your entry into service and marriage must have taken place about the end of Venus in Rahu when you were about 19 or 20. If this is correct then your time of birth rectified by me is correct." Chawla said that I was right.

Dealing with his longevity I said the Sun's sub-period in Saturn's Dasa would be critical and advised him to have some remedies performed. Elaborating further, "Saturn is the *ayushkaraka* and owns the 6th house. He is *maraka* from the Chandra Lagna. He is afflicted by his association with Ketu and aspect of Mars. The Sun is lord of the 12th and capable of causing *maraka*". Chawla, waving his land said "How can you say the Sun is a *maraka* to me when he is in the 9th. Why not we consider Mars as he is a powerful malefic and the relationship between the major and sub-lords is 6th and 8th". I continued, "I can concede your argument but I am aided by my intuition also. The Sun is also with Jupiter a *maraka* and hence I consider him a ruthless killer. I would advise you to have remedial measures performed. If through God's grace you can survive your 50th year" I ended the discussion. Chawla passed away in 1943 at the fag end of the Sun's sub-period in Saturn's major period.

The horoscope of Rai Bahadur Narain Das, boss of Chawla and owner of a big automobile concern was intriguing. The Rai Bahadur was said to be "very rich" but very tight-fisted also, though he was supposed to have helped many charitable institution.

From early years I had developed certain norms. Any person desiring consultation, irrespective of his social or financial position, should properly invite me to his place and treat me with due regard and without any air of patronage. There was no question of my dancing attendance on any high-ups of cringing for any patronage. In keeping with this practice, I called on the Rai Saheb. He was quite courteous and friendly. After preliminary exchanges of courtesies he gave me his *janma patri* – a scroll of paper which of course I recast in his presence. He was born on 4th November 1877 at Gh. 21-17.

The first impression of the horoscope (Chart No. 4) was that he was not happy in his private life. I told him, "Lord of the ascendant Saturn in the ascendant is a good point, but he is associated with Mars and Rahu, all the influences being concentrated on the 7th house. Lord of the 7th is debilitated in the 8th and conjoined with Mercury lord of 8th and 5th and the Moon, lord of the 6th. Methinks that your marriage is marked by enduring coldness on the part of your wife. Incompatibility, minsunderstanding and even scandal are all possible". Quoting a verse* from Satyacharya, I continued my interpretation, "Rahu is the karaka for *apasmara masuri,* a type of skin trouble, fear from poison, serpents and also diseases arising out of infection. It looks as though there could have been attempts to poison you but because of the presence of two benefics in the 3rd from the Moon, you were saved. The same combination in the 11th from the ascendant involving *Kalatrakaraka* must have brought sizeable fortune from your wife". When I paused for a while, the Rai Saheb interjected, "Your analysis is factually correct. Except when we desire physical contact, I and my wife, hardly meet, our thoughts seem to work on different wavelengths".

अपस्मारो मसूरीच शुद्रव्याधि क्रिमिप्रद:
विषपीडा सर्पपीडारा हुरेतान् करोति: ॥

"What I am interested to know is whether I could ever have a child. I am now 61 but am still quite virile". I pondered over the chart carefully and falling back on the dicta of Mantreswara that "when the 5th from the ascendant, Jupiter and the Moon are afflicted one will have no issues", and the Bija Sphuta theory, I observed "Lord of the 5th, Mercury is afflicted. The lord of the 5th from the Moon is Saturn and he is considerably afflicted by his association with Mars and Rahu. Mars, lord of the 5th from Jupiter is again afflicted. The Bijasphuta in your case falls in an even sign, viz., Pisces in the constellation of Saturn. All these afflictions indicate that you will have no issues. Narain Dass looked unhappy but said: "Pandits here say that by performing remedial measures and marrying another lady, I can get a son". But I had to tell him that even assuming that he had a second marriage, the disposition of Bija sphuta in his own case was such that he would not be capable of getting a child. He nodded his head and paid me as *dakshina*, the magnificent sum of fifty rupees!

The next morning I returned to Jullundhur and from there to Delhi and the next day left for Allahabad *enroute* to Varanasi.

Readers may be wondering whether all the predictions made by me in those days proved correct. Not all. While the majority, say to the extent of 70%, were successful, there were also failures.

22

On 2nd March 1938, I arrived at Allahabad. Leaving my luggage at a Dharmashala near the railway station I spent the day visiting places of interest.

As I was strolling near the Sangam, a *panda*, aged about 30, accosted me. Even in those days *pandas* were generally considered to be dangerous and intent on fleecing the moffusil pilgrims, but my panda-friend appeared to be different. He demanded Rs. 10 to help me get a dip in the Sangam-the confluence of the sacred Ganga, Yamuna and the "mythical" Saraswathi and to show me around the city. When he came to know that I was an astrologer, he agreed to take Rs. 2/- from me. Of course it was clear that he would like me to give him some predictions.

The perambulation round the city was in an *ekka*, an uncomfortable cart drawn by a horse. After a dip at the wonderful confluence which pious Hindus still hold as religiously significant we visited a few places of interest. I found Allahabad a fairly big city and intellectually active. I met one or two advocates but otherwise there was nothing significant to record.

In 1901, grandfather had visited Allahabad. The following extract from the August 1901 issue of THE ASTROLOGICAL MAGAZINE will make an interesting reading: "I met Pandit Auditya Ram Bhattacharji, M.A., Professor of Sanskrit in the college and a simple gentleman. I visited Vakil Madan Mohan Malaviya and he promised to arrange for a lecture and desired me to come to Kayastha Sabha Hall on a particular day and a particular time. When myself and Mahamahopadhyaya Auditya Ram went there at the appointed time, there were none to answer us.

These leading gentlemen had entirely forgotten their engagements."

On the 4th I reached Varanasi and was received at the railway station by one Srikanta Sastry, a *purohit* from the South settled in the city. I was lodged in a Dharmashala near the Dasaswamedha ghat. My first impression of Varanasi was disappointing. The old city dotted with innumerable lanes and byelanes was dirty and the people were generally somewhat rough. But from times immemorial Varanasi has been the most sacred city for the Hindus. It is this feeling of sanctity and the faith that one who bathes in the Ganga frees himself from all sins that has been attracting thousands and thousands of pilgrims from all over India.

Srikanta Sastry was a learned man, possessing a good knowledge of astrology. I had known him by correspondence. He was fairly influential locally and introduced me to some *pandas* and some South Indians. One of the gentleman introduced to me was Acharya, perhaps hailing from Tirupati. His horoscope almost undid my reputation as my analysis of his seventh house was totally disappointing. His question was quite simple. "How is my Kalatra bhava?" He was about 48 years old.

My analysis was simple. I said "The lord of the 7th, the Sun, is

			Sun Sat. Venus Jup.		Lagna	Mars
	Moon					
Lagna		Sat. Rahu				Ketu
	RASI			NAVAMSA		
Venus Mars Ketu			Rahu			
	Sun Jup. Merc.				Moon	

in a kendra (quadrant) in association with Mercury and Jupiter and otherwise unafflicted. The dispositor Mars is exalted but in the 12th house with Venus and Ketu aspected by the lord of Lagna Saturn. Thus while the 7th house is somewhat afflicted there is no denial of marriage." Acharya said, "Look here, my young friend, I am 48 and do you think I remain unmarried?" "But", I protested, "there could be persons who might not have married or whose wives might have died and who remain without getting remarried. In your case the influences are mixed. You will be a married man but the wife may not be alive. Since the Moon in a malefic sign is aspected both by Mars and Saturn, you will be highly restless, impulsive and quarrelsome. Because of these characteristics, your wife could have left you or even died. The combinations are unfavourable for a happy marriage."

As I was making the analysis I could sense he was getting restless and impatient. He blurted out somewhat rudely. "Young man, a sharp knife can be used to cut vegetables or to cut one's own throat. Which would you opt for?" I was amused and said his example was irrelevant. He retorted "No, it is quite relevant. Your analysis is totally out of tune with hard facts. What would happen to your reputation if you had given a similar analysis to one who does not believe in astrology? I pity you." I just could not understand why he was lecturing to me on irrelevant matters and wanted to know why he was beating about the bush. Acharya calmed down and observed, "No astrologer in India including Jyotish Samrats has succeeded in analysing correctly my 7th house. So I do not blame a young astrologer like you who has yet to gain experience. My first marriage took place in my 12th year and the wife died in my 18th year without nuptials. My second marriage was performed in my 18th year and my second wife bore two sons and four daughters. She died in my 41st year and my third marriage was performed when I was 43 and she died in my 47th year after giving birth to a female child who also died. I have now no wife and have come to this place to spend the rest of my life. Try to find out for your own information why I have lost three wives. I also know astrology but cannot figure out what combinations have caused these deaths."

It was as if a bolt from the blue had struck me. I went on cogitating as to what astrological factors could have caused the three marriages all of which resulted in the deaths of the wives. While my ego received a well-deserved blow, I also got an opportunity of learning astrology in greater depth.

The next day Srikanta Sastry arranged for my meeting with a *Bhrigu Samhita* astrologer. I had earlier in 1935 the experience of consulting Nadi Astrology and I was happy at the opportunity to learn something about *Bhrigu Samhita*.

Srikanta Sastry led me to the astrologer's house in a bye-lane in the old city. As we entered the house, the *Samhita* reader fairly advanced in age and supporting himself with a staff, greeted us with a smile and took us to a room stacked with soiled manuscripts arranged in a disorderly fashion. After preliminary enquiries and recording my birth details, the pandit asked me to meet him the next morning which we did. Unlike the majority of *Nadi* astrologers and *Samhita* readers, he appeared to be learned. He took out a few notebooks from out of a bundle and slowly read what purported to be my chart. The reading was in simple Sanskrit, and the clarifications, if any, were provided by Sastry, who himself was a scholar in Sanskrit and also knew astrology well. The reading began with obeisance to Ganesha, Siva, Vishnu, the Sun and the Moon.

The reading was said to give out losses and gains, happiness, sorrow, longevity, etc. The first sloka read

"जन्मपत्री शुभं दीपम् भृगुणापरिभाषितं, लाभालाभं सुखं दु:खं दृश्यति ग्रहमायुषं ।"

It began with the mentioning of my visit to the *Samhita* astrolonger with Sastry and my unsuccessful handling of Acharya's horoscope with the consoling remark that I had yet to master Jyotisha and gain divine grace. Then it said, giving the chart meaning the Sun

"कर्काकैयदाजन्म कुंभलग्नतथाप्रदि । वृश्चिके गुरु देवापि कोयोग: तस्य किं फलं"

is in Cancer, Langa is Aquarius and Jupiter is in Scorpio – what is the yoga and what are the results? A summary of the reading is herewith given for the information of the reader: "He will become a *sreshta.* He will unravel the future of persons. He will go into the subtleties of the *Sastra.* He will become world famous (विश्वेरव्याति मतां तया)   by his writings and will be engaged in planetary calculations (खेदगणानाद्धारा च देशदेशान्तरे तया)   He will be bold, dignified, generous and a man of characters (दैर्यगाम्बोर्यजोदायं गुणशालिनी तया)   . He will be the author of many books (तादा ग्रन्थ रचनादि स्थोत्माह एतीतया ।) . He is born in Bharat, in the south, having the name of Venkata   (जन्मतु भारतेचैव दक्षिण प्रांतिके तथा वेंकट इति नामाश्च नादि पितृके गृहे).

       . The *Samhita* went on: "His mother died in the second year. His wife whose name commences from *ra* is born in Makara Lagna (रकारेण ख्याति माता शुभेमकरलग्ने समुद्भय) . He will continue studies till he is 23 years old. He becomes famous by the art of *grahagananas* (ग्रहप्रहणनाविद्यश्च ख्यातिमान् घरणीतले).   . Fortunes increase day by day when he will be 35, 38, 48 and 58 (षाणरामे वसुरामे-वसुदेवे वसुताणगे तथा तयोत्कर्ष परचैव भाग्यवृद्धि दिने दिने).   . Because of past Karma, in the years 32, 34, 40, 52 difficulties occur. There will be loss of a close relative and fear from illness. At 48 and again in 58 he will have foreign travel, respect, felicitation and he follows pure *karma.* The world acclaims him as a pious soul (*subrhratma*)."

He took out another leaf and read: "Satyacharya was a great pandit in astrology. He had studied everything that was available in astrology but still felt he was lacking something. He did penance for twelve years. Lord Siva appeared and wanted Satya to ask for a boon. Satyacharya explained that though he knew astrology, he felt he was deficient in something. Granting a boon Lord Siva said, 'Hitherto you were a *Jyotishi* (astrologer) but from now on you will be a *Daivagna* (knower of the unknown)'. Immediately Satyacharya had a vision of all future births and patterns of planetary combinations and he compiled his famous *Satya Samhita.* This young man will also become a *Daivagna.* Let him practice humility." It indeed was an eye opener to me that knowledge and humility must go together.

The Sun was about to set when the pandit abruptly stopped reading further. He wanted us to meet him the next morning.

I was more curious to know the basis of *Samhita* reading rather than get a reading myself. To the several questions put to the pandit about *Samhitas,* he said: "These ancient *Samhitas* were written by sages thousands of years ago." Stopping him abruptly I remarked: "The *Samhita* in your hands appears to have been written on some sort of a parchment-like paper. How come you claim for it an age of thousands of years?" He calmly answered. "The originals were written probably two thousands years ago. They were copied from time to time by a select band of disciples who knew the secrets of *Samhitas.* The one in my possession could be about 300 years old." I examined the leaves carefully and thought it could not be earlier than 100 years. But the *grantha* characters could not be deciphered by me. He took us to another room where a number of old notebooks, said to be different *Samhitas,* had been kept in a ramshackle wooden almirah.

Thanking him for the reading, we took leave of the Pandit. Of course we could not meet him again as I had to leave for Calcutta the next night.

The forecasts, which abruptly ended, did not say anything about longevity, children etc. But whatever it said about the future, including the name and Lagna of my wife, could be considered fairly accurate differing by a year or two in the matter of foreign travel, etc.

Srikanta Sastry was also interested in our ancient history and culture and the material he had collected about the birth-data of some of the Mughal rulers were made available to me. In fact I have referred to Sastry's assistance in this direction in my book NOTABLE HOROSCOPES.

N.C. Lall, Editor of a monthly astrological journal *Celestial Messenger* and his son R.N. Lall, a high school teacher, called on me the same night and took me to their residence. I knew the Lalls by correspondence as I was an occasional contributor to *Celestial Messenger.*

Our discussion ranged over several aspects of astrology. The senior Lall, about 60 then, well-read and cultured, said that in calculating the ruling Dasa at birth, the constellation to be considered should be either the one occupied by the Moon or the Lagna was in depending upon, whichever was stronger. This was the first time that I heard about considering the constellation of the Lagna. Lall said, "This principle was revealed to me by my *Guru*. I have tried it in a number of cases and found it quite satisfactory. Take your own case. Your Lagna is about 11° Aquarius – Satabhisha 2 leaving a balance of about 11 years and 9 months in Rahu Dasa which ended about May 1924. In Saturn in Jupiter there was a break in your education. In Mercury's sub-period you were married. You are now having the Moon in Jupiter, enabling you to have dips in sacred rivers and establish your name. The end of Mercury which commences in your 65th year can prove fatal as Mercury is a *maraka*. I have tested scores of horoscopes and find the principle working". I nodded my head and asked him on what basis he considered my Lagna constellation, in preference to that of the Moon. He explained, "Because the Lagna is stronger than the Moon, as Lagna is aspected by lord of Lagna and three other palnets." I interjected, "Is not the Moon stronger than the Lagna?" He is exalted, is with the ascendant lord and is aspected by Jupiter causing *Gajakesari Yoga*. And what is the authority for your thesis?". Lall said the authority was *Brihat Parasara Hora*. The discussion ended there.

This problem set by Lall was always working in my mind, till I came in possession of *Satya Samhita*, wherein the Sage says:

बलिनान्दौ तत् स्थितर्षाम् जन्मनक्षत्रमुच्यते ।
गतनाडयस्तु विघ्नया: चन्द्रचारेण निश्चितः ॥
गतनाडीम् परध्निाय लग्नमध्य गतर्षकम् ।
जन्मर्ष कथयेत् श्रीमान् धीमान् दशा भुक्ति च योजयेत् ॥

The meaning is clear that the Dasas should be calculated on the basis of the Nakshatra of the Lagna or the Moon whichever is stronger. But my experience all these years and the innumerable *Nadis* I have seen have convinced me that the Moon's *Nakshatra* alone is to be considered. Vimshottari is also called Udu Dasa. The Moon is *Udupa* or the lord of constellations. Hence, it is my opinion, formed after decades of study and experiment that the Dasa should be based on the position of the Moon alone.

23

The railway journey from Varanasi to Calcutta on the night of 6th March 1938 was uncomfortable, what with all sorts of people crowded together in the third class compartment. At the Wheeler's railway book stall at Varanasi, I had picked up a copy of Dr. Alexander Cannon's THE INVISIBLE INFLUENCE, a remarkable book dealing with such subjects as "Mind over Master", "Psychology and the Occult", "Some Psychic Phenomena", etc. Those were the days when many an educated Indian had surrendered his ability to appreciate the uniqueness of his own culture to Western thinking. Forty-three years after the so-called political independence things do not appear to have changed. On the other hand they have deteriorated. Effects of dreams, psychic phenomena, astrology, etc., discovered by our ancient seers and sages and borne out in actual practice are being labelled as 'superstitious' in the name of scientific temper and rationalism, just because of the intellectual slavery we are still suffering from.

Dr. Cannon, an M.D., Ph.D., etc., asserts in the pages of this book that "Black Magic does exist and the Biblical doctrine of Demonistic theory of Insanity would appear to be more scientific than our 'lip-service' psychology of today". Giving a number of instances of black magic, control over the mind, etc., Dr. Cannon says: "The Western methods of hypnotism and telepathy, good as they are, in no way equal to those of the Aryan Hindu Masters who hold all the secrets ever discovered by man with regard to the control of the mind of another" and that "India and Tibet can teach us more about psychology and the workings of the mind than any Freud, Jung, Alder or the exponent of any other new thought movement".

A reading of the work during the journey again revived my interest in *mantra sastra* and recalled to my memory of my early experiences with Ibrahim. I arrived at Calcutta on the 7th morning and the first thing I did after leaving my luggage at a South Indian hotel in Chittaranjan Avenue was to visit Mr. Fakir Chandra Dutt with whom I had been in correspondence for some years. Engaging a rickshaw I waded through several lanes to locate Mr. Dutt's house at 69, Amherst Row. He was already aged and ailing. After a preliminary discussion about the merits of the *Sayana* and *Nirayana* systems – he was of course a follower of the *Sayana* – I expressed my desire to meet a genuine *mantric* as Calcutta was said to be famous for *mantrics*.

Mr. Dutt sent a guide who took me to the Kali temple. My first reaction was one of abhorence at the sight of innocent animals being sacrificed. After a reluctant *darshan* of Goddess Kali, I was taken to a nearby house and introduced to a *mantric* who was bedecked with all the paraphernalia generally associated in popular minds with such persons. To demonstrate his powers, he took two broomsticks each about 6 inches long, made them stand before the image of the deity and as he went on uttering some *mantras*, the broom-sticks began to dance. It looked as if they obeyed his commands. To "prove" his claim that he could read or communicate ideas through the media of thought, he wanted me to jot down whatever I desired on a piece of paper. I wrote down in Kannada script, half a dozen names of my ancestors. The *mantric* asked me to think what I wrote which I did. He revealed r˜y thoughts. For a moment I was simply flabbergasted. I asked him: "What are the processes involved in reading others' thoughts? How can we send messages through thought-waves?" His explanation was that by practising certain *kshudra mantras* and bringing the deity concerned under one's control one could easily read others' thoughts. I pressed him further to say whether his expertise in *mantra sastra* enabled him to predict the past, present and future. Almost apologetically he replied: "Yes, we can". I was mentally getting ready to counter his onslaughts by silently reciting Gayatri *mantra*. He said: "Your past is unhappy. You have no mother. You are embarking on a work which promises no success." It was my turn to speak. "Your reading is not correct. I know you will not be able to probe the past or look into the future. I had made my mind impervious to your thought-vibrations." He took the cue and dismissed me.

I narrated my experience to Dutt. He said there were several such fakes in Calcutta while real *mantrics* kept aloof from public gaze.

Dutt had specialised in Western astrological teachings. I had carefully read his *Predictive Astrology*. The last book *Astro-Palmistry* presented to me by Dutt "as a token of my sincere love and kindest regards" was on 7th January 1953. He revealed that though he practised Western Astrology based on the *Sayana* zodiac he relied much on the "old Hindu method of House Division, also advocated by Ptolemy." I differed from him in several matters including methods employed in *timing events*. He would emphasise on primary and secondary directions on which I have always had my own reservations. In fact, I could convince even Carter that the only reliable methods of timing events were the Dasa systems propounded in Hindu Astrology.

According to Dutt, the period by directing the cusp of the 8th house for instance to the place of the Sun in the 9th would show a breakdown of health. He would also employ the solar revolutions, etc. In fact Dutt worked out secondary directions for my 27th year (to commence on 8th August 1938) and predicted a windfall for me. Of course it did not happen. Dutt also said that important events of life very often could be ascertained by considering the zodiac from the ascendant indicative of 100 years. Thus 1 year measures 3° 36', and 1 month measures 18'. The chart is divided into 4 parts or quadrants – ascendant to mid-heaven (25 years), mid-heaven to descendant (26 to 50), descendant to the 4th house (50 to 75) and 4th house to the ascendant (75 to 100). For example say Mars is at a distance of 12° from the meridian. At the age of 28 years roughly (25 + 3) the native sustains an accident. With due deference to Dutt, I must say that the system has certain flaws and is not fool-proof. Why should 100 years be allotted to the entire zodiac instead of 120 years considered in *Vimshottari*? Of course factors like the *yogas*, afflictions, etc., cannot be ignored.

In 1941, I wrote to Dutt pointing out my apprehensions about the system suggested by him. Dutt was modest enought to agree. I fully endorsed his view that "astral factors only show the tendencies" and the exact effects "will depend on the heredity, environment and character of the native".

Dutt was of course the first in India in recent years to write a book on *Prenatal Astrology* though germs of the theory are to be found in classical works like *Brihat Parasara Hora, Brihat Jataka,* etc. Relying on Ptolemy and drawing liberally from Hindu astrology, E.H. Bailey brought out his *Prenatal Epoch* long before Dutt's book. The method has as its basis the theory that the ascendant degree and the longitude of the Moon at conception interchange with the longitude of the Moon and the degree ascending at birth, or their respective opposite points.

Over the years I experimented with this method and many articles have also appeared in THE ASTROLOGICAL MAGAZINE. I found that it was not quite reliable. But it does offer scope for research. These are of course my own views. It is interesting to note that even Ram Dayalu in his *Sanketanidhi* refers to predicting the nature of effects in the future on the basis of the Moon's position, prior to birth.

In the course of further discussions Dutt revealed that Mihiracharya, a pen-name assumed by a well-known palmist of those days, outlined the methods of tracing birth-details and the horoscope from the palm and these principles were adumbrated in a recent book *Astro Palmistry,* a copy of which was given to me. My first experience of my horoscope being traced from my palm was with a *Nadi* astrologer in Madras in 1935 and I was naturally interested in knowing more about the relation of palmistry to astrology.

The age of the Moon, the month of birth, the signs occupied by the different planets are supposed to be revealed by a certain manipulation of the vertical lines on the 2nd and 3rd phalanges of the different fingers. For example, the vertical lines on the 2nd and 3rd phalanges of the second fingers of both the hands are totalled. This is added to a basic number 32, the result multiplied by 7 and the product divided by 15, is said to give the age of the Moon or the lunar day of birth. The whole difficulty is in correctly calculating the vertical lines, as some will be well formed and some will be faint. I have already referred, in a previous chapter, to the methods suggested in Hindu palmistry to trace the birth chart. After carrying out much study and research in this subject, I felt that the results were not worth the time and labour spent. On the contrary, the methods suggested in *Prasna Marga* for finding out unknown horoscopes appeared to me to be more reliable.

In the 50's I met a palmist in Bangalore who was able to trace the horoscope by considering not only the lines on the palm but also the lines on the heels. He was successful in a number of cases. After some meetings, he said he was an *upasaka* of a *kshudra devata* which revealed the birth details. During my first visit to the United States in 1959 I was able to trace the birth time and Lagna from the palm of Charles Jayne, a well-known astrologer who died recently and Mr. Ernest Grant, the first Secretary of the American Federation of Astrologers.

It is for budding scholars in astrology and palmistry to make further research into the subject of astro-Palmistry and convince themselves.

I returned to Bombay for a further stay of one week, with a view to having some more consultations and securing subscribers to THE ASTROLOGICAL MAGAZINE. This time I rented a room (Rs. 30/- per month) at Matunga. Chubb, an officer in a Bank was the first to meet me, of course, at the instance of B.H. Ganoo. He was a young man of 36., fair looking and deeply interested in astrology. Placing his horoscope in my hands he said: "God has been good to me in all matters. But still I am suffering a lot mentally. Can you analyse my problem and advise me?" Hesitating for a moment, I asked him what his problem was. His reply was, "Well, you are an expert astrologer and it is for you to find out." I checked up the casting and reflecting on the chart for a few minutes I said: "You are born in *Kalasarpa Yoga*, all the planets being hemmed in between Rahu and Ketu. Rahu in Lagna no doubt gives you interest in occultism, astrology etc., but his being aspected by Mars leads to an obsession with those things. You are self-willed, sometimes eccentric and often changeful. The 1st, 6th and 7th houses are involved. This makes you highly sensual and I will

Sun Mars	Ketu				Merc		
Merc Venus		**RASI**		Rahu		**NAVAMSA**	
Jup Sat				Sat Ascdt			Ketu
	Moon	Ascdt. Rahu			Moon		Sun Mars Venus

not be surprised if you have a problem with your head, something like migraine, bouts of headache." Beaming with a smile Chubb said, "Yes, you have correctly said about my nature and about one problem. Is there any other problem that you think important "Yes," I proceeded, "lord of the 7th Mars is with the Sun, a malefic aspecting the ascendant, and in turn, aspected by Saturn. Ketu afflicts the 7th house. It is the marital problem." Chubb, waving his hand, observed: "But Venus is well-placed and can influence marriage for good." I retorted "No. Venus is with Mercury, an impotent planet, in the house of an impotent Saturn and subject to *papakarthari yoga*. Venus is weak." Quoting a stanza from a classical work –

शुक्रे बलहीनेतु लिंगरोगी भवेत् पुमान् ।
हुताव शत्रु ना भार्या परित्यकत्वऽयता भवेत् ॥

I said: "Venus is weak implying that you may be pre-disposed towards sex diseases. The wife may be an enemy and may reject you, unless both of you conduct towards each other in a manner that will conduce to mutual understanding."

Chubb became somewhat morose. Tears trickling down his cheeks he said: "The main problem has been pinpointed by you. I and my wife have never seen eye to eye with each other". I told him: "Ketu in the 7th threatens domestic troubles, jealousy, and even deceit."

Chubb met me several times after this first meeting. The husband and wife lived together but as strangers.

My stay at Bombay for a few days was fruitful. I could do some professional work besides enlisting a few subscribers for THE ASTROLOGICAL MAGAZINE, which, by then, eighteen months old, was suffering from strokes of *Balakrishta*. Ganoo introduced me to A.C. Mujumdar, Manager of Hindustan Life Insurance Company. He and his immediate assistant Patel were quite influential people and to some extent, knowledgeable in astrology too. Mukherji who, in 1944, introduced me to Sarat Bose, elder brother of Netaji Subhash Chandra Bose, was interested to know how by looking at a chart one could know the sex of the native. Somehow I had not considered this question important. According to the method suggested by Varaha Mihira (vide *Brihat Jataka, Nishekadhyaya,** verse 11), according as the Lagna, the Sun, and the Moon occupy movable, fixed or common signs or Navamsas the sex of the person would be male, female or hermophrodite. Actually this method is to be applied for ascertaining the sex of a child to be born on the basis of the conception chart. In actual practice however I applied it to birth horoscopes and found it useful.

According to a method given to me by Palaniswamy, to whom reference has been made in an earlier Chapter, the *Navamsa-Dwadasamsa* (N-D) one-twelfth division of a Navamsa (16' 40") should be the deciding factor. Here only odd and even signs are considered

---

* ओजर्क्षे पुरुषांशकेषु बलिभिर्लग्नार्कगुर्विन्दुभिः । पुंजन्म प्रवदेत्समां—
शकगतैर्युगेषु तैर्यौषितः ॥ गुर्वकौ विषमे नरं शशिसितोत्यक्रक्षः
युमोस्त्रियं । द्वयंगस्था युधवीक्षणाया यमलौ कुर्वन्ति पक्षे स्यकौ ॥

to indicate the male and female sexes. Suppose the Ascendant is Libra 10° 30'. The Navamsa will be Makara or Capricorn (10° to 13° 20'). The arc covered upto Makara N-D extends till 10° 33' 20'. Since the Lagna is 10° 30", the N-D will be Kumbha or Aquarius, an odd sign, indicating male sex.

In practice, this method has been found to be quite workable as the interval involved is 16' 40" (equivalent in time to approximately 1m. 9s). After I came into contact with *Nadi* literature and after having studied scores of horoscopes in the light of *nadi amsas* I came to the conclusion that a correct identification of the *nadi amsa* could enable one to hit at the correct time of birth, and of course, the sex of the person also. I expect to deal with this subject more extensively in the articles on *Nadi Jyotisha* which I am hoping to serialize in THE ASTROLOGICAL MAGAZINE at an early date.

Problems connected with THE ASTROLOGICAL MAGAZINE and an urgent summons from Rajeswari made me cut short my stay at Bombay and I returned to Bangalore on 15th March after an absence of nearly five weeks.

24

As the year 1938 advanced developments on the European political scene were disturbing and events had been transpiring with the rapidity of lightening. Deadly changes were taking place in Germany. Hitler's shadow was gradually falling on Europe. But his countrymen considered Hitler a patriotic German. He was not only in power but his cherished ambition of acquiring Austria had been fulfilled. The rejuvenation of German youth was in swift progress. Mussolini was anxious to safeguard his empire in Africa, but I had already indicated in THE ASTROLOGICAL MAGAZINE that the Negus, emperor of Abyssinia (Ethiopia) then in exile in London, would get back his empire. The League of Nations was impotent to check Mussolini who conducted his campaign in Abyssinia in a ruthless manner. In March 1938 Austria was militarily occupied by Hitler and Europe was confronted with a programme of aggression and Hitler was encouraged to pursue his designs against Czechoslovakia. The horoscopes of the countries threatened by Hitler were being duly discussed by me in THE ASTROLOGICAL MAGAZINE and predictions made about his future.

The danger to world peace was clear. Would there be a world war? If so, when? European astrologers, especially the British, were vague in their forecasts as their interpretations were highly coloured by subjective factors.

It was at this time that I decided to publish a small book entitled *World Prospects in 1939 and 1940*, to give a kaleidoscopic outline of the future of the world. How should I proceed? Where would I get the data needed to forecast world events? What methods should I employ. These were the thoughts then uppermost in my mind.

I had made an exhaustive study of *Brihat Samhita, Garga Samhita, Argha Jataka* and other collateral works. I was at home with the works of Ptolemy, Placidus Titus, William Lilly, Simmonite and Zadkiel. I had made a series of observations to correlate developments in the histories of India, U.S.A., etc. with the transits of major planets – Saturn, Jupiter, Mars and Rahu in certain zodiacal signs.

I had also experimented with the lunar year charts and the significance of planetary positions in respect of the signs ascending at the capitals of different countries. In fact, the well-known British astrologer E.H. Bailey for whose magazine *British Journal of Astrology* I was an occasional contributor since 1930, was all praise for the *modus operandi* employed by me. I would give pride of place to lunar new year charts, as just before entering Aries, the Sun and the Moon would be in conjunction significantly indicating trends in the year ahead. I would give equal prominence to the horoscopes of the rulers. The fact that I was also practising certain meditational techniques and a key-mantra not only energised my sub-conscious mind but gave me a confidence, which I now feel, was some thing unparalleled.

With all this equipment at my command I felt confident of making forecasts about world affairs.

By September 1938, Chamberlain was in complete control of British foreign policy. But he was dubbed as a man of appeasement. In his meetings with Hitler both on 15th September and 22nd September, 1938, for averting war he practically yielded to Hitler's black-mail. Chamberlain's verbal duels with Hitler had the aim of "Peace at any price".

Dealing with the effects of the solar ingress into Cancer on 16-7-1938, in the July-September 1939 issue of THE ASTROLOGICAL MAGAZINE published in the first week of June, I said, after discussing the astrological rulerships of different countries, "The effects of the ingress will be felt for a period of three months beginning with the day of the entry". The Ascendant has fallen on the cusp of Scorpio thereby extending the influences to Dhanus also which rules Spain, lower Italy, and a part of France. The Ascendant receives no other beneficial aspects. What wonder is there if we anticipate sudden political developments in almost all the countries mentioned above?

Aries rules England. It is not aspected by malefics but it is hemmed in between two of the worst malefics Ketu and Saturn thus causing *papakarthariyoga*. This will undoubtedly cause Britain to adopt a most unsatisfactory foreign policy which would provide much material for comment and criticism. Her powers of judgement will be marred and there will be further entreaties to maintain a closer contact with Italy and extolling of Anglo-Italian friendship as a stabilising factor. Further revolutions are indicated in France. A plot is being hatched by Fascist elements, according to astrological indications, to overthrow democracy. Mussolini certainly views with concern the sudden expansion of the German frontier right upto Italy. It is natural therefore that he is willing to free himself from German entanglement, but the time at which the Anglo-Italian Agreement was signed, does not seem to be propitious for him to get into better relations with England.

"Hitler is at present having a good time. He would have nothing to fear from either Britain or France to check his aggressive designs against Holland and Czechoslovakia, both of which Hitler seems to be bent on absorbing into Germany. Aquarius rules Abyssinia. Jupiter and the Moon are situated there aspected by Venus and Mars. The hands of Ethiopeans will be strengthened and Italy will suffer many reverses. Her authority as guardian of Ethiopia will be questioned and Ethiopia will be able to liberate a portion of the vast empire from the hands of the aggressor. The conjunctions of the Sun and Mars in Cancer increases the driving ambition for world power by dictator countries with actions furthering their private aggrandisement. Saturn's presence in *zeta piscium* will have grave consequences on Portugal, Spain and Egypt giving rise to assassinations and severe political struggles."

Again commenting on the Anglo-Italian Agreement in the same issue, I wrote as follows : "According to press reports, the Anglo-Italian Agreement was signed on 16-4-1938 at 6.30 p.m. at Rome. At this time Libra was rising with the Moon there, Rahu in the second, Jupiter in the fifth. Saturn in the sixth, Mercury, the Sun and Venus in the 7th and Mars and Ketu in the eighth. The very fact that Britain has entered into a pact with Italy hits a crushing blow to the principle of justice. That Great Britain being afraid of the strength of Rome-Berlin axis has played a painfully unworthy part, unworthy of its great traditions is a belief which every right-minded individual seems to share.

"As has been pointed out several times, this kind of degrading show which England has taken upon itself to run, is due to the presence of Saturn in the 12th from Aries ruling England. Lord of the Ascendant Venus is hemmed in between Saturn on one side and Mars and Ketu on the other. The sub-period of Venus in the major period of Jupiter remains with a balance of about 2 years. Venus is lord of the 8th. In the Navamsa Venus is the lord of the 2nd and 7th. In the 8th or house of death, there are Mars and Ketu aspected by Saturn. Therefore it is evident that there are many difficulties on the way preventing the smooth working of the agreement".

"To think that mutual interest and a sense of realism have been the dominating factors in bringing about this agreement is to betray one's ignorance. Planets clearly indicate that it is not compatible with international security for this recognition, sold as part of an imperialist bargain (Sun in the 7th) and that it undermines the foundations upon which international confidence rests. It imperils the security of the British Commonwealth (Saturn being in the 12th from Aries); and it shows lack of the most elementary sense of reality".

"There is no hope of Italy holding its authority over the Ethiopean people triumphantly. The League when it was alive was used by England as a lever for the paltry purpose of winning an election. Now its dead body is to be used for proclaiming the triumph of inequity and the stability of unconscionable prevarication. Planets do not indicate that Italy would adhere to the terms of the agreement".

The new year's chart for *Pramadi* (1939-40) carried adequate destructive elements to disturb the peace of the world. At Berlin 25° Scroprio rose and the lord of Lagna Mars occupying the war-like sign Sagittarius was powerfully aspected by Saturn. The Sun, the Moon and Mercury were all subjected to the powerful aspect of Mars, while the meridian point was aspected by Saturn. Rahu was in the 12th aspected by Jupiter but he was powerful in his constellation. Mars occupied Moola ruled by Ketu. Based upon the above astrological factors plus an intuitional perception, I made the following observations in the WORLD PROSPECTS IN 1939 and 1940 published in August 1938.

"In the scramble for world power, nations have begun to cut each other's throats. Diplomats and politicians have become thoroughly impotent to check the aggressive forces at work. The League of Nations has become a meeting place for treaty-breaking countries. 'What next?' is the question that each puts to the other. Will there be a next war? Will aggression stop? Will Providence take care of countries guilty of the most flagrant violation of international law, international justice and international morality?

"We are constrained to say that the so-called universal peace would be a delusion. Affairs in Europe will rapidly develop launching the world in a state of turmoil and chaos. The conjunction of Saturn and the Sun, Saturn and Mars will precipitate matters ultimately leading to a general conflagration. The attitude of Britain towards Indian aspirations will be unsympathetic... but owing to troubles at home and international developments British statesmen would be obliged to change their outlook towards Indian demands... The conjunction of the Moon, Ketu and Saturn in the 12th from the Ascendant (in the horoscope of the French Republic) augurs an unstable Republic.

1940 is one of the likely periods for any sudden developments in the French political world (France fell in 1940)... Mussolini's horoscope bristles with heavy afflictions and hence Italy cannot hold Abyssinia longer... While European nations begin to cut each other's throats, Abyssinia will have breathing time to compose her differences for freeing from Italian aggression... the Sino-Japanese war will not terminate easily and speedily... Russia will actively support China. The future action of this man (Hitler) will not be mild and peaceful. He uses his mind and personality to enslave fellow countries. An ultimate fall is indicated for the Nazi leader. The nativities of Hitler and Mussolini, full of aggressive elements, will drift Europe towards a dangerous one... Britain will be obliged to compromise under the influence of Saturn. Taking the world situation as a whole one feels from an astrological survey of the horoscopes of different nations that 1940 to 1942 are indeed critical years pointing towards a great clean-up. If statesmen can get through this critical period, then the world would be saved of terrible destruction of humanity."

The English went on appeasing Hitler and a wave of perverse optimism swept across the British scene and Chamberlain the British Prime Minister had thought that he, Hitler and Mussolini had together saved the world from the horrors of war! While statesmen misjudged facts and suffered from delusion Saturn's transit of Aswini was the signal for the outbreak of World War II on the unleashing of German armies on Poland.

Writing in July-September 1938 issue of THE ASTROLOGICAL MAGAZINE on "Europe's Fatal Year", I said: "it is highly significant that the months of August and September 1939 are fatal months for peace in Europe". On September 1, Poland was attacked by Germany. On the same day, a British ultimatum was given to Germany followed by a second and final ultimatum on 3rd September. And the world received with astonishment the declaration of war upon Germans of Britain and France.

The 2000 copies of WORLD PROSPECTS IN 1939 AND 1940 (priced at 8 annas or 50 paise) was sold within 6 months and resulted in several persons in different walks of life contacting me for horoscopic readings. I had not yet ceased to be a professional but considered myself as an adviser and consultant. One such person who met me was a City Magistrate of Bangalore. I shall call him Murthy for obvious reasons. The outbreak of war had upset him so much that he had almost become a nervous wreck and his mental state had even come in the way of his discharging his official duties. He considered himself a stick person and wanted to know whether there would be any relief.

Mars	Venus	Sun Moon Merc.			Saturn		Moon Ketu
Rahu			Jup.				Mars Merc.
	RASI		Lagna Ketu	Sun	NAVAMSA		
		Saturn		Rahu		Jupiter	Venus Lagna

Murthy said: "I want you to please check up the correctness of my horoscope and tell me when my marriage will take place." This was a ticklish question requiring not only astrological ability but also common sense. I was married when I was 18. Murthy was 16 years older than me and naturally he should have got married about my age according to the then prevailing practice. This was of course my reasoning. Would the ruling Dasa and Bhukti say at the age of 18 to 21, warrant the happening of this event? In this case the Dasa of Rahu ruled from August 1906 to August 1924. I said after explaining the chart, "Lords of Lagna and Kalatrakaraka Venus are near each other. This means marriage can take place early in life. Rahu is in the 7th and the lord of the sign occupied by him is exalted. Therefore the marriage can take place in Rahu Dasa." Murthy interjected: "You mean before Rahu Dasa ends in 1924?" I went on: "You should not be hasty. I can specify the exact period. Ketu is in Lagna. Moreover the Sun, lord of Lagna, will be transitting the 7th between 14th February to 14th March. Jupiter will be transitting Aries about the same time. Taking all these into consideration I dare say that your marriage will have taken place in February-March 1977". Surprised, Murthy expressed joy and complimented me for my "hitting the bull's eye".

Saturn was transiting Cancer and aspecting radical Venus. I ignored this phenomenon and took a chance in giving the probable month. He said he was married on 25-2-1917. Analysing the chart further I observed "Rahu should give the results of Saturn. Saturn is exalted in the 3rd. He is the Yogakaraka from Chandra Lagna. But he is in the constellation of Jupiter occupying the 12th house. Until the end of Rahu Dasa in August 1924, there is no chance of your entering service. As soon as Jupiter Dasa started you will have entered Government service. Jupiter though in the 12th is lord of the 5th and occupies the constellation of Saturn, a Yogakaraka, who aspects Venus, lord of the 10th" Murthy was so overwhelmed with joy at meeting with "such a great astrologer" that he burst out: "Yes, I joined Government service in September 1924."

My ego had been satisfied and I was confident that I would be able to identify his illness and advise him. Analysing the various combinations I said: "Your Lagna is Leo. Generally those born in this sign enjoy good health. But because Ketu is in Lagna inviting the aspect of Rahu, due to self-indulgence you are likely to suffer chronic trouble involving the digestive system. Lord of the 5th Jupiter being aspected by Saturn lord of the 6th, there is a tendency to consume rich foods resulting in digestive problems. Ketu's situation in Lagna causes trouble of some kind or the other through allowing the senses, feelings and emotions to sway the reason. The same position makes you consciously or unconsciously take on the conditions of the surroundings. Ketu rules weird feelings and gives a visionary trend of mind. The receptivity to psychic conditions may run to extremes allowing the feelings to get the better of judgement. There is a tendency to excitability, morbid imagination, wandering disposition and strange feelings."

Raising his hand Murthy remarked: "As a magistrate I can study the psychology of criminals. But you have analysed my mental disposition in such a way that I endorse every word of what you have said. But what about my illness?"

I explained to him: "You are now having Rahu's sub-period in Jupiter's major period. This goes under the name of Dasa-chidra.

Transit Saturn is in Pisces aspecting the Moon and Mercury, the planets ruling the mind and emotions. It looks as though your problem is psycho-somatic. You are readily affected both mentally and physically, by the psychic conditions of the environment. This also causes mental confusion, nervousness, fear and apprehension. The outbreak of the war need not worry you, as it does not affect your interests. If you take care of your digestive system and emotions, your problem gets solved."

Murthy was satisfied and was about to take leave of me when I interjected and cautioned him: "Rahu, whose sub-period you are having, is in the 7th house. This threatens domestic troubles, illness to partner and a feeling of sickness. Developments in the household cause you much misery. Astrology being a science of tendencies you should not take my analysis as deterministic. After Saturn's major period commences things will improve and you will get over your troubles." I dismissed Murthy after recommending suitable remedial measures.

25

The latter half of 1938, just about the time of commencement of Saturn's sub-period in the Dasa of Jupiter in my horoscope, saw my gradual emergence into literary activities, though financially things did not improve much. HINDU PREDICTIVE ASTROLOGY and VARSHAPHAL were ready for publication. I had completed GRAHA AND BHEVA BALAS. I started working on VARSHAPHAL and THREE HUNDRED IMPORTANT COMBINATIONS. But I had neither the resources nor any influential backing for getting these books printed.

One day in July 1938, when I was ruminating as to what to do R. Gopalakrishna Rao (Meena) unexpectedly called on me to seek my help for bringing out his book on *Nadi* Astrology. For me it was like a blind man leading another blind man. With a view to convincing me of what he called the "correctness of his *Nadi* System", Meena took up my horoscope and went on analysing the results of Saturn in Jupiter. He said: "Sir, I have found that *Nadi* Astrology as taught to me by my Guru is quite accurate. In your own case, lord of the 2nd Jupiter is situated in the constellation of *yogakaraka* Saturn, so your financial position throughout life will be good. Jupiter, *dhanakaraka*, is also well disposed indicating financial prosperity". I did not want to tell Meena that I was yet to reach a stage when I could say that I was well off. I was also not much interested in his reading of my horoscope. But we met a few times discussing his manuscript on *Nadi* Astrology. Though I expressed frankly where I dissented from his theory, I told him that the book was worth publishing and that I would help him to get a good printer.

Meena, then probably about 45, was a signaller in the Railways drawing about Rs. 80 per month. He had a large family. There was no family planning in those days and poverty never came in the way of begetting, God willing, as many children as possible. He would also earn Rs. 20 to Rs. 30 per month by way of consultations. I found Meena unassuming, frank and friendly, and well-up in his subject. It was then that he explained to me the so-called *subs* dividing a constellation into nine parts in proportion to the ruling periods of the nine planets. The results of planets in different constellations and the timing of the nature of the results of a Dasa lord, on the basis of his situation in particular constellation etc., as given by Meena are worth study and research.

I applied these rules to a number of horoscopes and found the results fairly satisfactory. I arranged with the Modi Printing Press to get the I and II parts of his *Nadi Jyotisha* printed.

In 1958 when K.S. Krishna Murthy met me to explain his so-called 'paddhati', I reminded him that the germ of the theory was revealed by Meena and that mixing up Meena's *Nadi* system, some principles of Hindu Astrology and a few western theories would not constitute a new system! I suggested that he gave due acknowledgement to R. Gopalakrishna Rao, as he was the first to mention the so-called *subs*. Murthy apparently did not like my advice.

Meena's theory was that because Jupiter in my case was in the constellation of Anuradha, ruled by Saturn, Saturn would give the results of Jupiter. But I had my own reservations. The general principles of Astrology were enough to suggest that Saturn, because he is lord of Lagna and *yogakaraka* from Chandra Lagna, should improve my finances.

Banking on what I thought were favourable indications and strengthened to some extent by Meena's forecasts, I was contemplating as to how I could generate funds not only to get over my financial commitments but also to publish my two books and convert the quarterly THE ASTROLOGICAL MAGAZINE into a monthly.

Though aware that I would be coming under *sade sati* for the second time from about April 1939, I felt that this transit would not adversely affect the directional influences because of Saturn being my Lagna lord.

Sir Mirza Ismail was a good friend of our family. Even after grandfather's death he would now and then ask me to meet him and enquire about my welfare. At one such meeting when I told him that bringing out two of my important books could not be done for want of funds, Sir Mirza said: "Look here Venkata Raman, why not you publish a souvenir bearing on Mysore State? We shall give you advertisements and also buy one or two hundred copies." This suggestion appealed to me and I decided to publish the *Indian States Souvenir* dealing with the then important states – Mysore, Hyderabad, Travancore, Indore, Gwalior, Baroda, Jaipur etc. The response from the Governments of these states was encouraging. Sir Mirza gave me all the facilities to collect the material needed to prepare the Souvenir. In the preface to the Souvenir I wrote: "Recent events had revealed to a great extent the importance and complexity of the problem of Indian states. And the Souvenir is designed to supply a real and long-felt want by bringing to the notice of the readers, the progressive conditions obtaining in leading Indian states... I have not followed any order of precedence in the arrangement of states dealt with in this Souvenir. But I have deliberately placed Mysore as the first state because in actual achievements Mysore is easily acknowledged as a Model State."

The publication of the Souvenir resulted in my getting about Rs. 1500 as net profit and I was enabled to bring out the first editions of HINDU PREDICTIVE ASTROLOGY and VARSHAPHAL and made THE ASTROLOGICAL MAGAZINE a monthly from January 1940. Eversince then the Magazine continues to be published regularly and without a break, thanks to the encouragement and kindness of my readers.

Reverting to my forecasts about world affairs, Hitler's onslaughts were continuing unchecked. Poland was subjugated in a few weeks. Though for a time both France and England remained impassive, the transition of these two countries from peace to war was quick, thanks to the association of Ketu and Saturn in Aries, the sign ruling England. When England declared war, Libra was rising, the 7th house being considerably afflicted by all the malefics. When France declared war, Sagittarius was rising with Mars in the 2nd aspecting the 8th or house of destruction. How my own astrological thinking was shaping in the matter of this war, and how I anticipated *fairly accurately* the developments in Europe following the declaration of the war will become evident to any one who goes through carefully my editorials in those years.

Jup.	Sat. Moon Ketu			Lagna	Merc.		Sat. Moon
							Ketu
	RASI		Sun Merc. Venus	Rahu Mars	NAVAMSA		
Mars							
		Lagna Rahu			Jupiter		Sun Venus

There were unfounded rumours that the Allies might sign an armistice with Hitler. I wrote in the January 1940 issue of THE ASTROLOGICAL MAGAZINE: "It seems to be astrologically advisable that so long as Saturn continues to be debilitated in Aries, the Allies sign, no armistic whatsoever as it may simply meet with the same fate that the Munich agreement did."

Within hardly two months after the declaration of war by Britain and France, Molotov denounced the Non-Aggression Pact between Finland and Russia, and Russia invaded Finland on 30th November 1939 at about 9.15 a.m. Hardly a couple of months earlier the Russian Dictator Stalin had declared, "we stand for peaceful, close and friendly relations with all the neighbouring countries, which have common frontiers with the U.S.S.R. We stand for the support of nations which are the victims of aggression and are fighting for the independence of their country." Yet Stalin committed the act of unabated aggression on a small and peaceful neighbour. This shows the utter disregard nations have for moral values; and this also showed that Russia had

Jup.	Sat. Ketu		Moon	Lagna		Sat. Ketu	Moon Venus
Mars				Mars			
		RASI				NAVAMSA	
Venus	Sun Lagna	Rahu			Sun Rahu	Merc.	Jup.

proved that it was as imperialistic and covetuous as any of the Big Powers which it frequently denounced.

Editorially dealing with the "Destiny of Finland" in the February 1940 issue of the A.M. I observed: "The presence of the Sun in the ascendant, Mars in the 4th, and Saturn and Ketu in the 6th and the ascendant being aspected by Jupiter are all factors favourable to Russia, Jupiter, the most powerful planet in the chart is about 5 signs away from the ascendant suggesting that this war would continue for some more time. The Finnish resistance, admirable as it is, will show signs of weakness and collapse. Planets are in a frowning mood and sonner or later almost all nations of Europe will become involved in the war that is now going on. Finland may ultimately win back her independence."

There were often conflicts in my mind between the astrological factors and the common-sense factors, especially because I was cautioned by some well-meaning friends that forecasts pertaining to the war might land me in trouble and invite action against me according to *Defence of India Rules.* This warning, given in all good intention, made me for a time, somewhat uneasy whether I should at all air my forecasts in the A.M. boldly, forecasts which might be considered adverse by the Allies.

I met the Chief Secretary to the Government of Mysore, B.T. Kesava Iyengar, who was well-known to me and who had sought my astrological advice about his daughter's marriage. He sent word to the Law Secretary one Narayana Rao, who had also consulted me in regard to his service some months earlier.

After some mutual discussion – the Inspector General of Police Sundar Rao had also joined us – Narayana Rao said: "Look here Mr. Raman, you base your predictions on astrological factors. You can write what the chart warrants, and not to please the authorities. The British government cannot initiate any action against you without the consent of the State government. But see that you avoid sensation-mongering language."

This assurance from the Law Secretary emboldened me to interpret horoscopes bearing on the war, without any reservation.

My first observation in the January 1940 issue of THE ASTROLOGICAL MAGAZINE on the outcome of the war were no doubt fairly accurate but the timing of the termination was somewhat vague. I had said: "Suffice it to say that till at least Saturn emerges out of his fall the war may not end. Hitler's own horoscope points to his downfall. The aggressive forces at work will be on the increase and destruction of life will be colossal indeed. The affliction of Mercury in Hitler's horoscope will pull him down as speedily as he rose to power."

Continuing the analysis of the war chart, I had said: "The Germans may launch an offensive on the Western Front when Mars conjoins Saturn in Aries in the course of the next few months". The conjunction took place on 12th February 1940. It was clear that at the beginning of 1940, Hitler had a detailed plan for the invasion of Belgium, Holland and France. Internal politics in France was confused. It was said that in reaction to growing communism, important elements in

France had swung towards Fascism lending a ear to Goebbel's propaganda. Hitler's assault on Norway followed on the heels of this sinister conjunction. Ketu was also close by. What havoc such malefic combinations can play in shattering peace and in causing great historical events become too obvious by a close study of the various vicissitudes of the second world war.

It will be seen that early in May 1940, all the German forces sprang towards France across the frontiers of Belgium and Holland. And by 15th May France was defeated. About this period Mars was in Gemini aspecting Rahu in Virgo and aspected by Saturn from Aries. The situation of Jupiter in Aries had a feeble effect in the sense the Allies had realised their weaknesses. The fall of France in 1940 as per the forecasts given in my WORLD PROSPECTS IN 1939-40, to which reference has been made earlier, brought me a number of letters of appreciation and I was being often referred to as a "great astrologer", a compliment which I liked then, but which I feel now, was somewhat unmerited.

Kasturi Srinivasan, proprietor of THE HINDU was not only a good friend but a well wisher of mine. He took much interest in my work and predictions. He used to visit Bangalore at least once a week and would invariably meet me. He was also seeking now and then my astrological counsel in his family matters. In one such meeting Srinivasan said: "Your predictions about the war and especially the developments in France have come to the notice of the British Resident here. Italy and Germany are at the throats of the Allies. The whole of Europe is open to Hitler's power. And Japan is glowering in the East. Naturally the Resident must be anxious about the future of the war and England. he desires to meet you. If you have no objection I shall take you to him." I thought for a while and replied: "Sir, it is not so easy to indicate the final outcome of the war. I have to study the horoscopes of the Monarchs who had ruled England and the countries at war with her in the past. In particular I need the horoscopes of Queen Elizabeth I, Charles II of Spain, George III of England and Napolean Bonaparte". Srinivasan nodded his head as if he agreed with me and said, "Most probably the birth data of these monarchs may be available at the British Museum, London. I shall speak to the Resident and see whether they can be secured".

I was not very particular to meet the Resident. I told Srinivasan that after the required details were obtained I would study the horoscopes and give my findings. Three months later, the great Editor was able to secure the birth details required by me and I started working on them.

In those days the role of many British and some American astrologers was somewhat suspect. They started with the assumption that there was nothing that was not known to them in Astrology. Most English astrologers were of the view that the war would not come in 1939. R.H. Naylor, an English astrologer, well known for popular forecasts in the press, had assured me before the war started that Britain would not be engaged in a major conflict in 1939. The following is reproduced from my editorial article in the March 1940 issue of THE ASTROLOGICAL MAGAZINE.

"The very same worthy now comes before the public with the prediction that a 'determined thrust by other powers (Russia in particular) towards India' is indicated. He expects the thrust to be made through Mongolia and not through Afghanistan. He further expects that Germany and Japan will also aim at the penetration of India. The Russian and Japanese threats are much more immediate' thus concludes the english astrologer. He asserts that 'India will never be in a position to defend herself but always be controlled and exploited by stronger nations. Hence as an Englishman his advice to India is, we presume, to remain a subject nation. The conclusions of this astrologer, which are of course coloured by feelings of political superiority deserve our careful attention.

"History tells us that no empire or nation can perpetually exist or be powerful. Change is the Law of nature. It is only a matter of Time. When creative forces are issued by planets, empires are founded; When destructive forces operate, they are destroyed. The same rule applies to Russia also. Let us consider the astrological possibility of Russia invading India. Russia is supposed to be ruled by Taurus and Aquarius. India is ruled by Virgo. Saturn at present is in Aries, the 8th from

Virgo. But the lord of Russia's **ruling sign** Saturn is an intimate friend of Mercury, lord of Virgo, ruling India. At the time Russia invaded Finland Scorpio was rising with its lord Mars aspecting India (Kanya). Since Mars also happens to be the lord of the 6th or house of enemies, diseases and debts, any schemes by Stalin to invade India will meet with failure and such steps if taken by Stalin are bound to bring disaster to Russia. Jupiter aspecting India's sign at the commencement of the Anglo-German War spares this country the evils of modern warfare. The real ambition of Stalin as revealed by planets are indeed interesting and we shall study them in our future issues. We may assure the Indian public that there is no likelihood of Russia invading India according to astrological considerations.

"Of course Russia continues to steal the limelight making important gains at the expense of other countries. The Jupiter-Saturn conjunction to occur in August of this year will have great repercussions not only on Russia but on almost every country, pointing to a climax of violence which will create great changes in the political future of Europe."

Though my public activities had started moving favourably I could not give much attention to the Magazine work due to some personal matters. My eldest son **Surya Prakash** and daughter Saroja had severe attacks of whooping-cough. **My third issue** (Suryanarain Rao) born early in May 1940 was a sickly child and suffered for nearby 9, months from what was locally called *pakshiroga*. He had to be tended very carefully as even a slight pressure on his body would result in the peeling off of the skin. The health of all these three children caused me and Rajeswari much anxiety and demanded full-time attention.

In October 1940, we shifted to a newly constructed house in New Extension, Seshadripuram, on a monthly rent of Rs. 25/-. It was situated in an isolated place; it had a hall, two bed rooms, dining, kitchen and a small compound. It was my office-cum-residence. A typist was employed on Rs. 40 per month. Today the prices have gone up by 75 times. These personal matters, though not of astrological interest, would give the reader an idea of the golden age prevailing under the rule of the Maharaja when the rulers were concerned with the welfare of the people, when life and property were secure and not threatened by dacoits and goondas, unlike today when rulers styling themselves as people's representatives and in the name of democracy are interested in helping themselves and exposing the public to all kinds of dangers.

My quest for *nadigranthas* continued unabated. It was, I think on 4th April 1940, that a distant relative of mine introduced me to one Srinivasacharya, the possessor of *Budha Nadi*. I had a number of sittings with him. Sreenivasacharya claimed infallibility for his *Nadi* but I had my own reservations. *Budha Nadi* had a peculiar method of interpretation.

26

My involvement in Mundane Astrology became deeper as developments in the European war took different turns. Though I had been assured by the Law Secretary to the Government of Mysore that I could publish my predictions without fear, yet there were certain problems I had to contend with, viz., frequent visits to my place of military personnel, Indian and British, and their veiled threats that publication of predictions not favourable to the Allies could land me in trouble. This made me uneasy, though the same officials would also seek my astrological advice about their own future.

The collapse of France and Hitler's agreement with Stalin and Mussolini's declaration of war on England also put me on guard that forecasts bearing on the war should be made with a greater sense of responsibility.

About June 1940, the heavens showed a strange array of planetary situations — Saturn from Aries aspecting Mars in Gemini and Mars aspecting Rahu in Virgo. Except Rahu all the planets were arraigned from Pisces to Gemini. This was the time when Germany, fresh with victory in France, was gathering for another attack. Italy was seeking the destruction of the British forces in the Meditarranean and Japan had started giving pinpricks to the British. Russia was bound to Germany by a war pact. This situation seemed to have alarmed even the United States.

It was at this time that I made a careful study of the horoscope of the German National Socialist State which came into existence on January 30, 1933 at 10 a.m. at Berlin ushering Hitler into power. It will be seen that the Nazis got into power through the betrayed of the German Republic by President Hinderberg. Hitler and Goebbles seemed able to make the isolated Germans believe anything they wished.

I found the chart of the National Socialist State intriguing. The Lagna and the Moon being aspected by the lord Jupiter could be a strong point but the most important factor viz., both the Lagna and the Moon being aspected in addition by Mars and Saturn introduced a destructive element revealing the psychological structure of the persons at the helm of affairs, viz., Hitler. There was plenty of nationalism in the world before Hitler and Mussolini, but deification of the State began in Germany, the Dictator claiming that he alone represented the nation, not indeed in its millions of *epheral* individuals, but in imminent and permanent will. My analysis of this chart was somewhat on the following lines: "The 10th house is occupied by Venus, lord of the 3rd and 8th, and the 10th lord is aspected by an afflicted Moon. Therefore Hitler's activities would find expression in destructive channels." This inference was further strengthened by his birth horoscope where Mars dominated the 7th house signifying aggressive designs and actions. The affliction of the 6th house by the situation of Mars and Ketu indicated not only peculiar psychological fixation of the rulers but also danger and disgrace for them.

Ascdt. Moon				Ascdt. Rahu	Mercury	Saturn	Sun
Rahu		RASI			NAVAMSA		
Sun Merc. Sat.			Ketu Mars	Jup.			
Venus			Jup.	Mars Venus		Moon	Ketu

The purpose of Hitler's activities was to break the League of Nations, isolate France and Britain, foment insurrection in the surrounding states and organise anti-semetic bands. I reflected, "Venus lord of the 3rd and 8th ruling the 'length of life' no doubt occupies a Kendra, which is not quite recommended. But the Lagna and the Moon are blemished" and I felt that Hitler would not continue in power for long. I figured out that Mercury as lord of the 7th in association with two malefics, though placed in the 11th, could be a *maraka* in his Dasa. Juxtaposing this chart with Hitler's horoscope and other connected charts bearing on the war, I concluded that Hitler's state might collapse in the Sun's sub-period.

What was most depressing and causing terrible anxiety to the Allies was Hitler's agreement with Stalin just before Hitler started his aggressive compaigns.

In one of his meetings with me in the latter half of 1940, Kasturi Srinivasan wanted me to examine carefully the future of the Russo-German pact and whether Russia would join Germany in mounting a powerful assault on England. While the military implications of such a development could not be discernible to a lay person like me, I nevertheless took up the matter seriously. Though I had read a lot about European history and tried to understand the forces which shaped

Jup.	Ketu Saturn (R)					Sun Venus Moon	
	RASI		Merc. Ascdt.		**NAVAMSA**		Ketu
Mars			Sun Venus	Merc. Rahu Mars			
Moon		Rahu			Jup.	Sat.	

history – and my understanding had been mainly derived from a careful study of Gibbon's *Roman Empire* and Alison's *French Revolution*. My knowledge of communism was almost nil. Of course some of the newspapers described communism as the devil incarnate! So I thought within myself that after all the difference between Nazism and Communism was very thin. Both held that the state was everything and the individual was subordinate to the state and hence deterimental to religion and spiritual values. Both the systems believed in the abolition of individual rights and spreading doctrines of atheistic materialism.

Analysing the chart of the Agreement I told the exteemed Srinivasan, "At the time the treaty was signed a formidable array of afflictions is focussed on the 10th house from the rising sign. Saturn and Ketu are in the 10th aspected by exalted Mars in the 7th. Jupiter's aspect on the Ascendant suggests that both Russia and Germany may co-operate with each other to defeat the British but at the same time each will do all it can to weaken the power of the other." Commenting on this subject in the May and August 1940 issue of THE ASTROLOGICAL MAGAZINE, I had said: "The significance of the Russo-German Pact is being overestimated by most people who will place the wrong values upon it. In due course it will prove valueless. The Russo-German agreement is not likely to last long. Stalin is under 7 1/2 years Saturn influence and before Saturn leaves Aries the Russo-German Agreement will have been practically dead." It will be noted that Saturn entered Taurus on 7th June 1941 and Germany declared war on Russia on 22-6-1941.

The fulfilment of this prediction tempted me to make the following observations in the August 1941 issue of THE ASTROLOGICAL MAGAZINE: "The above prediction was not made by us without adequate astrological reasons. No other art or science in the world could have dared or claimed to anticipate such a contingency at the time the pact between Russia and Germany was signed in 1939. Astrology is therefore the most sublime of all sciences". Of course in these remarks there was a streak of egoism.

In Mundane Astrology, the time at which a pact is signed is highly significant. The data collected by me during the past half a century bearing on different countries, when different types of political changes and establishment of different systems of government occurred, will be gradually revealed in these pages and in a book on Mundane Astrology, now under preparation.

How rulers and political leaders eat their own words and often treat important treaties as scraps of paper can be of great consequence to students of Astrology interested in predicting political events.

Reverting to my war predictions, the following observation extracted from the August 1941 issue of THE ASTROLOGICAL MAGAZINE will be found to be significant:

I had said: "Speaking on September 1, 1939 in the Reichsteg Her Hitler declared 'I am particularly happy to be able to tell you of one event. Germany and Russia have resolved to conclude a pact which *rules for ever* (italics mine) any use of violence between us. Astrology said that this eternal (?) pact of friendship would be torn into pieces within two years. But still the so-called scientists will not admit the claim of Astrology to the rank of a science. They may go a step further and say that Astrology is all quackery and humbug and that its principles have been exploded. Such vituperation if thrown at Astrology, does not give any colour of reason or argument and we leave our numerous learned readers to draw their own inference after they peruse our logic and marshalling of facts.

"Why did Hitler invade Russia? To save Europe and the world from the evils of Bolshevism? Realist that Hitler always is, the catalogue of 'reasons' he has given for this atrocious invasion cannot fool any sensible man to take Hitler at his word. It is becoming increasingly clear that Hitler wants to dominate the world. No nation has ever said it began war for personal aggradisement. The Nazis want the world to believe that in attacking Russia they are only fighting communism. German propaganda had even gone to the extent of describing the war against the Soviets as a crusade against Bolshevism. Hitler has put forward this canard to comoulfage his real objective. He thought that in giving a pious objective to his new aggression he could keep Britain and America off the scent. But both these countries saw through

the German game with the result the Anglo-Russian alliance has been
signed and that America has promised all aid to Russia.

"Every nation which enters into war with its neighbours cooks
up strange logic in its favour, flourishes it with saintly phraseology,
glosses it with the velvet of political webs and charges the other with
breach of promise, aggression, tyranny, insult etc.

The world has seen enough of this tom-foolery and statesmen are
not ignorant of these expressions of diplomatic codes. These facts are
too glaring to escape the notice of even the casual observers of human
psychology. World is what it had been and the world will continue to
be what it is now. Germany is no exception. Hitler's 'treacherous
attack' on the Soviet Union is yet another instance of his insatiable
thirst for world mastery and world domination. At the time Germany
declared war on Russia the following were the planetary positions.

Ketu Mars		Saturn Ascdt. Moon Jupiter	Sun Merc. Venus
	RASI		
			Rahu

"An examination of this chart suggests that Hitler commenced his
attack at a time declared auspicious by his astrologers. Lord of Lagna
is in the 2nd with lords of the 5th and 4th. In Lagna itself Jupiter is
present with the Moon. In the 11th are posited Ketu and Mars.
Astrologically these planetary positions seem to be good for the
invader. But Hitler cannot be successful in defeating Russia according

to his *blitzkrieg* methods just because Stalin has also a powerful horoscope.

"The potential of each horoscope is capable of being increased by bringing into contact with it another powerful horoscope by way of marriage, partnership or alliance. Thus it happens that individuals are lifted in position and affluence through their association with persons whose horoscopes are in sympathy with theirs. Therefore it follows that on account of the Anglo-Russian alliance, the horoscope of Stalin gets added strength. In the Chart given above, as the Lagna is a fixed sign and as Mars aspects Lagna lord, the fight would be a tough one and both sides are likely to suffer heavy losses. Till November 1941 Stalin will be having the sub-period of Venus in the major period of the Moon. The major and sub lords are in the 2nd and 12th from each other. This is a bad combination...

"In the coming years there will be economic troubles and misunderstandings. Russia will present a stiff resistance to the invader. The Red army will gain in prestige and power. We have several times examined the horoscopes of Hitler and the third Reich. Russia is governed by Aquarius, Saturn is transitting Taurus the 4th sign which, in astrological language goes under the name of *Ardhashtama*. This is bad. This blemish is moderated just because Saturn happens to be lord of Russia's ruling sign. Though directional influences are not quite favourable till November 1941, yet because Saturn and Jupiter are transitting the third from Stalin's Janma Rasi, the German expectation that Russia would be 'liquidated' soon cannot be fulfilled. Added to this, however, Russia's good fortunes have become fortified by the Anglo-Russian alliance. Owing to unfavourable directional influences there may be surprises in store for the world but the ultimate outcome of the struggle will be favourable to the Allies. According to Gochara, Saturn and Jupiter are in the 3rd from Stalin's radical Moon. This is favourable and helps Stalin to present an united front to the invader.

There are several conjunctions occurring in 1942. Their influences should be carefully watched. Russia will also collaborate with Britain in peace negotiations. Though planetary influences are somewhat unfavourable, yet with the help the U.S.A. and Britain have readily offered to Russia, it is hoped that Russia will throw back the invader and rid the world of Nazi tyranny. Planets only indicate and they do not compel. Astrology expects man to put forth his best efforts to counteract the evil indications so that success may be ensured. There are peculiar forces at work affecting Germany".

It will be interesting to note that in June 1932 in the British press, Britain's Astronomer-Royal Dr. Harold Spencer Jones had written an article "challenging" astrologers to say in advance "What was going to happen" when "on 11th May 1941, Mercury will be in conjunction with Venus, Saturn and Uranus; Venus will be in conjunction with Jupiter and Uranus; it will be full Moon. Saturn will be in conjunction with Venus and Mercury and Jupiter will be in conjunction with Uranus a few days previously. Mercury, Venus, Jupiter, Saturn and Uranus will all be close to the Sun."

Like many astronomers of today his attitude towards Astrology was unscientific. Ignoring Uranus and Neptune which do not come within the purview of Hindu Astrology, the Sun and Saturn and Mercury, Jupiter and Venus were in conjunction respectively in Aries (ruling England) and Taurus; Rahu placed in Virgo and the combination in Taurus was subject to the powerful aspect of Mars from Aquarius. There was also the *parivartana* (interchange) between Mars and Saturn. The British astrologers referred to the planetary situations mentioned by the astronomer as "the constellation of the heavens the like of which the world has not seen very often." Of course, my approach based on the Nirayana zodiac enabled me to forecast the developments in Europe and the attack of Germany on Russia. It was evident that in about a month's time from the date of this configuration, the German aggression would become a fact. On 27th May the President of U.S.A. declared a state of emergency and American troops occupied Iceland.

The nearness of Saturn and Jupiter in Taurus plus the mutual aspects of Mars, Rahu and Ketu, coinciding with Hitler's invasion of Russia suddenly altered the values and relationships of the war. The Russians were taken by surprise and initial disaster fell upon them but the powerful horoscope of Stalin and the malefic directions in the chart of Hitler enabled the Russians to face the new struggle with confidence. While western astrologers speculated about the outcome, Indian Astrology indicated that Hitler would not succeed in his attempts to subjugate Russia.

27

Nadi Astrology is a unique system of horoscopic inter-pretation but most *Nadigranthas* available in the market are unreliable so far as the future predictions are concerned. The basis of Nadi Astrology was revealed to me by a Nadi itself in 1952-53 and I shall elaborate on this at the appropriate time.

Some of the Nadis are too vague. Under cover of Astrology they claim to deal with the future while in reality, no astrological discussion is found. The emphasis is more on past births which cannot be verified. The same individual gets different details from different Nadis, so that at best they could be treated as of only academic interest. To enable my readers to have an idea of the approach of the various Nadis, I have no option but to refer to the delineations given by them in respect of my own horoscope.

According to its owner Srinivasachari, the approach of Budha Nadi which is the subject matter of this chapter, has a certain distinctiveness of its own. My contact with him continued till about 1958-59 when he was leading a miserable life in a choultry at Mysore. When I first met him in 1936, he was overbearing and dismissed me as of no consequence. He even refused to tell me anything about my horoscope. But life's experiences, pleasant and unpleasant, have their own lessons to teach. If an arrogant person in dizzy heights is thrown into the abyss he may realise the transitory nature of name, fame, position, wealth and influence and understand that wisdom consists in developing from the beginning humility, love and sympathy for the poor and those in distress. By 1958, Srinivasachari had become completely mellowed and he was the personification of humility, friendliness and helpful attitude.

From the series of meetings I had with him from 1936 onwards I gathered the following information about Nadis. Nadi astrologers in general are in distress mentally and financially in the closing periods of their lives. One should never own a Nadi as it would only spell disaster for him and his family. He never revealed why he had come to such a conclusion. He had married three times. Excepting the last wife with whom he was then living, the first two wives died under tragic circumstances. He felt that many of the popular Nadis were based on *kshudra mantras* and unless the ordained practices were correctly followed the guiding spirit would curse the possessor of the Nadi! He cited the example of an astrologer by name Narayana Sastry who hailed from Chikmagalur. Sastry was rigorously practising a certain *kshudra mantra* to get 'control' over the Deity associated with Saturn. If he had succeeded in this, he would have been able to correctly say the past and foretell the future accurately upto one year from the date of consultation, just on the basis of a Rasi chart. In the last stage of his penance, when Sastry was reciting the *mantra*, standing knee-deep in the village tank, he saw a beautiful young woman who came there to wash clothes. Her charming looks disturbed him and his attention was so diverted that he could no longer concentrate on the image of the Deity in his mind. Soon after, Sastry lost his power of speech and the use of a leg due to paralysis, although he never obtained the boon of prophecy for which he had worked so hard.

Of course, I cannot vouchasafe for the authenticity of this story, but could not also disbelieve Srinivasachari who in the last years of his life would not lie. He was of the firm opinion that the propitiated Devata controlling the Nadi would harm the reader.

The reading given to me was in fits and starts. A description of the planetary positions was followed by some deaths, not quite relevant to the chart, but nevertheless containing interesting information.

According to Srinivasachari, "the horoscope has *Sanyasa Yoga* because lord of Lagna and the 12th viz., Saturn is in *neechamsa*. This is due to a *sapa* (curse) current in the native's family for the past 17 generations. This will disappear in the native's 47th year." The nature of the curse is narrated thus: "Seventeen generations ago the native when aged 16, wanted to serve a Guru. He created a KASHTA on the order of the Guru. Without knowing that the Guru's wife was sitting there, he dropped the bundle on the lady injuring her head. She was in agony for one *muhurta*. Even though she interceded and pleaded with the Guru not to harm the native, the Guru cursed him. And the effect of this curse will be lifted now."

I found that the delineation was marked by several contradictions. My Ascendant was given as Poorvabhadra 2 and the Navamsa Lagna as Kumbha, a mathematical absurdity. When I questioned the contradiction, the Nadi reader took another leaf and exclaimed: "These calculations are according to Agastya. However, the exact position of Lagna 'as revised' is Satabhisha 3".

This was immediately followed by information not bearing on the chart by saying "that this *grantha* was written 2400 years ago by a disciple of Agastya, 48th in succession, on the basis of Tatwasastra. The total number of Tatwas is 108. The 46th refers to *rasayana sastra* (chemistry?) and the 96th to Vedanta. Budha Nadi authors knew all the Tatwas while Varahamihra wrote his book without a knowledge of the Tatwas. In *Bhrigu Samhita* 2646 horoscopes are given with permutations and combinations. In Budha Nadi, for each Rasi 1800 horoscopes are given."

Then there were again some remarks, which were not quite relevant. "Kaliyuga 5001 corresponding to Sarvari — actually this will be Vikari, 1899 A.D. — saw a dispute among Saurashtrian Brahmins. They divided themselves into three sects and the reader of this Nadi belongs to one such sect. Saurashtra belongs to Cancer."

The Nadi continued: "The native in his previous lives completed study of the 96th Tatwa – Vedanta. When he was studying the 45th there was obstruction. In his past life he was taught only 48th and not the 46th and 47th because of his birth is an *apasavya* star, viz., Mrigasira 1. When the 48th was about to be taught the native died by snake-bite. Because the serpent (Rahu) is in Guru's house (in his horoscope), Agastya could not save him." These details were all in Tamil poetry, sonorous to listen but sometimes contradictory and not bearing on the horoscope.

Now begins what purports to be the reading. The Nadi fixed the time of my birth as ghatis 34, vighati 1 and para 3 stating that "11 3/4 ghatis have passed in Mrigasira". the duration of Mrigasira was given as gh. 57.8 and the balance of Mars Dasa as years 5-7-17 1/2. According to this 'Nadi' "as Mercury is in the 6th – Mercury is actually in the 7th – the longevity stops with Mercury lord of the 8th. His longevity will be 74 years 7 months and 16 1/2 days.

According to this Nadi I should have died by 24th March 1987!!

"In Navamsa Mars aspects the 4th, 2nd and 3rd and is in the 8th. Therefore the native did not die in Mars Dasa." Some of the astrological reasoning was interesting: "Jupiter lord of the 2nd and 11th is in the 10th and aspects the 2nd. If he is in the 1st Amsa, his mother shall be a widow. The Lagna is the 95th pada." At this stage Goddess Parvati is said to intercede and say: "Then we should take Mrigasira 1. This is the 17th pada. The 63rd from this is *Kalagnana*. If there were a planet in *Kalagnana*, he would have died after marriage. As lords of the 12th and the 6th are in one sign, the former behind the latter and as there is no mutual aspect between them in the Navamsa, the native has *purnayus* or full term of age. The Nadi suggests that a planet in the 84th pada from Saturn's position and 97th pada from the Moon gives Balarishta. "Venus is lord of the 4th. He is in Makha 3, i.e., the 39th pada. The 83rd from this is Vainasika. Saturn is in Rohini 1. When Saturn enters Rohini 2, the mother dies. The native's point of death (*Ayus*) is in Hasta 2. When marka planets transit this point the person dies".

Then there are several statements followed by a reference to grandfather's death. "When Saturn enters Uttarabhadra 4, grandfather dies on a Friday. Before the native completes Jupiter in Jupiter every property will have been lost and the grandfather will not have a single pie to give. The native will have all the children born to him before he completes 42 years of age."

The mode of directions employed appears to be based on the transits of major planets in certain *padas* as reckoned from the *padas* in which the planets and the Lagna are situated.

The wife will pass away in his 57th year and at this age he gets Brahmacharya. My wife, now 73, is quite hale and healthy.

Then there is a general delineation of the Bhavas employing the standard astrological combinations often spiced with humorous observations. For instance "Lords of 5 and 8 and 9th in the 7th, lord of 8 *vakra*, lord of 7 in the 12th from the 7th must make some one in the family blind. Who could it be? Though Sun is in the 6th, he is aspected by Jupiter, but his beneficence is lost. Why? Because he is in the 5th from Rahu who caught hold of the native's father."

There is in abrupt reference to *Mahabharata*. "Bhima's wives are Hidambi and Draupadi, Arjuna had Subhadra and Draupadi, Draupadi dies. Bheema and Arjuna mourn. But Hidambi and Subhadra are alive. All the Pandava brothers have Kalatradosha. Abhimanyu did not have it. Ghatotgaja died a *Brahmachari*. On account of Mercury's retrogression and association with lords of 3rd, 10th, 4th and 9th, the native's grandfather, father and the unless had two marriages. But the native will have only one. The native's father will have lost his sight."

According to the Nadi, the 84th pada from Saturn's position is significant in the sense planets transiting it give adverse effects befitting their *karakatwas* or ownerships. Thus Mars transiting this point may produce very bad results so far as brothers are concerned. The reading continues: "Any planet in the 97th pada from the Moon gives Balarishta. Goddess Parvati says, Venus being lord of 4 and 9 (indicating father) is in Moola 3-39th pada. The 63rd from this is Uttarabhadra 2. There are no malefics here. Hence no *dosha* for wife." The Nadi proceeds "Astrologers do not know where Venus is strong. Taurus or Libra. According to me (Agastya) he is more powerful in Libra." What is the significance of Rahu's transit of the radical point of Jupiter? The sage says "When Rahu, after his Dasa, transits for the first time the exact point of Jupiter's situation he gives much gain of a permanent nature." Actually no gain had been caused under this planetary set-up. On the contrary, I was passing through a very disturbing phase of my life.

"The native faces a serious danger in his 48th year. He will suffer for 31 days from excruciating pain in his right knee. This will be a serious *ganda* and he will escape it."

The general description of the future year-wise was vague and has not proved quite correct. But the delineation about the birth of children upto the year of consultation was fairly accurate. There is again a jump giving some information not bearing on the chart. The Nadi explains: "There are 84 Rishis. The 6th is Kasyapa. The 72nd is Agastya. He has 48 pupils. The last one named Seshagireesa is the compiler of Budha Nadi. He has made a thorough study of *Tatwa sutras.*"

The Nadi says, "Though by *yugadharma* the native has learnt *hoona bhasha* (English?) he is not ambitious. He does not want to earn money by foul means. Because Jupiter is in the 10th *karmasthana*, he will never become evil-minded. Before Jupiter comes to his birth position for the 4th time, he will realise his mission in life and gets the grace of Agastya.

"Agastya's writings will reach him within 6 days from the day of Jupiter's return to his radical position. He should practice the instructions given in the writings for 270 days. On the 273rd day, after the native completes repeating of the special mantra for 7200 times, another disciple of Agastya meets him and clarifies all doubts. By this time he gets a special yoga, mental poise and some auspicious indications. Supplementing this yoga, the yoga caused by Mars-Venus combination in the 7th house will begin to manifest when his age is 49 years 6 months and 18 days. His proficiency in *Kalagnana Sastra* becomes widely known and admired after his age is 50 years. This will enable him to lecture uninterruptedly for 3600 days. He will get a palm-leaf manuscript which contains the 46th and 47th kalas. After his death he will go to *Rishimandala.*"

The above delineation while quite interesting does not throw any astrological light on the future or elaborate any astrological principles. From the readings given to others by Srinivasachari, I could gather that Budha Nadi appears to hold Jupiter's cycle, especially he 4th round, as very important. In my case Jupiter entered his radical position (in his 4th cycle) on 6th November 1959, when I had entered my 48th year. The only event of importance was my first trip to Europe and America. I delivered a series of lectures, made the Americans take real interest in Hindu Astrology and the Nirayana System and impressed on them the transitoriness of western culture and the need for appreciating ancient India's life-values. I must say that my trip to the West was remarkable in its own say, as before me, no astrologer from India had presented the case for Hindu Astrology. This apart, no Agastya disciple met me, no manuscript reached me except that eversince my first trip to the West, I embarked upon a long programme of lectures in different parts of India and the world. For details about my work in the West reference may be made to my book HINDU ASTROLOGY AND THE WEST.

Then there was an abrupt switch-over to my wife's horoscope. "The wife has *putradosha* because Ketu is in the 5th. But the *dosha* is neutralised because Saturn is posited in Makha 1, ruled by Ketu and aspecting Ketu. As Ketu is the 9th planet, the lady will give birth to 9 issues, out of which 7 may survive! All the children will be born before her 37th year. As Saturn lord of the 2nd is in the 12th (from the 9th), in an inimical place, and in the 5th from the 4th and as the native was born in Rahu Dasa and Rahu is in conjunction with Mars and as Mandi is in the 12th, the native will be denied happiness from parents as soon as Saturn Dasa commences. As Mercury as lord of the 6th is in the 10th, the native suffers from inflammation of *vayu* till the end of Saturn Dasa. There will be *bhagyavriddhi* (increase of fortune) during Saturn's Dasa."

Upto this point, the delineation is fairly accurate. Then there is a reference to the children's prospects, etc. But they are all off the mark and are not relevant.

Gathering some gems here and there in Budha Nadi, it occurs to me that the emphasis laid on the transits of major planets in certain *Nakshatra padas,* Vainasika, Kalagnana, etc., merit further study and research.

28

My experiments in Mundane Astrology kept pace with the progress of the second world war. To assist me in my researches, I engaged a pandit, well-versed in Sanskrit and Astrology, and a statistician-cum-astronomer who could analyse the collected data properly. My contacts with the British and American astrologers enabled me to secure important data bearing on the war.

Though grandfather had made a number of astounding forecasts-the most astounding being his prediction made in the March 1914 issue of THE ASTROLOGICAL MAGAZINE, that the European War would break out in March 1914 due to the assassination of a prince, his approach to Mundane Astrology was not that systematic. I tried to make good this deficiency by a systematic analysis of the data in the light of astrological factors.

I had keenly studied the forecasts made by the Zadkiels and had a thorough acquaintance with western astrological classics like *Tetrabiblos* by Claudius Ptolemy, *Primum Mobile* by Didacus Placidus de Titus, *Christian Astrology* by William Lily, the *Celestial Science of Astrology* by Sibly and *A Text Book of Astrology* by Zadkiel, not to speak of our own ancient classics like *Brihat Samhita, Garga Samhita, Argha Jataka* and appropriate extracts culled out from *Dhruva Nadi* lent to me by late Dr. R. Nagaraja Sarma.

The more I tried to delve deep into these great works the more I felt small before the astrological giants, Hindu and western. Of course I have my own reservations about the methods employed in the West today, which are superficial and cannot stand comparison with the Hindu methods. My admiration has been for the Western classical writers and not to the present-day astrologers in the West who have commercialised the subject in a manner that smacks of exploitation. Of course, there have been exceptions like Tucker, Bailey, Elizabeth Aldrich, Robson and Sepharial, all dedicated souls.

The following passage extracted from Sibly's book on Astrology will be found to be interesting.

"The building of Rome was begun when the Moon was in Libra, the Sun with Mercury, and Venus in Taurus, Jupiter in Pisces, and Saturn with Mars in Scorpio. The Archbishop of Pisa consulted several different professors of Astrology concerning his destiny, and they all calculated his nativity at different times, and without any communication with one another; but they all foretold he would be hanged. It seemed highly incredible at the time, because he was in so much honour and power; but the event justified the predictions; for, in the sedition of Pope Sixtus IV, in the sudden rage and uproar of the people, he was seized and hanged. Petrus Leontius a celebrated physician and astrologer of Spoletanum, cast his own nativity, and foretold that his death would be occasioned by water; and many years afterwards he was found drowned in a pond, into which he had fallen the preceding night, by mistaking his way. Josephus tells us he cast the nativities of Vespasian and his son Titus, and predicted that they would both be emperors; and so it turned out. R. Cervinus calculated the nativity of his son Marcellus, and foretold that he should come to great preferment and dignity in the church; and, his mother afterwards entreating him to marry one Cassandra Benus, he very resolutely declined it, saying, he would not with the bonds of matrimony bind himself from that better fortune which the stars had promised him if he continued to live single and unmarried. And he was afterwards really made Pope. Picus Mirandula was a severe writer against Astrology, insomuch that he was termed, *Flagellum Astrologorum,* the Scourge of Astrologers; and, to stop the malignity of his pen, Lucius Bellantius, and two other astrologers of eminence, procured the time of his birth, and calculated his nativity, which they afterwards sent him, and with this prediction enclosed, 'that he would die in the thirty-third year of his age.' This exasperated him so much that he began to write a new tract, with inconceivable asperity, against the poor astrologers, attempting to prove their calculations a mere bubble, and themselves a set of impostors.

"But when the fatal appointed hour arrived, he saw the folly of his own conceits; recanted his opinion, and sealed by his death a standing memorial of the inerrability and truth of this science. Many other extraordinary circumstances of the kind might be related from different authors, were it not already sufficiently obvious that the intellectual faculties of man, when cultivated by study, and improved by observation and experience, are capable of obtaining very extensive degree of knowledge and skill in this art. We will therefore dismiss this argument and endeavour to explain what the subjects are that the science of Astrology naturally comprehends."

It will be noted that these ancient astrologers in the West made their predictions without the extra-saturnine planets then not yet 'known'. What struck me in the author's introduction was that his observation, "The intellectual faculties of man when motivated by study and improved by observation, and experience are capable of obtaining a very extensive degree of knowledge and skill in this art".

Ancient astrological classics have always held the mutual conjunctions, oppositions, *shashtashtaka* of Mars, Saturn, Jupiter and Rahu as highly mischevous indicating "famines, war-like activities and war, panic amongst the public, mutual hatred amongst rulers, revolutions, strife, outbreak of violence and epidemics and destruction of crops".

A study of the Indian and European history in the light of the movements of Saturn, Mars and Jupiter and Rahu, has revealed valuable clues which I have tried to make use of in all my forecasts bearing on national and international affairs beginning from the outbreak of the second world war. Of course I have never claimed infallibility, but the educated public who have been watching my work for more than five decades feel that by and large the forecasts have been satisfactory.

Switching back to the war, from the time Hitler invaded Russia, moulds had been shaped for the occurrence of great events in Europe.

Great military disasters fell on England. There was the fear that Japan would also jump into the war on the side of Hitler. This fear arose because of a pact signed between Germany, Italy and Japan on 27-9-1940. Would Japan dominate the Pacific? This was a pertinent question to ask then in view of important developments in the Far East. With the occupation of important air and naval bases in Indo-China, Japan had given clear proof of her aggressive designs. But the Allies were trying to avoid war with Japan. The thinking of the British was that Japan might not declare war unless Germany could successfully invade Britain, but Germany could not win the battle of Britain. Two cardinal points seemed to be in the forefront of Japanese foreign policy, viz., the expansion of Japan on the mainland of Asia at the expense of China and the recognition of a "Japanese Munroe Doctrine" which would leave Japan as the virtual and undisputed mistress of the Pacific. Commenting on these developments I wrote in the September 1941 issue of THE ASTROLOGICAL MAGAZINE thus:

"What part will Japan play in the new division of the world? Perhaps the signing of the Berlin-Rome-Tokyo axis on 27-9-1940 at Berlin will be as important a turning point in the history of Japan as was her adhesion, on March 31, 1854 to the first formal treaty with any Western country.

Ketu	Jupiter Saturn			Venus	Sun		Rahu
	Berlin-Rome-Tokyo Axis **RASI**	Moon Venus			**NAVAMSA**		
			Mars				
Ascdt.		Mars Sun Merc. Rahu	Moon Ketu	Ascdt.		Jupiter Saturn	Merc.

"At the time this pact was signed, there was a balance of 8 months and 25 days of Saturn's Dasa. Then Mercury's Dasa commenced. The sub-period of Mercury in his own major period lasts from 22-6-1941 to 19-11-1943. A careful examination of this chart reveals quite interesting details. Every one agrees that Nazism should be destroyed once and for all, so that the world may be made safe for humanity. Nazism and all the ugly doctrines it stands for cannot be destroyed if its evil nature is minimised. If the enemy is strong then resistance to him should be also proportionately strong. Similarly if elements favourable to Japan are to be seen in her horoscope then greater effort is necessary on the part of those who wish to check her aggressive designs.

"The Lagna is Scorpio and its lord is in the 11th or house of gains with the Sun, Mercury and Rahu – all malefic planets. This combination is suggestive that Japan which has learnt the methods and the language of nineteenth century imperialism and which faces needs which brook no delay, is scarcely likely to reverse a policy pursued with grim determination for 30 years merely in order to propitiate a group of powers who have in the past shown little sympathy with or comprehension of Japanese problems. On the other hand the situation of the lord of the 7th in the 9th with the Moon is suggestive that Japan, like her partner Germany, will try to create the impression that she is the standard against the dangers of Bolshevism. The 7th house rules foreign relations while the 9th indicates fortune in general. The conjunction of Venus and the Moon in the 9th is a good Rajayoga. Members of the Rome-Berlin-Tokyo triangle will try to cooperate with each other but for reasons already discussed in the previous issues, Japan will have to pay dearly for her expansionist policy. Mercury's inter-period will last till about 19-11-1943. Mercury is the lord of 8th and 11th and though exalted is practically in the end of Kanya. Japan will continue her present programme of bluff. Relations with England and America will of course be sensitive and may develop into a conflict unless Japanese statesmen become more sensible and avoid hostilities. The possibility of a conflict between Japan and the U.S.A. has been hinted at often in our previous writings on the subject. Because an event may happen however it does not follow that it will. It can be prevented. Till at least 1943, Japan adheres to her present dreams of hegemony in the Pacific. Her dreams of course will always remain dreams. In the Mikado's horoscope the sub-period of Jupiter in the major period of Jupiter lasts from 29-8-1940 to 17-10-1942. Jupiter is in the Ascendant in conjunction with Saturn. Lord of the 2nd and 3rd Saturn is transiting the 9th from Mikado's radical Moon. Added to these there will be two eclipses occurring within a fortnight—rather a rare phenomenon — this month. About this time Japan is likely to make some surprising moves. We said in the July 1940 issue of THE ASTROLOGICAL MAGAZINE that astrologically Italy's entry into the war would be favourable to the Allies. Recent events have justified this deduction. Likewise if Japan enters into the war it would be highly favourable, astrologically of course, for the Allies. When it is astrologically favourable it must be so otherwise too. Notwithstanding the fact that Jupiter is the Ascendant lord his conjunction with Saturn, lord of the 2nd and 3rd, is so unfavourable that in the event of Japan embarking upon any fresh aggression she is likely to sustain severe setbacks the effects of which would be so disastrous that her national progress would retrograde for generations.

"In the long run the Rome-Belin-Tokyo pact will prove a liability not only to Germany and Italy but also to Japan. The disposition of Saturn in the Emperor's horoscope may make the Emperor willing to take a desperate gamble and inaugurate violent action. Japan is not going to be able to dominate the pacific. But she is going to strive and may fight also to do so. It is therefore advisable for Japan to enter into a genuine *rapproachment* with peace-loving Democracies and modify her aims and rescue herself from the bondage of slogans concerning *Asia Alone*. By so doing the Japanese people will have been saved from a position of considerable national peril. Till October 1942 as Jupiter's sub-period will be ruling in Jupiter's Dasa in the Mikado's horoscope, Japan will wait to see the progress of war in the West. She may also strike at Russia (because Jupiter is transiting the 9th) at an opportune moment. Should war come, Japan would suffer the same consequences as did Italy and naturally the Allies will be benefited. As long as Saturn continued in Aries, Democracy was to fail. Now that Saturn has entered Taurus, things will somewhat improve for Democratic countries. The China war is not easy to liquidate and Japan knows that she would not be able to undertake an adventure in Siberia. But the planetary rays act on the glands of men at the helms of affairs in Japan and excite warring elements in them. Japan should realise the disadvantageous position in which she has put herself through her axis partnership. Astrologically, however, a push towards the south is also probable in addition to an attack on Siberia. In Jupiter's Bhukti which will rule till about 1942 internal troubles and great difficulties from without are indicated for Japan. The Western Democracies have rightly remembered that issues like security in the Far East are as important as the fight against Nazism and Fascism, in the destruction of which lies the ultimate peace and prosperity of the world. The solar eclipse occurring on 21-9-1941 will have grave repercussions on Japan. Important political decisions, earthquakes and volcanic eruptions may follow close on the heels of this eclipse. It is hoped that the firm stand taken up by Britain and U.S.A. will prevent Japan from pursuing her aggressive designs."

Just before the end of Jupiter's Bhukti and within three months from the date of the solar eclipse, Japan attacked Pearl Harbour on 7-12-941 when Mars was opposing the eclipse sign and America was at war with Japan. It was at 3 a.m. on December 8, 1941 that Admiral Hart intercepted a message giving the staggering news of the Japanese attack on Pearl Harbour. Britain, Soviet Russia and the United States were now bound together to defeat Hitler. The coming conjunction of Mars and Saturn in the beginning of Taurus involving the constellation of Krittika indicated terrific forfeits in the East. The aspect of the Moon, Ketu being aspected by Saturn, and the disposition of the two major planets Jupiter and Saturn in the 12th from the Moon (at the time of attack on Pearl Habour) indicated that disasters mounted swiftly. The American air force was destroyed and Germany and Italy declared war on America.

Almost every editorial in THE ASTROLOGICAL MAGAZINE would deal with the war and its course, analysis of mutual pacts of friendships etc. By and large the majority of the forecasts proved correct.

It was clear from the dispositions of planets at that period that major disasters awaited the Allies. **Singapore** and Penang fell into Japan's hands even though Indian troops put up stubborn resistance.

Apart from Mundane Astrology, personal consultation, book-writing, discussions with fellow-astrologers and replying to the heavy mail I was receiving, thanks to the publicity my forecasts on the war received, kept me busy. Added to this I had another work entrusted to me by Kasturi Srinivasan viz., to pick out likely winners in the Bangalore races!

Thanks to the Papakartari Yoga, the 5th house and the 5th lord in my horoscope are subject to, I have had no interest in gambling or any type of speculative activities and least of all horse-racing. But because of my close association with Kasturi Srinivasan and because of his keen interest in racing I had to devote time to astrologically picking out the prospective winners. Srinivasan owned some race-horses and for him it was just a hobby. During all my life I have visited the race course only twice - once at Bangalore with Kasturi Srinivasan and once at the Mahalakshmi Race Course at Bombay as my good friend N. Saliwateeswaran, then THE HINDU representative at Bombay, wanted me to keep company with him.

I had picked up the methods of racing Astrology mostly from Sepharial's "Silver Key" and by my discussions with late Bh. Satyanarain Rao and T.G. Butaney whose methods did not appeal to me much, I was also dabbling in market forecasts, my mentor being one Swetaranyam of the editorial department of THE HINDU. In fact the Market Forecasts published in the 1940 issues of THE ASTROLOGICAL MAGAZINE were written by me under the pen name of "Astro Economist". My toying with commercial Astrology and racing did not last long as I felt that it would be unethical to employ Astrology for speculative purposes and Astrology should always be used for guiding people on right lines. A horoscope should clearly indicate success in speculation if one were to expect any windfalls.

I had to tackle with all sorts of problems in the course of my astrological consultations and this would bring me into contact with different strata of society. Since most of my forecasts bearing on the war proved correct and the circulation of THE ASTROLOGICAL MAGAZINE had also been gradually improving I had already become "famous".

About this time a well-known person met me wanting to know about the health and longevity of his only daughter. He said she was brought up with all care and affection. I narrate these happenings from my memory.

			Ketu		Ketu		Sun	
Moon			Mars		Moon Sat.			Merc.
	RASI				Jup.	NAVAMSA		
Sun Merc. Rahu	Venus Saturn	Jup. Ascdt.			Mars	Ascdt.	Venus	Rahu

I said, after glancing through the horoscope, "Kalatrakaraka Venus is in the 2nd (family) with Saturn. The lord of the 7th Mars is debilitated in the 10th in the constellation of Saturn aspecting Lagna. Jupiter, lord of the 6th, is in Lagna in the constellation of Rahu. In the Navamsa the 7th and 2nd are spoiled. It seems to me that the lady could be very unhappy." The father butted in and said: "Yes, Sir, her miseries started the moment she stepped into her husband's house, because of the ill-treatment inflicted on her, not by her mother-in-law, as she is dead, but by her husband's aunt. She is made to practically starve due to the menial jobs she is forced to do and much mental cruelty is being inflicted on her and she often thinks of committing suicide. What about her health?" I said: "she is having the sub-period of the Sun in the major period of Mercury. The Sun and Mercury are both in the constellation of Ketu and in conjunction with Rahu in a common sign. Mercury is with two worst malefics Rahu and the Sun, in a common sign. Mercury is lord of the 8th and the Sun a *maraka*. This makes me feel that she should be suffering from the end of Ketu Bhukti, a disease connected with the lungs". The father of the lady shot back. "Doctors say she is having tuberculosis of the lungs for nearly 2 years and are treating her accordingly. Will she recover?" I paused for a while and said: "according to Satya's dictum since the lord of the 8th Venus is not free from affliction as he occupies an inimical sign, the constellation of a malefic and is associated with a malefic she has only Madhyayu." I had to reluctantly say:

"Both the Sun, the major and sublords in the 3rd become *marakas*. They are mutually in association. Therefore the period may prove fatal unless powerful remedies are undertaken". The lady died because of tuberculosis of lungs just before the end of the sub-period of the Sun. As I looked back, after some years at this prediction, I felt that my analysis was not quite adequate. I banked on the affliction of the lord of the 8th Venus and the situation of Mercury and the Sun in a common sign – The 3rd which rules the lungs – *runabadha cha patiya kshaya samudbhavaha*. Of course good luck must have favoured me.

29

One fine morning in November 1941, as I was getting ready to start writing the editorial article in my small office room, sparsely furnished with a table, two chairs and reference books scattered on my table, a well-built middle-aged man dressed in spotless white khadi *dhoti* and long coat entered my room.

"Hello my friend, so you are the astrologer who has been making astounding predictions about the war, which I have followed with great interest and which have become the subject of discussion amongst many people", he said greeting me with a *namasthe*. I smiled but kept silent. Continuing he said " I am also a student of Astrology and have my readings done by many astrologers.

Taking out from his brief-case a scroll of paper, he laid a Rasi chart on my table with the request that I must "tell something about the chart so that I can get convinced". This offended me a little and I retorted: "If you want to test my astrological abilities I would politely ask you to withdraw from the room". He was patience incarnate and was not upset by my somewhat brusque manner. "No, Mr. Raman, I know your abilities. That is why I wanted you to say something about the chart".

As I have mentioned in the earlier chapters, in those days, to satisfy my ego I would generally try to demonstrate my "abilities" by giving some predictions about the past of the consultor. Examining the Rasi chart, I said, "Sagittarius rising and the lord of Lagna exalted in the 8th makes the person inclined towards corpulence and gives an inclination for philosophical and occult studies. Somewhat impulsive the native is generally enterprising". The gentleman who had yet to reveal his identity, lifted his hand as if to indicate "you are correct so far. Proceed further, please".

I continued, "Fullness of figure characterises the native. Lagna is occupied by Mars and Venus. This is not an altogether favourable combination for domestic happiness as it highlights differences between the native and his wife. Moreover Venus in a common sign afflicted, denotes more than one marriage especially at the fag end of Venus Dasa. The Moon-Jupiter conjunction in Cancer is an asset in the horoscope. Mental disposition will be of a high order. The native is not moved by harshness, jealousy or vengeance. This combination also strengthens the vitality, inclines the native to benevolence and to spiritual and occult studies and given a jovial disposition. The affliction of Lagna by Saturn and Mars has its unfortunate shades. Lord of the 2nd well placed, the 2nd being occupied by the lord of the 9th and aspected by Dhanakaraka Jupiter indicates powerful Dhana yogas. Lord of the 10th Mercury in the 3rd with Rahu denotes a business which involves dealing with metals like aluminium etc. Ketu in the 9th and lord of the 9th subject to Papakartari Yoga and the lord of the 10th from the 9th Venus afflicted suggests humble beginnings in career".

						Sat. Sun Venus
Merc. Rahu		Moon Jup.	Moon			Mars Ketu
Sun	RASI	Ketu	Rahu	NAVAMSA		
Ascdt. Mars Venus	Saturn			Merc.		Ascdt.

As this stage, I stopped my delineation and awaited his reaction. Beaming with a smile, the gentleman said, "Your analysis is brilliant. The horoscope belongs to me. I am Himchand K. Shah, an industrialist manufacturing aluminium and stainless steel utensils. I have a number of friends who are eager of consult you". With these words Shah immediately became a patron to THE ASTROLOGICAL MAGAZINE.

Shah said that he had lost his first wife in 1926 and married again in 1927. Joining Jeewanlal in 1921 as an ordinary employee, he had organised an independent branch in Madras in 1923, stayed in Calcutta as Secretary till 1934, purchased a small factory in Bangalore in 1936, shifted the factory to Madras in 1939 and became the Managing Director of Jeewanlal in 1940.

In due course Shah became my staunch admirer and our friendship lasted until he passed away in 1966.

What was most annoying to me was his addiction to astrological consultations. He would consult every astrologer that he came across and then would send the interpretation to me for my opinion I did not wish to sit in judgement over the findings of other astrologers. I told Shah bluntly that it would be unethical on my part to sit in judgement over what others said. From then on he would seek my astrological advice in all his personal and business matters and he did in his own way much good for the cause of Astrology.

Of the several astrologers he had introduced to me, one gentleman interested me much. He was V.S.N. Sastry, an astropalmist from Rajahmundry. He had given a reading of Mr. Shah's horoscope from 'Bhrigu Nadi' which he claimed to have in his possession. As usual the past was correct in many ways. The Nadi's analysis of the horoscope was in simple Sanskrit verses. Shah said that the reading was accurate upto the time of consultation. When we met in 1965, a year before Shah died, he was of the opinion that the reading in general was fairly accurate but failed in timing events.

My interest in Nadi Astrology continued unabated until the sixties, when I decided not to waste time or money on hunting after the Nadis.

Surprisingly within a month from Shah's first meeting with me Sarma asked for my birth details and sent to me what he called my "test reading".

After giving the birth details and a description of the mental disposition, etc., the reading (as translated by Mr. Sarma's English knowing friend) said "close to famous leaders after 35th year (प्रसिद्ध प्रमुखात्मीयं पंचात्रिंश वयोगते), a man of principles earns money by trade (विघवान् गुणंशाली च व्यापारे धन संचय:), endowed with riches (these predictions were said to apply only after my 35th year), thick hair and capable, ऐश्वर्य धनसपन्नो कंबकेशी समर्भय: good natured, wavering, and religious (सुशीलाचंचलान्चित: । धर्माचारादि संयुत:)   scholar, capable of grasping other's mind, polite and good natured (विद्वान् सर्वगुणाग्रही विनीतश्च गुणप्रिय:) respect from rulers and influx of money through them (राजद्वारेतिमानंच नव्द्वारा धनप्तय:),   , he will visit foreign countries and has a beautiful wife of character   (विदेशे गमन भूयात् भार्याप्ति सुंदरी शीला)   allegations from relatives, and the family a little bit afflicted (बन्धुवर्गापवादींच कुटुंबं पीडितं खलु),   fearless and truthful, proportionate body and attractive   (निर्भयो सत्यवादींच सुगात्रो सुमुखोसिद्ध:), good friends amongst other castes (अन्यजाति सुमित्रता),   , helpful to others, learned and respected by rulers (परोपकारकर्तांच विद्यावान् नृप पूजित:), talking well in assemblies and pleasant towards all   (सभामध्ये सयक्ता च सर्व संतुष्टकारक:),   before the end of Mars Dasa bodily affliction, sorrow due to mother's passing, chance of getting a step mother (भौमशेष दशापूर्वे स्थीयदेहे प्रपीडनं मातृ खेटममेकत्वं सपत्नी मातृसंभवं ॥)   , Rahu Dasa important for education, blamed by relatives   (राहुर्विद्या प्रधानत्वं ज्ञातिवर्ग प्रनिन्दित:), in the 3rd year suffers a lot (जन्मादींच ततीयब्धे पूज्यकष्टं विधीयते)   . When 18, he gets married अष्टदश वयोकाले पत्नीभिग्रस्य लभ्यवान् at 21, break in education (एकविंशद्वयोकाले विद्या विघ्न प्रतप्तत्यं)   , becomes a family man at 24 and starts earning (चातुर्विंशदि गर्हस्य स्वयंभाग्य प्रपार्जितम्) probes into the effects of planets and leads a happy life (खगप्रज्ञ स्वशास्त्रांगम् शोधयेत सखजीवनम्). at 27, probes into the meaning of *sastras* (सप्तविंशद्वयोकाले दिव्यशास्त्रार्थ शोधनम्),, earns two to three thousands when he is 32 and in Jupiter Dasa children will be born (द्वित्रिसहस्रमादायं जीवे सन्तान सौभाग्यम्)   , in Saturn in Jupiter Dasa earnings will be expanded (जीवस्सौरि समरभे स्यार्जितर्थ प्रयोजनम्)   , in Jupiter-Venus benefic results will happen (जीवश्शोक्री शुभोदयम्). in Sun in Jupiter, enemies will be destroyed and goods results will happen.

The above was supposed to be the preliminary reading. The

general analysis was fairly correct. Later on Sarma sent me another reading analysing the various Bhavas and giving the results of Dasa. The delineation of all the Bhavas was general, sometimes capable of more than one interpretation and often wrong in respect of age at which the Bhava indications would manifest.

As I do not wish to burden my readers with a delineation of my horoscope I shall give brief extracts regarding the 8th and 10th Bhava analysis so that readers can have an idea of this Nadi's approach and performance.

Regarding the Ayur Bhava "At the end of the Sun's sub-period in Mercury's Dasa the native suffers from dysentry and weakness of the heart (रक्तातिसारव्याजेन हृद्बले दुर्बलान्वितं)   In the same sub-period his death is certain ¡सौम्ये सुर्यान्तरे काले निर्याणं ध्रुवमेवच);   before he is 67, the native is to contemplate on the Divine (सप्तषष्टितमो पूर्व देवतत्वार्य चिन्तनम्)   ). The Nadi said that according to Satyacharya longevity can be earned till Rahu in Mercury by daily recitation of Sivamantra (अथ सत्याचार्यः | सौम्ये स्वभर्गानुपुच्छस्ये जीवमायुष्यमार्जितम् | शियमन्त्र जपेन्नित्यं पुष्कलायुर्नसंशयः). Again quoting what it calls the view of Satyacharya, the Nadi concludes: The maximum span of life is 76 (षट् सप्ताशत् परमायुष्यं)

It will be seen that the Nadi anticipated my death in the Sun's sub-period in Mercury's Dasa. Theoretically this is feasible because as posited in the 7th Mercury could be considered a *maraka* and the Sun is of course the lord of the the the 7th house, a *maraka* place. Again the next fatal period given in the Nadi was Rahu Bhukti in the same Dasa. Mercury is no doubt a *maraka* and Rahu occupying the 2nd is also a *maraka*. The major and sub-lords are *shashtashtaka* and the period could be considered critical.

In fact just about the end of Rahu, all of a sudden, I took ill for 48 hours, which the doctors said could have proved fatal. But I did survive the crisis. The Nadi then extended my life upto 76. Of course that period is also over and Budha Dasa has also ended.

In longevity determination certain special combinations peculiar to *alpa, madhya* and *poorna* terms of life are to be considered.

In my twenties when I used to suffer from the obsession that I might die at the end of my Rahu Dasa, grandfather had assured that I would live long because of *Chatussagara* Yoga etc.

I also visited Pandit Siva Sankara Sastry, to whom I have referred in the earlier articles of this series to get further confirmation. He gave me the following combination for long life which he said "was generally applicable to me". I have found this combination fairly correct in a large number of persons who have lived over and above 75.

केन्द्र त्रिकोण निघ्नेषु न यस्य पापाः ।
लग्नाधिपः सुरगुरुश्च चतुर्पूयस्य ॥
भुंते क्षयानि विविधानि सुपुण्यकर्म ।
जीवेच्छ यत्सर शतंस सयिमुक्त रोगः ॥

The Bhrigu Nadi, inspite of the generalised nature of predictions can be considered in accuracy next to Markandeya Nadi about which I have written in the earlier chapters. Bhrigu Nadi's forecast about my longevity can be considered approximately correct though I have survived the maximum longevity indicated by it.

Shah's friendship enabled me to meet a large number of professional astrologers, most of whom were found to be wanting in their knowledge of Astrology and astrological experience.

A year or so after Shah met me, he came with a then well known ICS officer "who is anxious to consult you about his 5th house".

I cast the horoscope and after a casual study applying a simple method which in later years I have explained in my HOW TO JUDGE A HOROSCOPE, I said, "The native has five children." Mr. Shah being a keen student of Astrology, wanted to know how I gave the number. I said "Jupiter, *putrakaraka*, is in the 5th house. Mars, lord of the 5th has Neechabhanga and has covered 8 Navamsas which means 8 issues. Three malefics are situated between the first and the eighth Navamsa. Deducting this the remainder viz., 5 represents the number of issues." Mr. Shah and his friend nodded their heads in approval. My reasoning, as I look at the horoscope now was somewhat elementary. "How many sons and how many daughters?" queried the friend. This was a tough question. I pondered thus, "Lord of the 5th

				Merc. Venus			Jup. Ketu
Ketu			Moon Mars	Mars			
Sat.	RASI		Rahu Sun Venus		NAVAMSA		Ascdt. Sat
Ascdt.	Mandi			Merc.	Moon Rahu		Sun Mandi

Mars is in a feminine sign in association with a feminine planet Moon. Mars is aspected by Saturn, a feminine planet. In the Navamsa also, though Mars is in a male sign he is aspected by a female planet Saturn. The 5th from Lagna is also occupied by the Moon and Rahu. Therefore, he should have more daughters. But how many? Putrakaraka Jupiter is in the 5th. What is the significance of this? After a lot of cogitation, the following verse came to my mind.

मन्देकर्किणि बहुसुतः । सौम्ये तथाऽल्पात्मजः ।
शीत्रांशौ बहुकन्यकाल्पतनयो । जीवेतु कन्याप्रजः ।
शुक्रे ऽर्के सुचक्षितीयदाचितलब्ध्यात्मजः स्याभ ।
व्यस्य: मन्दगृहे फलं सदसतं मित्रेलाडयाम्रबेत् ॥

"If Cancer happening to be the 5th house is occupied by Saturn one will have many children; if Mercury, few children; if the Moon, more daughters and few sons; If Jupiter, only daughters; if Venus,

the Sun or Mars – issue through second wife; if the 5th house belongs
to Saturn, the results are reversed. Benefic and malefic influences
should be balanced and results given."

In some texts instead of *manda gruha*, the words used are
indugruha, which means the Moon's sign. Obviously *indugruha* is a
contradiction in terms because the first line itself is clear meaning
Kataka or Cancer which of course is the Moon's sign. Therefore when
years later this was brought to the notice of Pandit Sivasankara Sastri,
he at once said *mandagruha*.

In applying this stanza to the chart concerned I found that the
5th house did not fall in the Cancer or Capricorn. However I felt that
a literal interpretation of classical dicta was not called for and banked
on *jeeva kanya prajaha*. Jupiter in the 5th indicates only daughters
and accordingly said that the native has only five daughters. He was
anxious to know whether he would get a son in the near future. The
native was only 40 years old and his wife 37.

I continued my interpretation thus: "At the moment your friend
has Venus Dasa and Saturn Bhukti. Venus extends upto October 1946.
Then commences the Sun's Dasa. Venus as lord of the 6th and 11th,
a functional malefic, in association with Rahu and the Sun denies male
issues."

I felt Shah and his friend were satisfied with my prediction and
before taking leave of me Mr. Shah said, "My friend whose chart
you have seen is Mr. H.M. Patel, Secretary to Government of India".

I have often reflected why the predictions of an astrologer however
experienced do not click at certain times while at some other times
they just work. Is this phenomenon due to incomplete knowledge of
Astrology, want of a spiritual base, or just accidental? I now feel —
many may not agree with my views — that the correctness of
astrological predictions could rest on (1) the astrologer's experience,
(b) a disciplined life, (c) faith in God, (4) intuition and a clear
psychological perception of the event and (5) favourable directions in
the astrologer's horoscope.

The following extract from "Notes" to my English translation of
PRASNA MARGA will be found to be appropriate.

"Qualifications of an astrologer have been laid down in stanzas 15 to 18. In this connection, reference may also be made to similar qualifications laid down by Varahamihira, in his *Brihat Samhita*. One, who wishes to be a correct predictor, should not only be an adept in Astrology, Astronomy, Vedas and Mantra Sastras, but also must be a man of character, religious, righteous and must have obtained *siddhi* of certain secret *mantras* which would confer on the astrologer the uncanny power of correct predictions.

"The astrologer should be of noble birth and agreeable appearance. Humility must characterise his behaviour. His personal habits must be disciplined and above opporbium. He should be well versed in ritual and expiatory ceremonies. He should be gifted to resolve independently any tough problems. Disciplined life, faith in God, a helpful nature and scrupulous adherence to certain types of austerity would enable him to develop his power of intuition considerably and this would be a great asset to anyone who aspires to be a successful astrologer."

If we are to be a judged on the basis of the rigorous qualifications laid down by the seers, I am afraid most of us may not be considered as astrologers at all.

Whether or not I am capable of intuitional perception, my predictions have mostly come correct when favourable Dasa and Bhuktis operated in my horoscope. During unfavourable periods, my forecasts have sometimes been disappointing. Of course these thoughts never occurred to me fifty years ago when my ego dominated my thinking and when inspite of well-wishers cautioning me I often entertained a high opinion about my predictive abilities.

In the next chapter I shall deal with my predictions bearing on the course of the second World War and how I was able to anticipate things which no western astrologer could. This remark should not be construed as boastful, but only as an objective narration of facts then.

30

As the year 1942 was progressing the tumult of the war was increasing. The scale of events grew larger as Saturn journeyed through Taurus and greater military disasters fell on the Allies. America was moving more closely towards British.

While the British empire seemed to be reeling to a collapse and France was prostrate, the Italian empire in Africa under Dictator Mussolini had spread far and wide. Consistent with the structure of his horoscope, Mussolini felt certain that a vast area of the earth's surface – Egypt and other British colonies in Africa – would be added to his empire, the like of which had not been seen since the days of the Caesars. But this gleaming vision got abruptly dimmed, thanks to the Allied onslaughts on Abyssinia and the entry of the Negus into his own territory.

Developments in the East meanwhile were taking a different turn. Japan declared war on Britain and U.S.A. on 8-12-1941 at about 6 a.m. (Tokyo) and Britain declared war on Japan at 12-30 p.m. (GMT) on the same date. The positions of the planets in both the charts were the same. But Scorpio rose at Tokyo and Aquarius was the Ascendant at London.

Commenting on these two charts in the February 1942 issue of THE ASTROLOGICAL MAGAZINE I observed thus:

"In Chart No. 1, the Lagna is Vrischika, an insect sign and lord of Lagna Mars is in the 5th unaspected by benefics or malefics. Lord of the 11th Mercury is in Lagna with the lord of the 10th, the Sun. Jupiter and Saturn are aspecting the Lagna while Rahu is in the 10th. These favourable combinations explain the initial successes of Japan in the Pacific War. Did not Hitler reach the gates of Moscow securing victories after victories for a period of 4 months until his hordes were driven back by the gallant Red Army of the Soviets? Planets were unfavourable for Russia till November 1941 (to which we made reference in the August 1941 issue of THE ASTROLOGICAL MAGAZINE and said that after this, favourable period for Stalin would set in) and the stubborn resistance of Russia coupled with the will of her people to oust the invader did minimise the evil indications of the planets.

Stalin's well-calculated and successful transition from the defensive to the offensive against a formidable and experienced foe will not only remain a masterpiece of military achievement but a demonstration of how events become favourable consistent with benefic angular dispositions of planets. When planets occupy certain angular positions (such as 4th and 10th, and 5th and 9th), they simply stimulate the resistance power while in unfavourable situations (6th and 8th and 2nd and 12th), they will introduce a feeling of inaction or dejection. A student of Astrology will do well to compare the horoscopes of Germany's attack on Russia and Japan's declaration of war on Western democracies. He will come across convincing proof that initial successes are often the fore-runners of great reverses as is the case with Germany and is likely to be the case with Japan.

"In Horoscope No. 1, the sub-period of Venus (in the Dasa of Saturn) lasts till 29-3-1942. The sub and the major lords are in the 9th and 5th from each other. After this, the sub-period of the Sun will set in. The Sun and Saturn are mutual enemies. They are aspecting each other. In Navamsa they are not mutually well disposed.

"In the Mikado's horoscope Jupiter in Jupiter lasts till 17-10-1942. Jupiter is in the Ascendant in conjunction with Saturn, lord of the 2nd and the 3rd. This is again harmful. Therefore, a bad time for Japan is likely to commence from about the middle of 1942. From this period onwards she will sustain reverses and setbacks, the effects of which on the future of Japan will be disastrous.

		Saturn Jupiter	
Mars			
Ketu		RASI	Moon
Venus			Rahu
	Ascdt. Sun Merc.		

"In Horoscope No. 2 the Lagna is Aquarius occupied by Ketu while the lords of the 5th and the 7th are in the 10th. Ketu's presence in the Ascendant is not desirable. Sani Dasa rules till November 1942. Sani is no doubt lord of Lagna but he is with Jupiter, lord of the 2nd and 11th and hence, bad. As a result of these malefic influences the British have suffered reverses in Malaya but this is not going to be a permanent feature. From November 1942 Budha Dasa will commence. Budha is lord of the 5th (and 8th) from Lagna and is in the 10th with

Mars		Jup. Saturn	
Ascdt Ketu		Chart 2 RASI	Moon
Venus			Rahu
	Sun Merc.		

the lord of the 7th. In Navamsa he is in Upachaya. Added to these, influences in the horoscope of King George VI will become favourable so that Britain will be able to stem Japanese aggression.

"Summing up the above observations, planetary influences will be favourable to the Allies in the Pacific war till about the middle of this year. Even though there is no direct threat to India the planetary movements are unfavourable for Burma and Bengal."

Japanese air raids on Rangoon had begun by the beginning of 1942, causing havoc and many casualties, Japanese advance into Burma had also begun. Fierce fighting ensued between the Japanese and the British Indian army. Rangoon fell and in a sense Burma was lost. Many perceived that the threat to India was real and in the view of the British "the security of India was now directly endangered".

The Indian national opinion was that India should remain neutral in this war, while the British Indian Government, to help it in the war, busied itself in raising an enormous Indian army. The stresses latent in Indian politics – Gandhi to start the independence movement in August 1942 – grew and Subhas Chandra Bose had come on the scene. It was suggested that if India could somehow throw off the British connections, the Japanese might not invade India. The Cripps mission arrived in April 1942 and Pandit Nehru is said to have observed that "Japanese must be resisted. We are not going to embarass the British war effort in India". And Gandhi wrote in HARIJAN, "The presence of the British in India is an invitation to Japan to invade India. Their withdrawal should remove the bait."

When things were in such a state of confusion there was some sort of panic in India about Japan bombing Madras, Calcutta etc. Even THE HINDU wanted to shift the paper to Bangalore. At this juncture I assured Kasturi Srinivasan that Japan would not be able to invade India or bomb Madras and wrote in the February 1942 issue of THE ASTROLOGICAL MAGAZINE that "There is no need for panic about the war developments in the Far East... the conjunctions of planets occurring in the first half of 1942 release energies unfavourable to India. But this does not warrant in the least the exodus that is taking place from Madras, Calcutta and other towns... India at this juncture should effectively and willingly co-operate with the war effort and stem the evil influences of planets while Britain on her part should readily concede the Indian demand for a truly national government, without repeating the miserable inadequate 'august offer' so that India's war efforts may be completely nationalised."

I continued, "the study of national Astrology has special difficulties of its own. It is not always possible to find a moment in a nation's history for which a horoscope can be cast in the same way as for the birth of an individual. Therefore much of national Astrology has to be based upon Gochara movements, horary charts and horoscopes of rulers. Hence we have attached due importance to the horoscopes of King George and the Mikado.

"While not wishing to encourage wishful thinking as regards Japan, a study of the relevant data gives us the impression that we shall hear in the near future some more unpleasant news; but in the long run, that is, after the period suggested above, the Japanese war machine will receive serious blows. This effect will be realised by the combined action of the Allied forces in the Far East – but it will also be a confirmation of the astrological principles... after all the Allies are fighting a righteous cause and by the time Jupiter reaches Cancer, the Allies will certainly have gained an upper hand".

I have never claimed that all my predictions about the war had been fulfilled. But the spate of letters received by me during this period and subsequently after the termination of war, were generally flattering.

Even in those days there was a breed of so-called "rationalists" who had the knack of bracketing some unfulfilled forecasts with those that happened slightly before or after the indicated time and gleefully declaring "Astrology is irrational". But many of these poor fellows lacked intellectual integrity, as later on they visited me to "know their future".

Typical of the letters complimentary to my "achievements" was one dated 18-2-1942 from Prof. Christian Paul of Colombo, "Ceylon's Premier physical culture expert" which read: "Your predictions relative to the present state of affairs are quite accurate uptodate and I have every confidence that the same will be true to the very letter in the future.

"As a matter of fact predictions by several western savants have proved futile. Astrologers like Naylor have actually misled the reading public with their fanciful and false predictions. It is no flattery when I emphasise that – you are not only an astrologer but also a prophet of the present day.

"I have been in constant touch with your movements and I am a regular reader of your magazine. What you predicted long ago regarding the non-aggression pact between Germany and Russia had come to pass. You stated that such a pact would not last long. Very correct in every detail. Analysing the Mikado's horoscope you stated that the Emperor's planetary positions have aggressive tendencies and Japan would be dragged into the war and that she will score victories over victories upto the end of June 1942. I believe that your scientific analysis would score another victory for you all over the civilised globe. According to your predictions, I also emphasise that the Japanese will get defeated in due course.

"I am at present engaged in the A.R.P. Movement and am longing for the time when I shall be able to meet you face to face and gather knowledge at your worthy feet – Sd. Christian Paul."

Most of the Western astrologers, especially the British, were partisan in their forecasts and I often had digs at them and their predictions. Unfortunately, the English media in India, with rare exceptions, would publish the forecasts of western astrologers and ignore those of the Indian astrologers while the language press in general carried my forecasts. But unlike a few Indians who gloat over the Western system of Astrology and still dub the Hindu system as obscurantist, the Western astrologers never gave – and even today, they never give, (with very rare exceptions) – any credit to the superiority of Hindu Astrology.

This attitude of the English media and the arrogance coupled with the pontifical attitude of Western astrologers often provoked me to highlight how most of the forecasts made by them about the war flopped exposing their pretensions.

Under the heading "A Fault with Western Astrologers" I wrote in the March 1942 issue of THE ASTROLOGICAL MAGAZINE thus: "Some people suppose it impossible to predict the future. Some others suppose that the future can be exactly predicted; while the majority of thinking men, rightly hold, that whilst it is possible to predict the future, a certain margin of error should be allowed because of human limitations. But most of the Western astrologers have a tendency to predict exactly (?) and most often hit off the mark in their predictions. Many of these prophets predicted a slow-up or defeat for Germany during the third quarter of 1940. Vincent Lopez said in an American astrological journal (October 1941 issue) that America would not declare war in 1941. Several English astrological journals expected the end of war in 1941. Their own anticipations were further strengthened (?) by prophecies made by seers like Nostradamus. Many of the Western astrologers went on interpreting (I hope not misinterpreting) the quatrains of Nostradamus to suit their pet theories and pet expectations. They interpreted Hister as Hitler. Clarence Reed observes thus: 'The details Nostradamus gives about the defeat of Germany are not very conclusive, *but it is quite clear* (italics mine) that he did not foresee the present situation'. In the imagination of these astrologers, Nostradamus expected the end of war in 1941 September. The translation reads thus: 'Arms and Plagues cease, death of the seditious, wine will not be abundant. France will be more victorious than ever'. Then there are Naylor, Lyndoe and Blake – who have all made (or marred) history. Clarence Reed observes thus: 'In this country we have several well-known writers on Astrology, and it is remarkable that two of them fix on September 1941 for the end of hostilities'. He further says that 'the September date, if we look back, coincides with a suggestive stanza from Nostradamus, while December has the support of another stanza from Nostradamus as well as St. Odile and the Pyramid; it also accords well with Polish prophesy'. We are in February 1942 and have yet to realise the above predictions!

"I do not for a moment suggest that the great Nostradamus has failed as a prophet. Far from it, I would only like to impress that Western astrologers – English as well as American – are infected with a psychosis. They have a knack to explain away things. Most of them seem to be still under the delusion that it is below their self-respect or dignity to refer to predictions made by Indian astrological journals and admit their own failures. Surely it requires greater nobility to give credit to those who deserve it. The Western astrologers will do well to forget that they represent the sum total of astrological wisdom."

Commenting again on the Pacific War in the May 1942 issue of THE ASTROLOGICAL MAGAZINE, I said: "From 29-7-1942 to 26-8-1942 excepting the period of the Moon's transit from Leo to Capricorn, Kalasarpa Yoga will manifest, the effects of which on the present world crisis will be considerable. This forebodes evil for the entire world and the war is not likely to terminate in the course of this year.

"As we have said several times, astrological evidence points to the conclusion that when Jupiter enters Cancer, he becomes exalted and releases Jupiterian forces and therefore things are likely to assume a turn favourable to the Allies and the dream of peace is likely to be a reality."

About this time, a Bombay astrologer – unfortunately I have forgotten his name – who had specialised in market forecasts and who used to meet me whenever I visited Bombay, predicted in a local paper that the Allies would meet with reverses in Europe. He was hauled up for the "offence of causing panic amongst His Majesty's subjects by predicting reverses for the Allies". I was in Bombay about this time. The astrologer was on bail and I told him that according to my understanding the case against him would not stand.

At Bangalore I discussed the matter with the I.G. of Police and the Chief Secretary to the Government of Mysore. The I.G. while cautioning me not to make any "sensational forecasts" was of the opinion that the case against the Bombay astrologer would not stand. When the case was taken up in the Magistrate's Court at Bombay, I was present. The Magistrate dismissed the case and let the astrologer at liberty with the remark, "Astrological predictions are based on the science of Astrology and they cannot be tailored to please the authorities". This episode increased the popularity of the astrologer and added in a sense a feather to the cap of Astrology.

By this time, the whole of Malaya, Hongkong, Siam, Dutch East Indies and Burma were all under Japanese control. But Astrology did give the hope that Japan's ambitious policy would be thwarted and that she was bound to lose the war.

Moon		Ketu				Venus	Mars Merc.
Venus			Rahu				Sat. Moon
Sun Marc. Merc.		**RASI**			**NAVAMSA**		Ketu
Sat. Ascdt	Jupiter Rahu				Jupiter		Ascdt.

During a subsequent visit of mine to Bombay, about the end of 1942 and beginning of 1943 I again met Majumdar, a Bengali gentleman, quite influential and deeply interested in Astrology and philosophy. Our discussions covered several subjects including, of course, the war, its outcome and the future of Subhas Chandra Bose, who by then had left India and was perhaps organising the Indian National Army. The chronology of events in my life during these years is largely drawn from my memory. Therefore it is likely there could be some jumbling of dates mentioned in these "Experiences".

Majumdar's only ambition was to become the General Manager of the Hindustan Insurance Company he was then heading at Bombay. The time of birth mentioned in the so-called horoscope given to me was vague. Applying some snap-shot methods I found that it would be about 4.03 a.m. which meant the Lagna would be Sagittarius. He said: "I know your reputation and I am not interested in my past but you have to tell me if at all I would head this organisation as Chairman and if so when". But I had to first convince myself that my finding of his birth time was at least approximately correct.

I glanced through the chart and said, "You are born in Dhanur Lagna and Kanya Navamsa. Lord of the 9th, the Sun, who is also the Pitrukaraka, is in the 2nd (with Mars and Mercury). The Moon is in the 4th. Under such a planetary set-up* the native is said to lose his father in the 2nd Dasa own Bhukti, which in this case, is Saturn in Saturn. This mean the father might have died before you were three years old."

In giving this interpretation I look cover under a stanza said to be from Jamini Nadi. I had developed the practice of jotting down such *slokas* from astrological scholars whenever I chanced to meet them. In 1954-55 I saw what was claimed to be us *Jamini Nadi* with one Gupta, a Nadi reader, then living in Madras. The Nadi was in Telugu script, the language being Sanskrit. But this particular stanza could not be traced.

Majumdar exclaimed, "Yes, yes, my father died before I completed my 3rd year". This gave me the confidence to answer his question. I went on "You are now at the fag end of Ketu. Saturn has entered Taurus where Ketu is placed, depriving him of the power to confer any real elevation. The sub-period of the Moon in Venus Dasa lasting from June 1947 to February 1949 may elevate you to the position you are aspiring for. Venus is a functional malefic because of his ownership of malefic places both from the Ascendant and the Moon. But he is the Atmakaraka, and in Navamsa as lord of the 11th from the Moon." Majumdar appeared to have felt satisfied.

As I was about to depart, Majumdar said "You know the country is facing a crisis with Japan knocking at our doors in the East. Subhas Bose may attack the British in India, any time and make India free. His elder brother Sarat Bose on parole from his detention in Ooty is now in Bombay. He has heard of you and wishes to meet you."

The next day I was taken to Majumdar's place when I had the honour of meeting Sarat Bose. After exchange of greetings, Sarat Bose

---

* भाग्येशे कुज संयुक्तश्चन्द्रमा हिबुके तथा ।
संपद्वाये पितृनष्टस्य स्वभुक्तौ न संशय: ॥

said, "Japanese are planning to invade India and Subhas is in the vanguard. Here is his horoscope. Can you tell me whether he will be successful in his patriotic mission of liberating India with the aid of Japanese army? I am sure you know that every true Indian wants him to succeed."

The next day I met Sarat Bose again with the chart of Subhas Bose recast, rectifying the time of birth on the basis of some of the past events in his life. My analysis was largely confined to the 8th and 10th houses. I explained: "The Lagna Aries is a fiery and positive sign aspected by Jupiter and the lord Mars, an aggressive planet in the 2nd aspected by Saturn, denotes a frank, open, outspoken and free-handed disposition, qualities which to a large extent shaped the life of Subhas Bose. The Moon in a benefic sign devoid of malefic aspects gives the native a fertile mind and makes him just and precise. The situation of Jupiter and the fact that the Karakamsa is aspected by Saturn are indications that whilst he is moved by the highest impulses of partiorism, there will also be a sense of frustration. Enormous suffering is indicated by the conjunction of the Sun, Rahu and Mercury. Rahu's presence in the 10th is unfortunate as it does not indicate the native becoming a ruler. The 8th lord Mars (happening also to be lord of Lagna) is in the 2nd while the 8th is occupied by the Ayushkaraka Saturn. The latter combination can indicate good longevity; but because lord of Lagna and lord of the 8th are in fixed signs and because Lagna and Chandra Lagna are in moveable and common signs respectively only *madhyayu* is indicated which according to Jaimini would vary from 33 to 66 years.

"Jupiter could be construed as a *maraka* as he is not only the lord of the 12th but also owns a *maraka* place from the Moon. Though Mars is lord of Lagna he can be considered as a *maraka* as he occupies the 2nd and is aspected by Saturn. This could be a critical period for his life."

Summing up, I said "The Sun-Rahu combination in the 10th afflicts the political career and his mission might not succeed."

He thanked me for my forecast and I took leave of him.

31

The years 1942 to 1946 covered by the sub-periods of Mercury, Ketu and Venus in the Dasa of Jupiter in my horoscope were of much significance. It was during these four years that I became fairly well-known not only in India but also in other countries probably because of my many successful forecasts bearing on world affairs. And it was during this period that my financial position also began to show some signs of stabilising. I could now sign with some relief that the days of penury were over.

Mother died when I was slightly less than two years old. Father, mostly immersed in spiritual practices, did not concern himself much with family cares. Yet I had a fairly comfortable childhood until 1924-25 under the care of grandfather. Thanks to his over-generosity grandfather was soon in dire financial straits and the family had to pass through much hardship. Poverty was a part of my life throughout my Rahu Dasa which lasted till 1936. I had often wondered why Rahu should have proved so adverse to me especially in regard to financial matters.

An astrologer who used to occasionally visit us was emphatic that Rahu's position in my horoscope was responsible for the poor finances our family was in. I did not agree with his astrological views. I felt since grandfather was the head of the family, his horoscope alone could explain the state of the family at that time. Eversince Saturn Dasa began for him in 1924, Saturn being in the 2nd house in the constellation of Mars, who in his turn, is in the 6th with Ketu, poverty had plagued us.

For Aquarius, Jupiter as lord of the 2nd and 11th is no doubt, not quite a benefic, but during his Dasa as *Dhanakaraka* aspecting the

2nd, Jupiter did confer on me the blessings of his innate nature apart from the effects of Gajakesari Yoga which unfolded as the Dasa progressed. Contrary to the views held in some quarters, Venus in Jupiter bestowed on me mostly favourable results, but for one event, considered calamitous then, viz., birth and death of my 4th son, Sri Krishna. Venus the sub-lord in association with Mercury, lord of the 5th, in Makha ruled by Ketu, who occupies the 5th from the Moon caused this event. In fact I had anticipated it astrologically also. However, this being my first experience of the death of an issue disturbed me and Rajeswari quite badly but we soon recovered from the shock.

The conviction that I had to play an important role in the future to procure for Astrology its rightful place in the heirarchy of sciences and in the minds of the educated public began to grow in my mind. My main aim which I pursued with missionary zeal was to eschew Astrology from charlatanry and refute through my writings, stale objections against Astrology raised in some 'scientific' quarters. I also planned to bring to light so far unpublished literature on the subject and do research in the science. I had a great desire to make the Magazine and publications an Institution and not just a business concern. Looking back I feel Destiny has graciously led me to fulfil this ambition. My literary activities increased and a research section for the collection and codification of astrological data was also started.

Father died in September 1943 when I was having Ketu Bhukti. Jupiter and Ketu (major and sub-lords) have reference respectively to a *maraka* place (2nd) and house of loss (12th) from the 9th house.

I was also under the grip of *sade-sathi* for the second time. In the first round mother died. And I expected that in the second round there would be a bereavement on my paternal side. Inspite of his heavy leaning towards spirituality, from a worldly point of view father's was a tragic life. Unmindful of the tragedy that had befallen him by way of loss of sight and an unhappy domestic life, he pursued with unabated zeal the task of performing more than 21 lakhs of Gayatri Japa – and created around him a spiritual halo. Rajeswari who had a special place for father in her heart served him with devotion. She took great care to ensure him comfort and that nothing came in the way of his attending to his daily religious practices. He died in Mars sub-period of Saturn Dasa. In his chart Saturn as lord of 12th is in the 3rd, while Mars, a *maraka* is in the 12th.

During those days consultations formed only a minor part of my activities. My third son Suresh (now Dr. Sureshwara) was born in 1942. Family responsibilities further increased. At the same time there was also a steady increase in the readership of THE ASTROLOGICAL MAGAZINE. The small house I was living in since 1940 and which also housed my office was no longer adequate. Three rooms and a big verandah closeby were rented on a monthly rent of Rs. 60/- which today may fetch anything between Rs. 2500/- to Rs. 3000/- a month.

Additional staff had to be employed – a stenographer on Rs. 30 a month, a despatching clerk on Rs. 25, and editorial assistant on Rs. 60 a month and a Sanskrit Pandit on Rs. 50 a month and 2 attenders on Rs. 15 a month each.

These details though not relevant are given so that young friends of today may have an idea as to how plentiful the times were and what the real worth of a single rupee was.

The printng of THE ASTROLOGICAL MAGAZINE had to be shifted to Bangalore Press, then considered to be the best equipped printing house in Bangalore. The composing work was done on monotype and lino type machines. The appearance of the Magazine no doubt improved but the cost of production became equally prohibitive. The manager of the press, one Srinivasa Rao, was a stickler even in regard to small matters, and he would insist on an agreement on stamped paper being entered into every year. The change of printing press was also a blessing in disguise because I was not required to visit the press everyday as I used to do in the previous place and this gave me enough time to do astrological work and reimburse my income. My literary work also was progressing satisfactorily. My popular title "The Next Five Years" giving forecasts of world events from 1941 to 1945 underwent several reprints and secured wide circulation almost throughout the English-knowing world. As I learnt later, during the war years, a large number of copies were being smuggled into Burma, Malaya and other Japanese occupied territories.

The nature and type of horoscopic work handled by me was generally to do with occupation, yearly prospects, health and diseases, litigation involving landed estates – especially of the zamindari type and marriage. Today in view of the number and diversity of occupations an astrologer's task becomes formidable. In this respect we were perhaps more fortunate as we had to deal with less number of professions.

Questions bearing on marriage hinged mostly on the nature of married life, the longevity of the couple, whether the couple would continue living together and prospects of children. The Indian woman had not yet been "liberated" then and she lived in the shadow of her husband. Sometimes situations would arise when a husband would have a *upa patni* and in many such cases seen by me, on this score, the relations between the *dharma patni* and the husband would naturally go sour. Of course, such instances were rare. There were also cases of separation of the couple but they were far and few. In fact, I had to deal with some cases of ladies indulging in extra-marital relations clandestinely but much fuss was never made.

Unfortunately today, in the name of "progress", a dangerous term which we have blindly borrowed from the West, even the sanctity of marriage is being questioned, thanks to the sponsored programmes and serials of the T.V. and the "progressive" ideas publicised in the media by those calling themselves as champions of "women's rights". Life values so fondly cherished for generations and forming the foundations of family life in India are as a result being threatened and disruptive forces given freeplay. Sometimes the couples rush to astrologers just a few months after getting married to know when they would be able to divorce their partners. Some marriages hardly last even a year. Something must be done to halt the sense of alienation gripping the modern Indian generation. These remarks are by the way.

Before discussing a horoscope, I would first deal with verification of the birth-time. One such horoscope dealing with birth-time and longevity as done by me decades ago is reproduced below from my archives for the information of my esteemed readers.

"Before going into a study of the horoscope, it is necessary to have a check-up on the birth time on the correctness of which the entire structure of the horoscope is to be erected. There are several well-known methods to see whether the Lagna arrived at is the correct one. One test is the Mandi test. Note the Rasi occupied by Mandi at birth and note also the place where the lord of the sign containing Mandi is located. The Lagna at birth will be a position triangular to that of the aforesaid lord or one triangular to the Navamsa occupied by the owner of the sign representing the Navamsa occupied by Mandi. In this horoscope Mandi is in Virgo and the lord of this sign Mercury is in Satittarius. As the Lagna is Leo which is trine to Sagittarius, this test indicates the Lagna to be correct.

"There is another test called Pranapada test by which also the correctness of the Lagna can be determined. Multiply the *ghatikas* after birth by 4 and divide the *vighatikas* by 15. Add the two and divide the sum by 12. The remainder will incidate the Lagna or its trine − (42 gh. × 4 (+ (55/15) = 168 + 3 = 171. This divided by 12 leaves a remainder of 3 and this indicates Gemini, or Libra, or Aquarius. As the Ascendant is Leo some rectification appears to be called for. Rectification by the method of Epoch (details of calculation of which

		Jupiter		Jup.	Moon	Rahu	Mars Merc. Venus
Sat. Ketu		**RASI**				**NAVAMSA**	
Moon Mars			Ascdt. Rahu				Ascdt.
Merc.	Sun	Venus		Sun	Ketu Sat.		

are too technical to be given here) will suggest the birth time to be 43 gh. 15 vigh. instead of 42gh. 55 vigh. as per recorded birth time, an increment of 20 vigh. or 8 minutes, we find that the Lagna will be Leo asper this test.

"(43 × 4) + (15/15) = 172 + 1 = 173. This divided by 12 yields a remainder of 5 and this number corresponds to the number of Lagna as counted from Aries. That we are correct in assuming this to be the correct birth time is confirmed by another test. For this, the birth *ghatikas* and *vighatikas* have to be multiplied by 2 and then the number 9 added to the product as a fixed sign ascends and then again multiplied by 4. This product should be divided by 27 and the remainder should indicate the birth star.

"That is, (43 gh 15 vgh × 21) + 9 = 95.50. This should be multiplied by 4 and the product 382 so got divided by 27 or 382 ÷ 27 = 14 and remainder 4.

"The fourth star is Rohini and the birth star being Sravana falls in the trine group Rohini, Hasta and Sravana. This double verification is eminently satisfactory and we can therefore take the birth time to be 43 gh. 15 vgh. after sunrise. The only resulting change in the chart would be that the Amsa Lagna would be Leo instead of Cancer and this makes the Lagna Vargottama and gives added strength to the entire horoscope.

"Regarding longevity: There are various method of determining the longevity such as by judging the strength of Lagna, 3rd and 8th houses, called the houses of life, also by determining the *maraka* lord and the period when he will function to cause death of the native. Again there are methods of judging according to certain set rules, and there are the mathematical methods. Experience tells us that not one method taken by itself proves satisfactory and that a harmonium blending of the various methods alone will give the desired results.

"The 3rd and 8th houses are deemed the house of life. Lord of Lagna is in a *kendra* in a sign that gives vitality to the constitution. He is also aspected by Jupiter who is a benefic and lord of 8th house (life) and by Saturn (Ayushkaraka). Venus is placed in the 3rd sign but actually in the 4th house. But Venus is lord of the 3rd house and strong in *kendra*. He is also in his own sign though the house he occupies is the 4th. There are no planets in the 8th house but Jupiter is the lord of that house and he is strongly placed in the 10th house. He is also retrograde and aspected by the Sun, lord of Lagna. In the Amsa we find that Jupiter is strongly placed in his own sign in the 8th house. These are testimonials for a fairly long life for the native. Jupiter and Venus in Kendras may be taken as another indication for long life. We shall next apply the method set out in *Phaladeepika* verse 14 of Chapter XIII. "Consider the following 3 pairs: (A) the decanate Rasis of the Lagna and the Moon; (B) the Navamsa Rasis of the lord of Lagna and lord of the sign occupied by the Moon; (C) the Dwadasamsa Rasi of the lord of Lagna and lord of the 8th house. The life of the native is long, middle or short according as (a) when one of the Rasis in the said three pairs is moveable and the other also moveable or fixed and common, (B) when one of the signs is fixed and the other is movable, or when both are common, (c) when one is common and the other is movable or when both are fixed. Applying this test in your case, we find the following results:

(A)   Lagna Drekkana Rasi – Common Sign
      Chandra Drekkana Rasi – Fixed Sign = Life Long.

(B)   Navasma Rasi of Lord of Lagna – Common Sign
      Navamsa Rasi of Lord of Janma Rasi – Fixed Sign = Life Long

(C)   Dwadasmasa Rasi of Lord of Lagna – Fixed Sign.
      Dwadasamsa Rasi of Lord of 8th house – Fixed Sign = Life Short.

"The majority indication according to this test is long life which confirms our former judgement according to the strength of the Bhava. Next the actual length of life has to be ascertained by the period of the *maraka* lord. As the life is long, the major period of Mercury, lord of 2nd house, occurring between 69 and 86 years of life is the most likely period. And as regards the sub-period, as we find no planets associated with lord of 2nd house, and there being also no planets in the 2nd house, we choose the planets found occupying the 7th house. There are two planets there, Saturn and Ketu. Saturn is simply lord of 7th in the 7th, whereas Ketu is in 7th and also associated with lord of 7th house. Ketu has apparently better claims and so the life may be judged to be about 72 years long".

Sri Krishna Sinha, a respected Congressman of Bihar had contacted me as early as 1940 desiring to have an interpretation of his horoscope, particularly about his political career. He was a regular reader of THE ASTROLOGICAL MAGAZINE and had once congratulated me on my successful forecasts. The war developments in 1942-43 resulting in the withdrawal of the British from Burma and Malaya seemed to have unnerved many Congressmen that Japan might overrun parts of eastern India. Sinha gave vent to these feelings lurking in his mind. I had assured him, on the basis of my humble knowledge of political Astrology, that Japan would not be able to invade India or occupy any part of it and invited Sinha's attention to my editorials in THE ASTROLOGICAL MAGAZINE.

Sri Krishna Sinha's elder brother, Deokinandan Sinha, an admirer of grandfather, was well versed in Astrology. In fact when grandfather visited Muzaffarpur in 1906 or so this gentleman had played host. The elder Sinha used to write to me now and then on important astrological matters. He was good enough to present me with a copy of his excellent book on Astrology in Hindi in which he dealt with the different branches of the subject extensively interspersed with his own experiences.

Krishna Sinha also knew Astrology well. He wanted to have my assessment of his political future. What was worrying him was the prediction given by some astrologers of Bihar and Bengal that his aspiration to attain a high political career might not be fulfilled. It seems that emphasis was on the situation of Rahu and Saturn in the 12th house and the debilitation of the Sun. Unfortunately there was some doubt about his birth time. Deokinandan Sinha had also advised him to consult with me.

After checking up some life-events in the light of directional influences, the time was fixed by me as 3.21 a.m. and in an introductory reading sent for the year 1943, I had hinted about the death of a close relative of his on the paternal side. Later Mr. Sinha wrote to me. "Since writing to you last another thing has happened which has confirmed one prediction made by you. In the course of 1943-44 you predicted a bereavement on the paternal side. My eldest brother died. So with some difference as regards time this prediction has been fulfilled. The next few years may be years of great political importance and I would therefore request you to keep in view my future political career in recasting the reading".

At the time I was consulted though Sinha was an M.L.A. there was no chance of his becoming a minister as the political conditions in India were still in a state of flux.

He was having Rahu Dasa from 1937 to 1955. It was during this period, covered by the sub-periods of Rahu, Jupiter and Saturn that Sinha underwent much suffering, participated in the freedom movement and was also jailed. Probably because of these happenings in Rahu Dasa, his astrologer-friends might have felt hesitant about Rahu's capacity to confer any Yoga. In those days, I would examine horoscopes of important leaders not only from the point of view of Parasara but also in the light of Jaimini, Yogini etc. This was the same yardstick that was used even in the cases of Mussolini and Hitler.

Prima facie Rahu's disposition in the 12th from Lagna along with

				Moon Jup.			Merc.
	Jupiter						
			Sat. Rahu				Mars Ketu
	RASI				**NAVAMSA**		
Ketu			Mars Ascdt.	Venus Rahu			
Moon		Sun Merc.	Venus	Ascdt.	Sun Saturn		

Saturn was not a factor to make him confer Rajayoga. I pondered for some time and wrote to him thus: "You are now having Mercury's sub-period till 1947 to be followed by Ketu and Venus in the major period of Rahu. Because he is associated with Satura who as lord of the 7th in the 12th, you have had enough of suffering till almost the end of Saturn's sub-period. In the Navamsa also the position of Rahu is equally unfavourable. But according to the dictum *Sanivad Rahu*, Rahu should also give the results of Saturn, whose situation as lord of the 6th·(and 7th) in the 12rh from Lagna could be considered a Yoga. For deciding occupation and success in it the Dasamsa chart is equally important. In Dasamsa, Rahu is in the Ascendant with Mercury and the Moon who should give the results of Rahu and who as also lord of Lagna is in the 10th. Your elevation to a ministerial post is likely in Mercury's sub-period". The arguments given above were in accordance with my line of thinking then. As good luck would have it Sinha became the Chief Minster of Bihar.

After sustaining an almost unbroken series of military defeats in the war all these days for which no parallel had been found in the past, the Allies appeared to have felt that with the end of 1943 some cheering events had taken place in the western theatres of war. But Hitler and Mussolini showed no significant·sign of defeat. At this point of time my analysis of the horoscopes of these dictators caught the attention of the world, as I had forecast, in a sense, their doom.

32

About the middle of 1942 stirring events affecting the whole course of the war were occurring in Europe as well as in the Pacific Ocean. After the collapse of France in 1940, the Allies had a long succession of military defeats which included loss of Hongkong, Singapore and Burma and a "chain of misfortunes and frustration to which no parallel could be found in history". Germany under General Rommel was triumphant, pressing forward in its victories. The Axis' plans had been revolutionised. Elated at the prospect of conquering Egypt, Benito Mussolini, the Dictator of Italy, planned to attack Malta.

As astrologically anticipated these significant developments started occurring when Saturn and Jupiter were in conjunction in Taurus. The conjunction and opposition of these two superior planets have always been considered highly significant in mundane Astrology. Great political changes and social revolutions, economic crises, violent attempts on leaders can all occcur under this configuration subject, of course, to adverse movements of Rahu and Mars.

In fact, the present Jupiter-Saturn opposition (1990-91) involving Cancer-Capricorn axis and the movement of Mars and the declaration of war in West Asia on 17-1-1991 can all be appreciated in the light of this opposition. Of course the association of Rahu with Saturn has had its own sinister implications.

The long expected Nazi spring offensive against Russia commenced on 8-5-1942, and I wrote thus in the June 1942 issue of THE ASTROLOGICAL MAGAZINE. "The fighting in Russia so far has shown that the initiative is no longer with Hitler. But what do the planets indicate? Herr Hitler has threatened a decisive offensive campaign and the Russians have with equal determination declared their readiness to meet and overwhelm the aggressor. We had said in the August 1941 issue of A.M. that because the planetary positions at the time Hitler invaded Russia were temporarily favourable to the invader he would make progress till practically the end of November 1941 and that because Saturn and Jupiter are transiting the third from Stalin's Janma Rasi, the German expectation that Russia would be liquidated soon cannot be fulfilled. Many people expected the fall of Moscow but we stuck to our prediction that the Nazis would meet with reverses in their Russian campaign."

Ketu Mars	Saturn	Ascdt. Moon Jupiter	Sun Merc. Venus	Moon Sat.	Mars	Ketu	
				Jup.			
	Chart I Germany invades Russia 22-6-1941				Chart II Stalin's Horoscope		
			Rahu	Sun Rahu	Merc.	Ascdt. Venus	

I further said: "The world is expectantly awaiting developments in the Russian theatre of war and an examination of the relevant charts is necessary to judge the prospects of Hitler's spring offensive. In the chart cast for the Russo-German war, the sub-period of Venus in the major period of the Sun lasts from 11-1-1942 to 11-1-1943. The sub and major lords are in conjunction in the 2nd house with the 2nd lord. They are aspected by debilitated Saturn. Mars, ruler of the 7th also aspects this combination. At present Saturn is transiting radical Moon. For Stalin, Mars Dasa commenced from May 1942 and Mars Bhukti lasts till the end of September 1942. Mars in the 7th from

Lagna is in his own house. From the Moon, Mars is in the 2nd. These are favourable indicating great success in foreign policy. In the Navamsa, however, the situation of Mars is not quite propitious. Rahu's sub-period commences about the end of September 1942 and continues right upto the end of 1943 October. Rahu is in the 3rd from Lagna, 10th from the Moon and 9th from the major lord. But in the Navamsa, Rahu is subject to Papakarthari Yoga. Rahu being a shadowy planet he should give the results of Jupiter who, by the way, is in the 5th from Lagna and 11th from Mars. Rahu's sub-period therefore will be much more beneficial to Stalin than that of Mars. As Mars is in the 7th (foreign relations) Stalin can expect Japan to commit aggression on Siberia.

Venus	Sun	Jupiter Mercury Saturn	Mars
Moon Ketu	Chart III Hitler's Spring Offensive 8-5-1942		
			Rahu

"Since the time of Hitler's spring offensive is not known, the Moon's position has to be taken. Lord of (Chandra) Lagna Saturn is in the 4th but he is hemmed in between the Sun and Mars. Lord of the 7th (foreign relations) Sun is exalted in the 3rd. Ketu's conjunction with the Moon and Saturn aspecting the Moon are not favourable. The position of the Sun in the house of Mars is suggestive of great battles and colossal butchery. The influences of this chart suggest that the invader will meet with some success till about September 1942, after which time, Russia will again hurl back the invader.

"Summing up the above, we have to observe that astrological evidence points to the conclusion that Hitler's spring offensive is likely to meet with some initial success but it is doomed to failure after about September 1942. Therefore in order to hasten Hitler's defeat, the United States will do well to aid Russia with all possible help. The United States will also succeed in a large measure in thwarting Vichy's collaboration with Germany."

M. Laval was the head of occupied France. Commenting on his role I said the in the same issue: "It is against the background of the spring offensive that the significant rise of M. Laval to power in France should be noted. Laval has four planets in the 10th, a powerful combination. There is a conjunction of Mars and Saturn in the 10th house. This indicates violent attacks on his person and a sudden downfall too.

"M. Laval has declared that his policy is to maintain friendly relationswith both Germany and U.S.A. Compare the charts of Hitler and Laval. In the former Saturn aspects Mars while in the latter Mars is with Saturn. As transiting Saturn approaches Gemini Laval's unpopularity will increase. Mars is the planet that rules over 'foreign policy'. Because Hitler's Mars is in the 12th from Laval's, Hitler will not derive any real benefit from Laval. The French will harass the German conquerors and Laval's attempts to take the country by slow degrees into an active alliance with the Axis powers will be frustrated.

"Italy becomes completely crippled and the Allies will be able to drive Italy from the war. During the coming three months sabotage may be expected to increase on a gigantic scale with executions and imprisonments through Nazi occupied Europe. Privation and hunger are also indicated. Britain is also likely to be bombed heavily but she knows how to take it. Continental Europe shows a very different picture where the civilian population is concerned. The iron heel of Nazism will be felt by all. Britain's strength will increase and the R.A.F. bombings on Germany and Nazi occupied Europe will be instensified. Turnkey will come to the limelight. Within Germany there will be secret plotting to overthrow the Nazi regime.

"As Jupiter approaches Cancer, the United Nations will grow in strength and this should supply fresh reason for confidence in the final victory of the Allies."

Again in a detailed discussion of the "Future of Germany" in the February 1943 issue of THE ASTROLOGICAL MAGAZINE, I had said that three turning points in the recent history of Germany were important: viz.,[1] (a) declaration of the new empire of Germany on 18-1-1871 at 12.15 p.m. (L.T) ;[2] (b) the proclamation of the Federal Republic of Germany on 9-11-1918 at 12.30 p.m. (G.M.T.) and [3](c) the coming into existence of the Third Reich on 30-11-1933 at 11.00 a.m. (CET) at Berlin; when the formalities of creatig Hitler as Chancellor of the Reich were completed. After analysing the chart in detail I concluded: "Venus sub-period in Budha Dasa began on 7-11-1940 and extends till about September 1943. Germany launched her attack on Russia during this sub-period but was thrown back by the Russians. Though Venus is good by location, he is afflicted by ownership and consequently Germany must face reverses. From 7-9-1943, the sub-period of the Sun in the Dasa of Budha commences and this will last till about July 1944. About August 1943, Saturn will have transited into Gemini the 4th from the radical Moon of German Reich and he will be aspecting radical Mars and Rahu. Added to these, transit Rahu who has already entered Leo is conjunct radical Mars. The major lord Mercury is in the 12th from the sub-lord Sun (according to Bhava) while the sub-lord (ruling the 6th from the Moon) is with Saturn. All these influences combined together will render Germany vulnerable for attack in the latter part of 1943. The trouble for this country will come from within also. Summing up the above the following predictions in regard to Germany may be ventured for 1943:

[1]Rasi: Taurus – Lagna and Jupiter; Virgo – Mars; Sagittarius – Moon and Saturn; Capricorn – Mercury and Venus; and Aquarius – the Sun.

[2]Rasi : Taurus – Ketu; Gemini – Jupiter; Leo – Saturn; Libra – the Sun and Venus; Scorpio – Rahu and Mercury; Sagittarius – Mars and the Moon; and Capricorn – Lagna.

[3]Rasi: Aries – Lagna; Leo – Mars and Ketu; Virgo – Jupiter; Sagittarius – Venus; Capricorn – Mercury, Saturn and the Sun; Aquarius – Rahu; and Pisces – the Moon.

"Germany can be expected to make drastic demands during this period. Strife will occur in regard to her newly acquired possessions as Rahu is transiting rasdical Mars. Manufacturing of armaments will be greatly stimulated. Finances are severely afflicted while the death of important persons will prove a loss to the country and a blessing to the Allies. Internal friction will be itense. Mars indicates coercion and violence which will do great harm to Germany. Uprisings against German authority will manifest in The Balkans and death plays an important role. The German financial structure will be badly crippled. Privation and oppression may drive many individuals to rebel. There is also evidence that Hitler's agents may put forth peace-feelers but they should be flatly rejected and ignored. About the time Saturn enters Gemini, German leaders will resort to new extremes of violence and destruction. As Jupiter approaches and advances in Cancer, Germany's troubles will increase till finally, she will be on the defensive."

About the same period, stirring events effecting the course of the war were occuring in the Pacific Ocean. Japanese troops controlled almost the whole of South East Asia. Their triumphs convinced the Japanese that the Allies were losing the war and that the time for the fulfilment of their destiny for Japan and the Axis lpowers had come.

At this moment in the world war, no one could be sure tht Germany would not vanqusih Russia and invade Britain and press forward through the Middle-East countries to join hands with the Japanese in India. When the Japanese had extended their sway right upto the Bay of Bengal and General Rommel's advance had assumed a threatening form, Astrology anticipated what would be the shape of things to come.

Dealing editorially under the caption "Will Japan Invade Russia?" in the August 1942 issue of THE ASTROLOGICAL MAGAZINE I had observed: "These events had certainly been anticipated by Astrology. If events have proved that several of our deductions purely based upon Astrology, have been correct, then we would only suggest that responsible men take up investigaton of Astrology and make use of them in national Astrology.

"On April 13, 1941, a Pact of neutrality between Soviet Russia and Japan valid for 5 years was signed in Moscow. Article I said 'Both contracting parties agree to maintain peaceful and friendly relations betwen them and to respect each other's territorial integrity and inviduality'.

"This was hailed as a great stabilising force in otherwise crumbling world and a great personal achievement of Stalin and Matsuoka.

"It is not our purpose to go into the history of Japanese-Soviet relations in the past. We shall endeavour to show astrologically whether peace would prevail between the two countries or a clash of arms is inevitable. In the absence of the times of the treaties we shall base our conclusions on the dispositions of planets with reference to the Moon."

After considering the charts bearing on a Russo-German Pact on 1939 and Soviet-Japan neutrality pact of 13-4-1941, I had said: "The above configurations incline us to the perception that the Soviet-Japan neutrality pact would meet with the same fate as did the Russo-German pact. In other words whether Japan would invade Russia first or Russia would invade Japan, a clash of arms between the two countries is most probable astrologically before Saturn leaves Taurus. Uptodate, the policy of Soviet Russia towards Japan has been one of moderation and rectitude. The aggressive tendencies manifest in the horoscope of the Mikado are likely to find further expression in the shape of a push towards Siberia."

What could be of interest to the astrological savants is the employment of the services of astrologers by the Allies to aid them in anticipating the moves of Hitler, which were based mostly on the astrological counsel tendered by Hitler's personal astrologers.

Years earlier i.e., probably in 1936-37, I was in touch with the well-known Dutch astrologer Karl E Kraft. He had written to me in

---

^a*Rasi:* Aries – Saturn and Ketu; Cancer – Ascendant and Mercury; Leo – Venus and the Sun; Libra – Rahu; Sagittarius – the Moon; Capricorn – Mars; and Pisces – Jupiter.

^b*Rasi:* Aries – the Sun, Saturn and Jupiter; Virgo – Rahu; Libra – the Moon; Capricorn – Mars; and Pisces, Mercury, Venus and Ketu.

one of his letters, enclosing a copy of his book on Astrology in German language, that Hitler had been interested in Astrology for a long time. It seems one of his astrologers Baron Sobotendoroff warned Hitler against undertaking "anything of major importance" in November 1923. Hitler appears to have neglected the warning and undertook his famous beer cellar *Putsch.* This occurred according to Hindu Astrology in the beginning of the Dasa of Mars in Hitler's horoscope. It was in the same Dasa that Hitler's party National Socialists adopted the Swastika as an emblem and organised the first storm troops. Their theme was anti-republicanism and ant-Jew. Hitler had great hatred for the Jews probably because of the conjunction of the Sun and Mars in the 7th aspected by Saturn and the coglomerations of evil combinations in Navamsa Lagna. It was in the same Dasa that he organised the *Putsch* to overthrow the government. This was a failure and Hitler was sentenced to five years for treason. He shared his prison cell with Rudolf Hess who reminded him of Sobotendorff's prediction. Hitler's interest in Astrology increased and he started studying the subject and from then on had a number of experts to advise him. It might interest my readers to know that the Fuehrer had Astrology officially recognised. In fact he sent a personal telegram of good wishes to the astrologers' congress held in Dusseldorf in 1937.

Thanks to the interest evinced by the well-known Paul Brunton, author of *A Search in Secret India* etc., a German translation of my book HINDU PREDICTIVE ASTROLOGY was published in 1938 under the title *Indische Astrologie* by Otte Wilhelm Bartherlog. I had sent a copy of this book to Hitler which was duly acknowledged. In 1939 Hitler attacked Poland, it seems against the advice of Krafft, who along with several noted German astrologers, was herded into a concentration camp and all the available astrological literature, including of course my *Indische Astrologie* was destroyed. My German publisher salvaged some copies which were sent to me along with the royalty due after the end of the war.

It seems one German astrological school had an erroneous conception of "Saturn conjunction Sun". They advised Hitler to invade Poland when transit Saturn was in conjunction with Hitler's radical

Sun, a planetary pattern which no Hindu astrologer would have approved. Experience shows that when any important work is undertaken under this transit there would be undue delay, disappointment and frustration.

It was under such circumstances that some astrologers in Britain tried to convince the authorities that "astrological warfare against Hitler was a necessity". They said that if they made the same calculations as Hitler's astrologer would do, that would be of advantage to the Allies, as Hitler planned his moves according to astrological advice. And for this purpose one Louis de Wohl, an astrologer, was commissioned in the British Army with the rank of Captain.

In his articles on "Astrological Warfare" serialised in THE ASTROLOGICAL MAGAZINE decades ago he has given details of his 'astrological advice' to the Allies to face Hitler's plans.

As is usual in Western Astrology the aspects between the transiting and radical planets were the basis of astrological interpretation. To Hitler, astrological aspects simply decided the factor of luck. And he got away with the occupation of Rhine-land and invasion of Austria and Czechoslovakia. And according to military experts "four French divisions would have been enough to stop him at that time". He made his peace offer to the Western powers after his occupation of Poland. If only the then British Prime Minister Chamberlein had not resorted to the tactics of appeasement, World War II could perhaps have been averted. At this distance of time it is, of course, wishful thinking.

Carrying this analogy further, and in the light of certain similarities present in the horoscopes of Hitler and Saddam Hussain, I must say that if Saddam Hussein had been appeased as HItler was the consequences to world peace would have been disastrous and India would have also been exposed to the danger of Saddam's aggressive designs aided and abetted by Pakistan. It is a pity that some of the political parties and peace-mongers in India, in their anxiety to create a vote-bank amongst the minorities, should have been indulging in cheap theatricals of anti-war demonstrations against the Allied forces. These advocates of 'Peace' at any cost must realise that in the final analysis, it is the *Danda* of the four *upayas* that can ultimately bring peace to the world.

I am now and then reminded by well-meaning friends why even in the delineation of horoscopes of political leaders and nations I do not consider the positions of extra-saturnine planets. I may not be able to give a satisfactory explanation to gratify the curiosity of my friendly critics. Decades ago I noticed that predictions on the Second World War made by noted astrologers in the West who relied heavily on the oppositions, squares, conjunctions etc., of Uranus, Neptune and Pluto were generally off the mark while my own forecasts based on the good old Hindu system of Dasa and Gochara proved fairly accurate even in regard to significant developments.

The so-called advances in modern medicine based on 'researches' involving the killing of numberless dumb creatures, have not made human beings more healthy. On the contrary these medicines themselves cause diseases to remedy which more medicines have to be taken. This is because of our belittling the foundations of Ayurveda based on thousands of years of experience and capable of tackling human suffering without causing any harm to the human system. Similarly those who swear by the effects of extra-saturnine planets have not produced any significant evidence in favour of their claim that these extra-saturnine planets enable one to make more accurate forecasts. However, there is no question of my looking down upon those who out of curiosity or conviction based on Western claims engage themselvgs in the study of the role of extra-saturnine planets in forecasting world events.

33

As I was about to enter my 31st year my urge to acquire more and more knowledge in Astrology grew further. I determined that I would make myself as competent as possible assiduously devoting myself not only to the study of innumerable horoscopes, but also in collecting data for the purpose of a statistical study. The thought of "statistical study" was spurred in me because of a communication I had from the famous psycho-analyst Prof. Carl Jung, in which he wrote:

"*Dear Prof. Raman, since you want to know my opinion about astrology I can tell you that I've been interested in this particular activity of the human mind since more than 30 years. As I am a psychologist, I am chiefly interested in the particular light the horoscope sheds on certain complications in the character. In cases of difficult psychological diagnosis I usually get a horoscope in order to have a further point of view from an entirely different angle. I must say that I very often found that the astrological data elucidated ceratin points which I otherwise would have been unable to understand. From such experiences, I formed the opinion that astrology is of particular interest to the psychologist, since it contains a sort of psychological experience which we call 'projected' – this means that we find the psychological facts as it were in the constellations. This originally gave rise to the idea that these factors derive from the stars, whereas they are merely in a relation of synchronicity with them. I admit that this is a very curious fact which throws a peculiar light on the structure of the humand mind.*

"*What I miss in astrological literature is chiefly the statistical method by which certain fundamental facts could be scientifically established. I remain, Yours sincerely,*" – Sd. C.G. Jung.

Of course as I gained in experience my ideas about statistical studies changed. I have now come to the conclusion that statistical studies would be a waste of time and resources as the ability to predict events correctly is a combination of experience and intuition, though statistical findings may aid us a little.

I was fairly well-acquainted with almost all the extant clasical literature on Astrology and had the added advantage of having had serious discussions with well-known scholars in regard to controversial passages in the texts.

At that time I was some sort of a professional astrologer too in the sense that a number of people would consult with me on their problems. I had not fixed any scheduled fees and it was left to the sweet will and pleasure of the consultor to pay whatever he wanted to or not pay anything at all. My finances had improved considerably and THE ASTROLOGICAL MAGAZINE had become self-supporting.

My clients varied from the common man and woman to the rich and those in high walks of life. My consultors knew that their approach to me had to be serious, devoid of a patronising attitude, respectful and that I expected they treated me as they would a specialist in any other profession such as medicine, law etc.

On one occasion an elderly family friend S. Venkatakrishnaiah, a retired District Judge, said to me: "You have considerable knowledge of the science and have already secured a good name as a successful predictor of national and international events and your forecasts bearing on the present war have been bringing laurels to you; has it not occurred to you to take Astrology as a profession?" I replied: "No, Sir, lately I have been thinking of doing only non-professional work and help people solve their problems. I have a profound respect for Astrology. And my dedication is to the cause of promoting it against the odds which are now staring in my face, make the educated public Astrology-conscious and seek a place for it in the comity of other sciences." Venkatakrishnaiah observed: "Your object is noble but you have to face several hurdles and suffer at the hands of what he called vested interests in education, science etc."

His remarks were prophetic in the sense that for decades I had to work against severe odds trying to maintain my own reputation and to remove the stigma attached to the very name of 'Astrology' amongst the so-called elite and the educated. The task ahead was no doubt, arduous, but my determination to uphold the dignity and the social relevance of Astrology was equally firm and unwavering.

Delineating character from the horoscope was somewhat difficult at first. Classical writers did not attach much importance to character-analysis as we do today for reasons best know to them; perhaps, the moral fibre which held society together was more strong and uncompromising. Of course, general results ascribed to birth in different constellations, signs and on different lunar days, etc., have their own importance.

I felt fairly satisfied with my specialisation in Mundane Astrology and my interpretation of personal charts. But character-delineation was of a different type, having a bearing on psychology. Sometimes I would exchange notes with Tucker, Carter and Bailey in England and with Elizabeth Aldrich in U.S.A. They had already a good opinion of my reputation as a correct predictor of political events especially bearing on the World War which was then raging in its full intensity. Taking the cue from Varahamihira's *Brihat Samhita,* I felt even physiognomy would be helpful in delineatig character.

I felt even physiognomy would be helpful in delineatig character. I shall come to these reflections in a future chapter.

I had a surprising experience one day at my office which was situated a few yards away from my residence. A middle-aged person dressed in a three-piece suit, accompanied by an elderly lady walked into my room. The geneleman had a distinguished appearance. Introducing himself, the gentleman said: "I am A.S.P. Ayyar, District Judge, Ramnad and the lady is Mrs. Lokasundari Raman, wife of Sir C.V. Raman. I have heard much about you. I am also a reader of your magazine and some of the predictions you have made on the war are amazing. I had my own reservations about Astrology and had often thought that it encouraged inactivity and sapped one's urge to work. The lady has some problems pertaining to her family." I had.

heard of A.S.P. Ayyar and had in fact read his interesting book "An Indian in Western Europe". Ayyar was an M.A., I.C.S., Bar-at-Law, F.R.S.L. etc. After the preliminary introductory remarks, I said: "At the time of your entering my room Gemini was rising. I think your Ascendant could be Gemini or the opposite sign Sagittarius and Mercury must be strong in your horoscope". Ayyar queried: "What makes you think Mercury is strong in my horoscope?" I replied; "Your educational qualifications are of a high order. Your writings show wide reasoning faculties, perceptive powers, boldness and an ethical approach, creative capacity, sense of humour and constructional ability". Ayyar pulled out a piece of paper containing what purported to be his Rasi chart which revealed that this Ascendant was Sagittarius with Mercury and Rahu. Mildly surprised, he asked me, "Do you attribute the characteristics you have delineated to Mercury?" I said: "Yes Sir". Probably satisfied with my preliminary remarks Ayyar nodded his head as if in approval, got up from the chair, had a few words (in Malayalam or Tamil) with Mrs. Raman and promised to meet me again after a few weeks. Taking leaves of me he said "Lokasundari Raman has some domestic problems and she will see you again shortly."

As I have often pointed out in these pages, to make correct predictions an astrologer should not only have the predictive capacity but also good luck, that is, directional influences in his horoscope should be favourable. Since I was having the major period of Jupiter, the confidence that my forecasts would be infallible, had gripped me so that I never hesitated to categorically delineate the past and the future. This over-optimism, however, did land me sometimes in tricky situations with the result in some cases the delineation would go wrong and I would become the butt of severe criticism.

Thanks to the advice that had been given to me by my grandfather, I would frankly own my failure instead of blaming it on want of correct birth time etc.

The next time Ayyar called on me was when he had been transferred to Bangalore as Additional District and Sessions Judge, Bangalore Cantonment. He would visit Bangalore twice or thrice a week and he would invariably call at my place. Our discussions would range from ancient history to astrological theories. Politics was not, of course, taboo but most Indians had never dreamt that within a short period India would be freed from the clutches of British rule to be thrown into the clutches of the Congress, a party that has brought this great and ancient nation to the abyss of political and economic collapse. He would give me instances of the Madras Government practising discrimination against Brahmin bureaucrats.

Once he asked me, "What do you foresee about the end of the war and how it would affect India". By 1934-1944, I had made considerable research into the role of the major planets in moulding the future of nations and the implications, often sinister, of Saturn-Rahu conjunctions. After explaining the various technicalities I said, "The war in all probability may end in 1945". As a well-known Judge and a legal luminary Ayyar could appreciate my astrological arguments.

He was an admirer of our ancient sages, statesmen and scholars and his thinking was gradually veering towards an appreciation of our cultural, philosophical and spiritual heritage. He would often quote from the *Bhagavad Geeta* and Lord Krishna's emphasis on Karma Yoga had appealed to him much.

One day all of a sudden Ayyar visited me in the evening and

			Ketu	Jup. Venus Sat.		Sun	
	RASI		Moon Mars	Ketu	**NAVAMSA**		Moon Mars Rahu
Sun							
Ascdt. Merc. Rahu Mandi	Venus Saturn	Jupiter			Ascdt. Merc.	Mandi	

said "Do you see astrologically any chance of my being elevated to the Bench of the Madras High Court? Before giving your finding, can you give a few past events so that you are sure about the correctness of the horoscope". I nodded my head in assent.

After studying the chart for a while and adapting a verse* from a classic, I said "The Lagna is afflicted due to Papakartari Yoga and the association of Rahu. The Moon, Karaka for the mind is not only in a saturnine constellation but in exact conjunction with Mars in the 8th house. In the Navamsa, the Moon is afflicted both by Mars and Rahu. No benefic aspects the Moon or Lagna. This indicates early death to the mother. Mercury's sub-period in the Dasa of Saturn ruled till your 2nd year. Saturn is a Maraka from Matrukaraka Moon. Mercury is lord of the 12th from the Karaka. Your mother's death could have taken place when you were under two". Ayyar exclaimed, "Very good! What about father?" Pondering for a while, I said "Saturn is lord of the 2nd from Pitrukaraka and is in the 12th from Lagna. Father's death would have occurred before the end of Sani Dasa, which means when you were about 15 years".

The correctness of my interpretation was a combination of asrological and intuitional factors plus a little bit of bravado as I had to take a risk also in boldly declaring the conclusion before a learned scholar and a great judge and luminary. "Some say that being born on a full Moon day is an astrological handicap. What is your own view in the matter?" queried my learned consultor. This provoked me into giving some sort of a lecture on Sun-Moon relations in a horoscope. I said, "The Sun represents the ego and Moon, mind. The degree of harmony existing between a person's mind and ego is revealed by the relative positions of these two bodies. On a full Moon day, the Sun and the Moon will be opposing each other. Naturally those born on a full Moon day have a natural conflict between their emotions and their ego. They act hesitantly and are unwilling to let

---

* क्रूरेषितौ चन्द्र विलग्नराशी सौम्यग्रहै वीक्षण योगहीनौ ।
केन्द्रच्युतो यघमरेश मंत्री जातस्य माता समुपैति नाशम् ॥

go of the past. They display an outgoing personality. The sign disposition of the Moon is important. In a watery sign like Cancer the Moon gives an emotional nature and strong affections and persistence. Such a Moon conjoined with Mars and also involved in Gajakesari Yoga not only indicates some sort of an inner turmoil and sensitivity but this is more than offset because Jupiter makes one unselfish and concerned for others. But the failing in such a person would be bestowing generosity on those who do not deserve it", I concluded.

"So in a sense Astrology is like psychology. I now come to the main point. Is there any combination in my horoscope indicative of my getting the position of a High Court Judge?"

I continued: "Prima facie the horoscope does not show any significant Rajayogas as such. Mars is debilitated in Cancer and the planet who gets exalted there, viz., Jupiter is in a Kendra from the Moon. This is a Rajayoga. The Moon and Jupiter are in mutual Kendras causing Gajakesari Yoga. This has reference to the 11th from Lagna and the 10th from the Moon. Venus Dasa lasts till 1957. Venus, the dispositor of Jupiter, though in the 12th from Lagna is well placed from the Moon and can raise you to a higher position especially that he is in the constellation of Mercury, lord of the 10th. Saturn, though lord of the 2nd is in the 12th and in the 5th from the Moon in the constellation of Mercury. Therefore, the event can happen in Venus Dasa and Saturn Bhukti".

Ayyar became a Judge of the Madras High Court and we were in contact with each other for a long time. Whenever we visited Madras, where Ayyar lived after retirement, we would call on him and enjoy the hospitality of Mrs. Ayyar, a noble lady. He presented me with some of his publications – Krishna – The Darling of Humanity, Tenali Raman and An Indian in Western Europe, revised edition, in which he had made appreciative references to me.

There are some persons who have an absolute aversion to working for others. Their mentality is such that they would be rather engaged in a small way on their own than hold quite a high responsible position in which others are above them. There are other types the reverse of this who do better in others' employ than on their own account. I came across an interesting example of this sort when at the instance of a leading personality, a man of medium stature, darkish in complexion with pock marks on his face, consulted me. He was serving in a private business concern and was never satisfied with his job.

The horoscope showed interesting features, all the planets being

Ketu							Merc. Moon
Moon	Ascdt. Mandi	Mars Rahu	**RASI**		**NAVAMSA**		Venus Ascdt.
Mars	Jup.	Sat.			Sat.		Ketu
Venus	Sun	Merc. Rahu	Sat.				Sun

disposed continuously from the 2nd to 8th house-Dhana Malika. I thought that Lagna aspected by Yogakaraka Mars in exaltation and Jupiter and the Lagna lord Moon forming a fairly strong Gajakesari Yoga involving the 2nd and 8th houses ruled out a position of subordination. Mercury the planet of business though subject to Papakartari Yoga was not much afflicted. I told him, "You possess a practical business mind, are enterprising, speculative, sociable, adaptable, truthful and resourceful". He was enthusiastic regarding all that I had told him and kept on exclaiming "Wonderful!", "Remarkable!" etc. "You have told me so correctly except that you have not said one thing which I have concealed from you".

I examined the chart once again "Mars dominant and placed in the 7th", I continued – "You mean about your private Life? It is not bad. Kalatrakaraka Venus, though in the 6th, subject to Papakartari

Yoga is aspected by Jupiter. You are not guilty of disloyalty to your wife though you may be sociable with other women". "Exactly so", he confessed. Satisfied with what he called my "clever interpretation" of his chart, he came again after a week, exhuberant with praise regarding my delineation. He said "I wish you examine my 10th house and guide me as to the nature of business I can undertake so that I do not fritter away my energies in doing things not warranted in my horoscope.

In deciding what line of business would suit him, I had recourse not only to the usual Parasari rules but also to Jaimini. My dilemma was, the 10th lord Mars, exalted and a Yogakaraka also, aspects the 10th, Lagna and the 2nd. The 10th is occupied by Ketu. Lord of the 2nd, Sun is in the sign of Mars aspected by Saturn. This conglomeration of saturnine, martian, solar and nodal forces should indicate the business he should take to. I had seen in some horoscopes of excise contractors, dealers in liquids and owners of bars and hotels, the impact of Mars and Ketu/Rahu on the 10th house. After such reflections in my mind I told the person, "Mercury in the 4th house aspecting the 10th is good for business, though worry and anxiety due to domestic maters will be a part of your life. Ketu and Mercury in the 7th from each other create unexpected difficulties with partners, if you have any idea of establishig a partnership business. Rahu in the 4th shows many ups and downs. The Sun is in the 5th house aspected by Saturn shows losses in speculation. Venus, Yogakaraka from Chandra Lagna, occyping the 11th from the Moon favours success through medicine, food articles, restaurants etc. Mars in the 7th while adding strength to the horoscope as generator of Ruchaka Yoga is adverse for partnership. There will be much strife in business. Ketu in the 10th aspected by Mars is the most significant combination so far as your occupation is concerned indicating gain through pursuits connected with liquids, arrack, hotels and eating houses.

Summing up, I feel that hotel business would suit you best. The Dasa of Mercury is about to start and throughout this and Ketu Dasa, your business will thrive well." Nettakallu, the consultor, appeared convinced by my analysis. He started a restaurant and a bar and built up good reputation and made good money also. He was in touch with me for a long time seeking my counsel whenever needed and lived upto a good old age. He studied Astrology and secured a working knowledge of the subject.

The above two are some of the typical instances of the astrological consultations I was giving in those days.

As days passed I tried to cut off the professional aspect of this consultation work though counseling astrologically friends, relatives and those facing difficult problems became a part of my life. Book writing, editing THE ASTROLOGICAL MAGAZINE and receiving visitors, holding discussions with scholars and of course attending to the needs of a growing family, kept me very busy throughout the day.

EPILOGUE

I propose to issue in due course one more volume of my Experiences covering the years 1945 to 1976, detailing the next phase of my crusade against contemners and denigrators of Astrology.

I resorted to a three-pronged approach: (1) Rebutting attacks by political leaders and so-called "intellectuals" in the press by suitable rejoinders; (2) building up a case for Astrology by delivering public lectures in educational, scientific and cultural centres and presiding at and inaugurating conferences on an all-India level and establishing personal contact with men at the top in intellectual, scientific and educational fields; and (3) making forecasts on outstanding national and international matters.

My financial position was satisfactory and the responsibility of rearing the family was almost entirely taken over by Rajeswari, I was therefore free to explore the avenues I then felt necessary to press forward the cause dearer to my heart and for which I had dedicated my life.

Pandit Nehru, despite his patriotic and national outlook, lost no opportunity in debunking Hindu traditions and beliefs-Astrology included, posing himself to be of modern "progressive" thinking; and the media, with rare exceptions, always highlighted his attacks pointing astrologers in bad light and making them look small. I would take up cudgels against such attacks by emphatically refuting in the press the stale arguments advanced by Nehru and his political *chelas*. Leading papers carried my rejoinders so that the minds of the educated public could be disabused.

Many communications appreciating my rebuttals were received from such notable men as H.V. Kamath, I.C.S. (Forward Block); Kala

Venkat Rao, Congress General Secretary; Gulzari Lal Nanda, a member
of Nehru's Cabinet; Dr. Sampurnanand and other well-known local
leaders like C.R. Reddy, M.V. Rama Rao, Veeranna Gowda, Vaikuntha
Baliga etc.

In fact, Dr. Sampurnanand and I would often join issue with Nehru
when he made disparaging remarks on Astrology. One such occasion
was the eight-planet combination in 1962, when both of us cautioned
him that the combination would hit his health severely and
permanently. On the eve of the combination he had arrogantly declared
that he did not see how "the planets were interested in our affairs".
My rejoinder exposing Nehru's ignorance of planetary influences
received wide publicity in the media.

Dr. Sampurnanand and I had worked on an important piece of
research on planetary movements enabling us to discover an intimate
connection between the movements of Jupiter and Saturn and Indian
affairs. Earlier studies carried out in my research section had revealed
significant facts as to how the major planets influenced world affairs
and this correlation was amply established in my forecasts on the War.

Leading personalities in different walks of life visited me seeking
my views (astrologically) on important political matters and their own
prospects.

Many of them took the initiative in organising my lectures in
different Universities – Mysore, Bangalore, Rajasthan, Lucknow and
Institutes of Science etc. These lectures were inaugurated and chaired
by eminent men like Dr. S. Bhagavantam, Prof. M.S. Thacker, Prof.
Mathur, Dr. Gokak and such others. The audience comprised of the
cream of the educated and intellectual class. The media gave good
coverage to my talks. I was therefore able to influence to a great extent
the thought-patterns of the intelligentsia.

In my presidential and inaugural addresses at various conferences
chaired mostly by the local Governors or Chief Ministers, no occasion
was spared to uphold the dignity of the astrological profession, though
I had ceased to be a professional by then. Many astrologers, quite
learned and experienced, who had been looked down upon as social
parasites felt that they received a shot in their arms. Such an aggressive

presentation was then found necessary to cry halt to the thoughtless denigration of Astrology and astrologers.

THE ASTROLOGICAL MAGAZINE had earned a reputation for its correct editorial political forecasts and exposition of Indian culture and Astrology. It commanded a wide readership. The unique role played by the magazine in popularising Astrology amongst educated Indians and in creating a genuine interest in it as a subject of social relevance is now a matter of history.

Some of the contributors like Dr. C. Kunhan Raja, Dr. R. Nagaraja Sharma, Prof. R.V. Vaidya, Dr. Arka Somayaji, and Mrs. Rukmini were persons of high intellectual calibre deeply interested in my work in the field of Astrology.

The years 1945-46 saw the fulfillment of some of my most important forecasts such as the collapse of the Dictators, end of the II World War, developments in the Far East, survival of the Mikado, Presidential elections in U.S.A., Developments in Russia etc., correctly, especially in regard to the timing of these historical events.

A complete list of such forecasts made by me and assiduously collected by K.N. Rao, I.A.A.S., just retired from an important Administrative position and himself a scholar in Astrology has been given in his book. "The Science of Astrology" (pages 39 to 77)

It was a matter or gratification the Astrology was beginning to be used openly and not stealthily for important public purposes, such as the taking over of the Associated Press by Kasturi Srinivasan and his colleagues, the laying of the foundation-stones for many of the National Laboratories and major dams (e.g. Sharavati etc.) and other projects of public and national interest. The Muhurthams fixed by me in all these cases were meticulously observed and more importantly, the men involved were frank and openly declared the fact of the Astrological Muhurtham. To cite an example: the *time* for laying the foundation stone of the National Aeronautical Laboratory at Bangalore was fixed by me as desired by Prof. M.S. Thacker, the then Director-General of Scientific and Cultural Affairs, who, without any hesitation or inhibition did the Puja in a nearby Siva shrine and laid the first brick at the correct moment. The then Director, Dr. Neelakanthan, well known as a scientist was an *asthika* and was aware of the importance of Astrology. Some of his successors, however, who had then occupied inconsequential positions, today air their unsolicited opinions on the 'superstition' of Astrology. Invitations to give lectures at Rotary, Lion and similar clubs and such institutions as the Air Force Officers' Associations, Universities, Institutions of Medicine, Law etc., were extended to me, so that I was able to place my views and enlighten correctly on the scope, limits and practical utility of Astrology on a wide and varied mass section of the discerning public in general. Men like Air Marshal Bhat was particular that the cadets and officers got a correct picture of Astrology without being carried away either by exaggerated claims or unbalanced criticisms.

The penultimate phase of my work concerned with taking Hindu Astrology to the West and making the Westerners, especially the Americans, appreciate the predictive potency of Hindu Astrology and make them Hindu Astrology–conscious. In fact, my lecture at the United Nations, New York, on the "Relevance of Astrology in the Modern Times" appears to have thrilled the American astrological fraternity that this subject could find a hearing in the World Organisation. My sharing a common platform in the West in places like Cambridge, New York etc., with scientists like John Nelson, Michel Gaqueline who turned astrological, from debunking western Astrology to scientific proof for the validity of astrology, could be considered as very important. The fruits of these labours are being felt increasingly today with a large section of Americans veering towards a study of Hindu Astrology.

My book (now before the public) HINDU ASTROLOGY AND THE WEST gives details of my humble work in the West.

Many of my own countrymen including friends, astrological savants and astrologers have not lagged behind in extending to me their moral support in my work and in spreading my message. Of course some critics have not lagged behind either in indulging in cheap gibes against my crusade, quite unbecoming of any one claiming to have academic or intellectual pretensions. I wish them also well. Such criticism is a sad for it does not stimulate discussion or inquiry but advocates superstitious rejection of *Jyotisha*.

The next volume will highlight some of my failures in prediction in not anticipating such events as the birth of Pakistan! The failure was perhaps due more to my emotional approach than a purely astrological perception.

However, I did caution our leaders, before Pakistan came into existence, that the creation of Pakistan would pose perpetual and unresolvable problems to India, which we are witnessing today! Astrologically the disappearance of Pakistan as a political entity cannot be ruled out.

It was unthinkable at that time that my motherland would be vivisected before my own eyes; and that some of the national stalwarts would have an unwilling share in this vivisection.

I wish to close the epilogue by quoting the following extract from an assessment of my work by K.N. Rao whom I have mentioned earlier. (vide: p.33 of his took "The Science of Astrology")

"What is my assessment? He is, in the history of the world, of at least the last four hundred years, the greatest among successful astrologers; the greatest among the successful teachers of Astrology; particularly applied Astrology, through his books and writings in THE ASTROLOGICAL MAGAZINE; and the greatest promoter of the cause of Astrology through the encouragement he has given to others."

I hope to be worthy of at least a part of this tribute before I close my mortal chapter.